"Women, if you really want to know why men are so bored, uneasy, and passive in church, this is the book for you. If you want to know why he'd rather play golf than meet with the God of the universe, read this book."

— **Florence Littauer**
Founder, CLASSeminar
Speaker/Author of *Personality Plus*
and *Silver Boxes*

"David Murrow has made a painful reality profoundly clear: most churches no longer connect with men. Of course, it doesn't have to be that way, and Murrow shows why. But until we acknowledge the problem, nothing will change and we will lose millions of sons, husbands, and friends—and the gifts they bring to the church in the process."

— **Dr. Robert M. Lewis**
Founder, Men's Fraternity

"*Why Men Hate Going to Church* encourages and enables women to dive deeply into the hearts of men and understand what motivates them spiritually. While exposing the reality and danger of churches overrun by feminine ideals Murrow offers theological brilliance grounded in richly biblical truths. This is an amazingly insightful book."

— **Ginger Plowman**
Author of *Don't Make Me
Count to Three!*

"I've often noticed that sermons on Mother's Day tend to gush over moms, while on Father's Day they tell dads to 'shape up.' I've always thought this strange, but David Murrow's book explains how common this attitude actually is. The modern church pushes men out of the pews by ignoring their needs and devaluing their strengths. For churches and individuals wondering where all the men have gone, *Why Men Hate Going to Church* gives us a much-needed diagnosis and a practical prescription to call the church back to effective, relevant ministry to America's men."

— **Sheila Wray Gregoire**
Author of *Honey, I Don't Have a
Headache Tonight: Help for
Women Who Want to Feel More
"In the Mood"*

"David Murrow has shined a bright light on one of the church's darkest secrets: missing men. Church history shows that when men return to church, its impact on society multiplies. Murrow documents the reasons men are absent, then provides practical suggestions to make church a place where both men and women feel at home. You may not agree with everything Murrow says, but you can't ignore it."

— **Dr. Woody Davis**
President and Head Coach,
TEAMinistries, Inc.

"The problem of missing men could be the most difficult challenge the church faces today. We try to fix this problem with minor program adjustments, then wonder why there is little or no change! I challenge every Christian to read this book, to understand the problem, and enter into the battle to build Spiritual fathers."

— **Dan Schaeffer**
Author, Speaker, and Director
of Building Brothers

"Women, if you're having trouble getting Bubba off the couch and into the pew, this is the book for you. In a fair, enlightening, and entertaining manner, Murrow shares how to stand by our men, releasing them to God's great adventure, instead of taming or redecorating them."

— **Becky Freeman**
Author and Speaker

"Finally, a book that helps women understand why our best efforts to get our husbands to church almost always fail. In *Why Men Hate Going to Church*, Dave Murrow shows how we—and the church—have tried to 'feminize' men and why they fight against it (and why they should). We don't want girly men! We want men of God! Murrow believes that's possible and that it's not too late for it to happen."

— **Nancy Kennedy**
Author of *When He Doesn't Believe*
and *Between Two Loves*

"For every female who has ever wondered, 'Why isn't my man more into church?' For every male who has ever wondered, 'What's wrong with me?' For every leader who has ever wondered, 'How can we reach and inspire men?' David Murrow has brought to us a fresh voice regarding the spiritual gender differences and some amazing insights and stunningly simple solutions to the complex problem of reaching and inspiring the male. Though it's not likely that men were dropped on their heads in The Fall, this book offers better explanations of what makes guys tick and what ticks them off. It should be a crime for the things of God to bore *anyone*, and David is a first-rate crime stopper for the spirits of the male species."

— **Anita Renfroe**
Comedian and Author of
The Purse Driven Life

"And where are the men? David Murrow asks why so many good men do not fit the molds and patterns offered by the contemporary church. So should we, if we are to proclaim the gospel in its fullness."

— **David Dobler**
Former Moderator,
Presbyterian Church (USA)

WHY MEN HATE GOING TO CHURCH

David Murrow

NELSON BOOKS

A Division of Thomas Nelson Publishers

Since 1798

www.thomasnelson.com

Published in Nashville, Tennessee, by Thomas Nelson, Inc.

ISBN 0-7852-6038-2

Printed in the United States of America

05 06 07 08 RRD 10 9 8

CONTENTS

Part 4: The Straws That Break Men's Hearts

Part 5: Restoring the Masculine Spirit in the Church

Part 6: Meeting Men's Deepest Needs

INTRODUCTION

WHY DO MEN HATE GOING TO CHURCH? IT'S A QUESTION I'VE pondered for years. I've worshipped in congregations of every stripe: Catholic, Orthodox, mainline Protestant, evangelical, and Pentecostal. No matter the name on the outside, there are always more women on the inside. The men who *do* show up for services often seem passive, bored, or uneasy.

One Sunday I was sitting in church, half listening to the sermon, when my wandering mind recalled a quote from business guru W. Edwards Deming: *Your system is perfectly designed to give you the results you're getting.* In other words, if every third car rolls off the assembly line with bumpers installed upside down, you don't blame the bumpers. You've got a system that's unintentionally designed to produce defective cars.

Hmm. So what was this system we call church producing? I looked around the sanctuary and counted noses. Just one-third of the adult attendees were men—most of whom were over fifty. I identified at least a dozen married women whose husbands were absent. With the tots dismissed for kids' church, there was a handful of teenage boys, but almost no men between the ages of eighteen and thirty-five. There were no single men.

What kind of involvement was our church system producing? I studied the bulletin: all of the midweek and volunteer opportunities were pitched at women and children. Each announcement ended with a woman's name: "For more information call Shari/Sarah/Andrea/Victoria/Lauren, etc." I looked around at the men. Most were present in body only. Truth be told, the only man in the room who was truly engaged was the pastor, who, as he clicked past the twenty-five-minute mark in his sermon, seemed to be picking up steam, even as the men in the crowd were losing theirs.

I began to wonder: Could Deming's theory apply here? What if Christianity's primary delivery system, the local church, is perfectly designed to give us the results we're getting? What if church is unintentionally designed to reach women, children, and elderly folks?

Somebody needs to write a book about this, I thought.

I expected to find such a book at my local Christian bookstore. Nothing. I checked online booksellers. Nothing. I searched the archives of the Religious Research Association. Nothing. Incredibly, no one had ever written a book or published a study suggesting how we might solve the church's perennial problem with missing and/or unmotivated men.

Then I dug deeper. I spent many nights and weekends at the library and on the computer. I studied men and masculinity. I spoke with men about their religious experiences. I found a consistent, disturbing pattern: men want to know God, but they want nothing to do with church. Trying to bring men into a genuine walk with Christ through church is like trying to play golf with a shovel—you might hit a lucky shot now and then, but you're not using the best tool for the job. *Truth is, the modern church is not designed to do what Jesus did: reach men with the good news.*

I am not a theologian, pastor, or professor. I'm a man in the pews who, like so many others, has struggled to find his place in the church. One night, after years of waiting for a theologian, pastor, or professor to write on this subject, I heard a voice in my head: *You write it.* Sounded to me like the voice of God. As you read, you be the judge.

In the meantime, be encouraged! Women, if you've felt guilty or distressed because the men in your lives won't go to church, *it's not your fault.* Men, if church bores you to tears, *it's not your fault.* Pastors, if you're having a hard time attracting and retaining men, *it's not your fault.* It's time to stop blaming the bumpers. The modern church system is getting the results it's designed to get.

Must the church be this way? Or can it be a place where men of all kinds can connect with God? I believe it can be. For years we've called men back to the church. *Now it's time to call the church back to men.*

PART 1

WHY MEN HATE
GOING TO CHURCH

My wife, Gina, and I enjoy living in Alaska. We try to take full advantage of our short but beautiful summers. So do mosquitoes. Trillions of these flying vampires bedevil our state from late May to early September.

I've noticed something odd. Mosquitoes rarely bother Gina, but they attack me like kids diving for candy under a broken piñata. Before hiking I must bathe myself in mosquito repellent; she slips on one of those coiled bracelets and goes unbitten.

Like those mosquitoes, there's something buzzing around our churches that is literally sucking the lifeblood out of our men. But women seem largely unaffected. In the next six chapters we begin identifying this pesky affliction.

1

Men Have a Religion: Masculinity

CLIFF IS A MAN'S MAN. ON THE JOB HE'S KNOWN AS A GO-getter and a very hard worker. He's a good provider who loves his wife and kids. He's well respected by his neighbors. Cliff drives a humongous four-wheel-drive pickup. He loves the outdoors and takes every opportunity for a little hunting and fishing. He enjoys a cold beer and a dirty joke. He does not go to church.

Ask him why he doesn't go to church, and he'll offer up words like *boring, irrelevant,* and *hypocrite.* But the real reason Cliff doesn't go to church is that he's already practicing another religion. That religion is *masculinity.*

> The ideology of masculinity has replaced Christianity as the true religion of men. We live in a society with a female religion and a male religion: Christianity, of various sorts, for women and non-masculine men; and masculinity . . . for men.[1]

Cliff practices his religion with a single-mindedness the Pharisees would envy. His work, his hobbies, his entertainment, his follies, his addictions, everything he does is designed to prove to the world *he is a man.* His religion also demands that he avoid anything that might call his manhood into question. This includes church, because Cliff believes deep in his heart that church is something for women and children, not men.

Cliff is not alone. Men have believed this for centuries. In the 1800s, Charles Spurgeon said, "There has got abroad a notion, somehow, that if you become a Christian you must sink your manliness and turn

3

milksop." Cliff sees Christianity as incongruous with his manhood. It's a women's thing.

CHURCH . . . A WOMEN'S THING?

We're only in chapter 1, and I know I'm already in trouble with a lot of you. I can just imagine what you're thinking: *Church is not a women's thing—it's a men's thing!* It certainly looks that way, doesn't it? After all, a man and His male disciples founded Christianity, most of its major saints and heroes were men, men penned all of the New Testament books, all of the popes were men, all of the Catholic priests are men, and 95 percent of the senior pastors in America are men.[2] Feminists have been telling us for years that the church is male dominated and patriarchal. Are they right?

The answer is yes and no. The pastorate is a men's club. But almost every other area of church life is dominated by women. Whenever large numbers of Christians gather, men are never in the majority. Not at revivals. Not at crusades. Not at conferences. Not at retreats. Not at concerts. With the exception of men's events and pastoral conferences, can you think of any large gathering of Christians that attracts more men than women?

Visit the church during the week, and you'll find most of the people working there are female. Drop in on a committee meeting, and you'll find a majority of the volunteers are women—unless it's that small bastion of male presence, the building committee. Look over the leadership roster: the pastor is likely to be a man, but at least two-thirds of the ministry leaders will be women.[3] Examine the sign-up sheets for volunteer work, prayer, Sunday school, and nursery duty. You'll be lucky to see more than a couple of men's names on these lists. One pastor recently told me, "If it weren't for the postman, every visitor to the church during the week would be a woman."

Male pastors come and go, but faithful women provide a matriarchal continuity in our congregations. Women are the devoted ones who build their lives around their commitments to Christ and His church. Women are more likely to teach and volunteer in church and are the greatest participants in Christian culture. The sad reality in many churches today is this: *the only man who actually practices his faith is the pastor.*

With so much female presence and participation, the church has gained a reputation as a ladies' club in the minds of men. Cliff does not attend church for the same reason he does not wear pink: neither is proper to his gender. Does Cliff know why he hates going to church? No. Can he offer a detailed explanation of his feelings? Of course not. He's a guy, remember? Cliff knows one thing: he hates going to church.

HOW THE GENDER GAP AFFECTS WOMEN

If you are a woman, you may have picked up this book because a key man in your life does not go to church, or if he does attend, it means little to him. You are not alone. Connie is a lifelong Episcopalian, a fifty-six-year-old mother of four boys. She says, "None of my sons goes to church anymore. Two of them are divorced, and now all four are living with their lady friends. It's sad." Bernice from Connecticut says, "I have a large extended family. Not one of the men goes to Mass, let alone confession." Vicki's husband, Ron, attends their local Baptist church. "But he's a total hypocrite," she states. "He screams all the way to church. Once he's inside the sanctuary, he puts on a smile and plays 'Mr. Charming.' Why won't he let God change him?" Caroline is a twenty-nine-year-old single woman who won't date non-Christian men. "But I'm beginning to rethink that," she admits. "I go to a small Pentecostal church. There are no single guys my age. This man at work was pursuing me, so I told him our first date would have to be church. He came, but I think it freaked him out. He never called again."

Connie, Bernice, Vicki, and Caroline know from personal experience: *the modern church is having trouble reaching men.* Women comprise more than 60 percent of the typical adult congregation on any given Sunday.[4] At least one-fifth of married women regularly worship without their husbands.[5] There are quite a few single women but hardly any single men in church today. Every day it gets harder for single Christian women to find men for romance or marriage. Step into any church parking lot, and you're likely to see an attractive young mother and her brightly scrubbed children scurrying to Sunday school. Mom may be wearing an impressive diamond ring on her left hand, but the man who gave it to her is nowhere to be seen.

WHERE ARE THE MANLY MEN?

Although males have not completely abandoned the church, *manly* men like Cliff have all but disappeared. Tough, earthy, working guys rarely come to church. High achievers, alpha males, risk takers, and visionaries are in short supply. Fun-lovers and adventurers are also underrepresented in church. These rough-and-tumble men don't fit in with the quiet, introspective gentlemen who populate the church today. The truth is, most men in the pews grew up in church.[6] Many of these lifers come not because they desire to be transformed by Christ but because they enjoy participating in comforting rituals that have changed little since their childhood. There are also millions of men who attend services under duress, dragged by a mother, wife, or girlfriend. Today's churchgoing man is humble, tidy, dutiful, and above all, nice.

What a contrast to the men of the Bible! Think of Moses and Elijah, David and Daniel, Peter and Paul. They were lions, not lambs—take-charge men who risked everything in service to God. They fought valiantly and spilled blood. They spoke their minds and stepped on the toes of religious people. They were true leaders, tough guys who were feared and respected by the community. All of these men had two things in common: they had an intense commitment to God, and they weren't what you'd call saintly.

Such men seldom go to church today.

Furthermore, of the men who *do* attend church, most decline to invest themselves in the Christian life as their wives and mothers do. The majority of men attend services and nothing more.[7] Jay is such a man. He's in church most Sundays, but he's not very excited about it. "I go mainly for my kids and my wife," he says. "Church is okay, but it really doesn't enthrall me like it does her."

Who is being touched by the gospel today? Women. Women's ministries, women's conferences, women's Bible studies, and women's retreats are ubiquitous in the modern church. Men's ministry, if it even exists, might consist of an occasional pancake breakfast and an annual retreat.

How did a faith founded by a Man and His twelve male disciples become so popular with women, but anathema to men? The church of the first century was a magnet to males. Jesus' strong leadership, blunt honesty, and bold action mesmerized men. A five-minute sermon by Peter resulted in the conversions of three thousand men.

Today's church does not mesmerize men; it repels them. Just 35 percent of the men in the United States say they attend church weekly.[8] In Europe male participation rates are much worse, in the neighborhood of 5 percent.[9] This hardly sounds like a male-dominated, patriarchal institution to me.

What's worse, nobody seems to care about the absence of men. Have you ever heard a sermon on the church's gender gap? I've never heard a pastor or church leader bring it up. Heck, I've never heard *anybody* bring it up. It's just one of those things Christians don't talk about.

WHO'S TO BLAME FOR THE GENDER GAP?

For decades those few people who noticed the gender gap have assumed that men are to blame for it. Sometimes they are. Many men intentionally reject the Christian faith. Some men are proud and want to be their own God. Men hate to admit weakness or neediness. Millions are captive to sin, unbelief, and other religions that preclude commitment to Christ. Men get distracted by the concerns of this world and lose interest in spiritual matters. Men suffer abuse at the hands of church people and fall away.

But let's be honest—women grapple with these same issues. Women are just as susceptible to sin, atheism, other religions, and pride. There's nothing in the Bible to suggest that women are more virtuous or less sinful than men. Women are just as likely to have father issues or be victims of abuse. So why do women seem drawn to the church when men are not? What's the difference?

Let me be blunt: today's church has developed a culture that is driving men away. Almost every man in America has tried church, but two-thirds find it unworthy of a couple of hours once a week. A wise Texan once told me, "Men don't go to church 'cuz they've been."

When men need spiritual sustenance, they go to the wilderness, the workplace, the garage, or the corner bar. They watch their heroes in the stadium or on the racetrack. They plunge into a novel or sneak off to a movie. Church is one of the last places men look for God.

More than 90 percent of American men believe in God, and five out of six call themselves Christians. But only two out of six attend church on a given Sunday.[10] The average man accepts the reality of Jesus Christ, but fails to see any value in going to church.

Men's disinterest in Christianity is so consistent around the world, it can't be explained by pride, father issues, sin, or distraction. Neither can we say, "Well, men are just less religious," because this is untrue. Male and female participation are roughly equal in Judaism, Buddhism, and Hinduism. In the Islamic world men are publicly and unashamedly religious—often more so than women. Of the world's great religions, only Christianity has a consistent, nagging shortage of male practitioners. What is it about modern Christianity that is driving men away? That's the question I hope to answer with this book.

NOW FOR SOME GOOD NEWS

Can the church turn the tide with men? Yes! It not only can, but it must. Jesus built His church on twelve Spirit-filled men who changed the world. We must do the same: *you cannot have a thriving church without a core of men who are true followers of Christ.* If the men are dead, the church is dead.

Fortunately, pioneering churches and parachurch organizations are enjoying remarkable success in reaching men for Christ. New forms of worship and ministry tailored to the needs of men are springing up in the unlikeliest places. Some of the fastest-growing churches in America are also those most successful in reaching men. To learn more about these ministries, visit my Web site, www.churchformen.com.

Can *your* church turn the tide with men? Yes! But please don't hand this book to the minister and say, "Pastor, you need to do this!" Many of the needed changes cannot be imposed from above, but must bubble up from the congregation itself. *Too often it's not what the leadership imposes but what the laity demands that causes the church to repel men.* If your church has a large gender gap, it's probably not the pastor's fault.

The people in the pews hold the steering wheel on this one. In the coming pages I suggest dozens of ways to make your congregation more attractive to men. Your job is to read, pray, and take action wherever you can. Individual churchgoers have more influence than they think.

ABOVE ALL, DON'T DESPAIR!

As you read the dire statistics on male participation, don't panic! This low ebb may be part of the church's natural cycle. Over time the church tends to get out of balance and lose its masculine spirit. Then God raises a lion—a Martin Luther, John Wesley, Charles Finney, or Billy Sunday—to drag the church back into balance. The men return. The great revivals of the past three centuries always transformed large numbers of men.

God has balanced His church many times before. He will do so again. Our job is to confront the current gender gap for what it is: a strategy of the evil one to weaken the church. We need to understand what causes the gap and have the courage to remove the barriers that discourage and demoralize men. God will call men back to Himself. Will the church be ready?

Dream for a moment. What would church be like if the majority of the worshippers were men? Not just males taking up pew space, but strong, earthy men who were truly alive in Christ. Men who were there not just to please their wives, to fulfill religious tradition, or to go on a power trip, but men who were there to rock their world. Can you even imagine what that would feel like? Imagine what such a church could accomplish for the kingdom of God!

Impossible you say? Just read the book of Acts. The church was like this once; it can be so again.

AUTHOR'S NOTE

Let me say this in the strongest possible terms: *the answer is not a male-dominated church.* I am not advocating the "submit to me, woman," brand of Christianity in which men are kings and women are pawns. Not only is this model unbiblical; it doesn't create spiritually mature men. The answer is a *balanced* approach: teaching, practices, and opportunities that allow for both masculine and feminine expression in the church.

Please read this book with an open mind. Some of my conclusions may upset or shock you. I've tried very hard not to stereotype, but you can't write a book about men without making some generalizations about the sexes. (For example, I say that men are more competitive; women are more cooperative. Not every man is more competitive than every woman, but considering the genders as a whole, the observation is true.) If you agree with 90 percent of what you read herein, please don't throw out the whole book based on the 10 percent that makes you mad. This book is not a perfect plan to bring men back. Rather, I hope it is the match that ignites thousands of conversations and millions of prayers about a problem we've ignored far too long. I pray God's people take what's written in this book and test it, refine it, and use it to bring multitudes to Christ.

There are hundreds of great Christian books written to help men come closer to Christ. This is not one of them. This book does not contain the usual calls to repentance, purity, and holiness. You won't hear me talking about the sins that commonly ensnare men. I'm working the other angle. As I said earlier, I am not calling men back to the church. Instead, I am calling the church back to men.

At times this book may not read like a typical Christian tome. I won't offer many suggestions such as "we need to pray more" or "we need to show men God's love." Nor will you find a Scripture reference on every page. Prayer and Scripture are vitally important, but in this book I focus on *practical* barriers to male participation, because so little has been written about them.

Nor is this another book about how men *ought* to be. It's designed to give you insight into men's hearts, to illuminate the chasm between men's needs and the ministry of the local church.[11] So let's make a deal: I'll give you the straight story on men, and as you read, you resist the urge to utter the phrase, "Well, men should just . . ." This is not a book about what men *should* be. If we can't start with men *as they are,* we'll never reach them.

You might be interested to know I pitched this book to a number of publishers who rejected it. One publisher thought Christian women couldn't handle my message because it wasn't "sweet enough" for them. Women, what would you rather have—a book that tickles your ears or a book that tells you how men *really* feel? I think you're tough enough to handle the truth about men, even if the message isn't sugar-coated. This is a prophetic message and may at times sound negative. Please don't take it that way. I'm confident the church will get back on course, and you will play an important role in this turnaround story.

Here's how I see it: imagine a ship leaving England for New York. If that ship is just a couple of degrees off course for the entire journey, it will land in Boston instead of the Big Apple. This is where most churches are today—a couple of degrees off course. We're doing the things Jesus told us to do. Great things are happening in many areas of the world. But we need a few gentle course corrections to bring men back. Only then will we reach the goal Christ laid out for us. The longer we wait, the more drastic the corrections will need to be.

With all this talk of changing the course of the church, you may have the impression that this book is for pastors and church leaders. Not true. It is really a book for *laywomen*. I truly believe women must play a key role if men are to return. Because women dominate in attendance, leadership, and volunteerism, they hold great sway in the local church (even if they don't realize it). Women must humble themselves, pray, and allow the men of the church to lead the body toward an adventure. A frightening adventure. A "we've never done it that way" adventure.

Women, will you allow yourselves to be swept into this adventure, or will you stick with the safe, predictable, tried, and true? Will you allow men to take risks, dream big, and push the envelope within your local church? God made men for adventure, achievement, and challenge, and if they can't find those things in church, they're going to find them somewhere else. But if you allow your church to embark on a great adventure, the men will return. Slowly but surely, they will return.

2

WHY JUDY'S HUSBAND
HATES GOING TO CHURCH

THE PIANIST WAS JUST CONCLUDING THE PRELUDE AS JUDY slipped into her usual pew. Smoothing her crisp cotton skirt, she took her seat, exhaled deeply, and tried to prepare her heart to meet with Jesus. It had been a stressful morning.

Her twelve-year-old son, Matt, had refused to get up. He said he hated church and never wanted to go again. Judy argued with Matt, but the young man played his trump card: "Why should I have to go to church if Dad doesn't?" In a moment of anger, Judy ripped Matt's covers off and ordered the rebellious boy into the shower. She left his bedroom fighting back tears.

Matt's attitude was beginning to affect his little brother and sister. All through breakfast they asked if they could stay home, complaining of mysterious stomachaches. With herculean effort Judy managed to get the three kids scrubbed, fed, and seated in their Sunday school classes on time. Judy won this battle, but she was losing the war.

For years Judy had invested heavily in her children's spiritual development. Her kids rarely missed church. She volunteered in their vacation Bible school and Sunday school classes. She prayed for each child daily, and she rejoiced as, one by one, they invited Jesus into their little hearts. But now the children were turning their backs on the church, following the example of Judy's husband, Greg.

Greg. At that moment he was sitting at home in his pajamas, remote control in hand. In their fifteen years of marriage he had attended church exactly thirty-one times: at Christmas and Easter each year, and the day they were married. Greg was a good husband

and a great provider, but he was not the spiritual companion Judy longed for.

Judy tried to turn her eyes upon Jesus, but she could think only of her spiritually dead husband. In that moment she was overcome with emotions: loneliness, anger, resentment, and an overwhelming sense of defeat. Tears welled in her eyes as she thought, *I knock myself out to develop the kids' spiritual lives. Greg does nothing, but still the kids are following his lead.*

She tried to hear the voice of God, but another voice whispered: *If only you were a better witness, Greg would be a Christian by now. Why did you lose your temper with Matt this morning? Now he'll never turn to Jesus. You never should have married Greg in the first place. It was a big mistake.*

Judy grasped for a Scripture. Her mind took her to the verse she'd claimed for the past fifteen years: *"Wives, in the same way be submissive to your husbands so that, if any of them do not believe the word, they may be won over without words by the behavior of their wives"* (1 Peter 3:1 NIV). That passage was food for her soul in the early days of her marriage, but now it pierced her like a dagger. Hadn't she been holy enough? Submissive enough? Tender and loving enough?

Judy looked up from prayer, trying to focus through her tears. She spotted several couples seated near her: Ed and Nancy, Tom and Erica, Chad and Bonnie. As Chad placed his arm around Bonnie and gently kissed her cheek, Judy felt another emotion: jealousy. She instantly confessed her sin to the Lord, but it was too late—the fantasy started again. *There is Greg standing next to her in church, holding her hand, singing praise songs with gusto. In act 2 of her fantasy Judy and Greg are sitting on the bed, sun streaming in the window, enjoying coffee and morning devotions together. In act 3 the family is gathered around a sumptuous turkey dinner, with Greg leading the family in prayer.* "God, I want a Christian husband," Judy prayed under her breath. "Will my husband ever come to church with me?"

The answer is no. Greg will never come to Judy's church. To understand why, let me tell you a story from my childhood.

THE STORY OF THE THERMOSTAT

I grew up in Houston, Texas. On a typical summer evening my father would come home from work, put down his briefcase, and bellow, "It's hotter than hell in here!" Dad would walk over to the thermostat and crank it down to about 68°F (20°C). The air conditioner kicked on, flooding the house with cool air.

This sent my mother to the hall closet, where she kept a Pendleton wool jacket. She was comfortable when the thermostat was set at 77° (25°C). My mother is the only woman in Texas history to spend the month of August in a wool jacket.

When Dad wasn't around, Mom was free to set the thermostat where she liked it. So it is in most churches. Men have been absent or anemic for so long that the *spiritual thermostat* in almost every church is now set to accommodate the people who actually show up and participate: women, children, and older folks. But men suffocate in this environment, so they leave.

When I say *spiritual thermostat*, I'm not talking about the temperature inside the church building. Rather, I'm talking about the culture of today's churches, a culture that values safety over risk, stability over change, preservation over expansion, and predictability over adventure. Ignore what's preached from the pulpit, and look at what actually happens on Sunday morning. Almost everything about today's church—its teaching style, its ministries, the way people are expected to behave, even today's popular images of Jesus—is designed to meet the needs and expectations of a largely female audience. Church is sweet and sentimental, nurturing and *nice*. Women thrive in this environment. In modern parlance, women are the target audience of today's church.

Why? Because they show up! Adult women outnumber adult men by almost two-to-one in a typical congregation. Women are much more likely to volunteer, and more often show up for church events.[1] Without the superhuman commitment of women, the church's programs would grind to a halt. Pastors know this, so they work very hard to recruit and retain women.

Judy likes the warm family atmosphere of her church. Every Sunday is like a big family reunion. But Greg hates it. He can't tell you why; he just knows he can't stand it. The last time he was in church, he felt as out of place as a ham sandwich at a bar mitzvah. So he offers the usual excuses: "It's boring. It's irrelevant. It's full of hypocrites." Press him and he'll say, "Church is pointless. I see no value in getting together once a week to say nice things about God and about each other."

Despite their spiritual differences, Greg and Judy have a good marriage. They see eye to eye on just about everything—except church and the kinds of movies they like. Greg likes action/adventure films, while Judy prefers romantic comedies or chick flicks. Maybe there's a clue here.

MOVIES HAVE THERMOSTATS TOO

If you're having a hard time understanding the concept of a spiritual thermostat, grab some popcorn and head for the movies. Every film has a thermostat that's set for a certain kind of audience. If a film-maker is trying to attract a male audience, he will pack his movie with the things men like: buildings exploding, cars crashing, guns blazing, and bodies flying. There will be tension, intrigue, and a hero who saves the world against impossible odds. Go to the action/adventure rack at your local video store, and you'll find hundreds of films with thermostats set for men.

If a filmmaker wants to set the thermostat for women, he'll include lots of clever dialogue, beautiful costumes, flowers, and scenery. The movie will star a handsome couple who, after a series of misadventures, end up in a happy relationship. Go to the romantic comedy section to find hundreds of these chick flicks.

Films reflect our fantasies. Men fantasize about saving the world against impossible odds. Women fantasize about having a relationship with a wonderful man.

So what does today's church emphasize? *Relationships*: a personal relationship with Jesus and healthy relationships with others. By focusing on relationships, the local church partners with women to fulfill their deepest longing.

But few churches model men's values: risk and reward, accomplishment, heroic sacrifice, action and adventure. Any man who tries to live out these values in a typical congregation will find himself in trouble with the church council in no time.

This is why Greg hates to go to church. He finds it boring and irrelevant because he doesn't see his values modeled there. He finds church dull for the same reason he finds chick flicks dull: neither one reflects his masculine heart. Greg has no desire to fall in love with a wonderful man, even one named Jesus.

So who is right, Greg or Judy? Should church be more like a romantic comedy or an action/adventure movie? Put another way, is the purpose of the Christian life to find a happy relationship with a wonderful man, or is it to save the world against impossible odds?

Men Always Want to Succeed, Even at Church

Men want to succeed at everything they do. Competence is very important to them. They never stop to ask for directions because doing that would call their competence as a navigator into question. Men are also competitive. They want to win in every situation.

But when it comes to doing church, Greg is incompetent. He's a dope. A loser. And the deck is stacked against him. Like most men, he does not possess the natural gifts that make a good churchgoer. He's not very expressive, verbal, or sensitive. He's not a very good teacher or singer. He's uncomfortable praying aloud or holding hands with strangers.

However, Judy is absolutely fabulous at doing church. Her caring heart, relational skills, and emotional sensitivity make her the ideal churchgoer. She knows just what to say in every situation. She naturally coos for newborns, easily nurtures young children, and always has a tissue ready for a hurting friend. In fact, the women in the church always outshine the men because their natural feminine gifts make them so much better at the spiritual work of today's church: relating, emoting, nurturing, and offering verbal expression.

Since women are so much better at doing church, Greg doesn't bother to compete. To really win at Judy's church, Greg would need more than a conversion experience; he'd need a personality transplant.

Men need to be needed. Today's church does not need Greg because it does not need his gifts. In fact, masculine gifts often gum up the works of the ministry machine. If only Christianity required risk taking, boldness, aggression, and heroic sacrifice, Greg might find his place in church.

Men like Greg turn away from the church, looking for environments where the thermostats are set to their liking. Sports, career, hobbies, outdoor recreation, wealth building, and even video games reflect men's core values. Competitive environments allow men to reach for greatness. Church does not.

Truth is, men need a relationship with God, but most guys can't get past the church's negative image. Dan Erickson and Dan Schaffer write:

> Most men who are not involved with a church believe that the church does not offer any lasting value to their lives. The typical adult male in our society is more likely to spend his Sundays watching sports on TV than attending a church service. A majority of unchurched men believe that participating in church life cannot be justified because the return on their investment of time, attention, and energy is too slim.[2]

Must we compromise the gospel in order to attract men? Certainly not. Jesus had no problem attracting men. Fishermen dropped nets full of fish to follow Him, but today's church can't convince men to drop their remote controls for a couple of hours a week. The good news is, Jesus is alive today. He wants to speak to men. If only the church will let Him.

3

MEN AREN'T THE ONLY ONES MISSING FROM CHURCH

IN THE FIRST TWO CHAPTERS, WE MET GREG AND CLIFF, MANLY men who hate to go to church. Doesn't it seem the more masculine the man, the less enthusiastic he is about Christianity?

But men like Greg and Cliff aren't the only ones who are absenting themselves from weekly worship. Research shows that young adults of both genders are the generation least likely to attend church on a given weekend.[1] Cameron Strang notes, "Look inside most churches and you'll notice something about men and women in their 20s: you won't find many. To most 20-somethings, the church is irrelevant."[2]

On the other hand, Christianity has a bumper crop of women and older adults. The church has an attendance pattern that looks like this:[3]

Who's Most Likely to Be in Church	Who's Least Likely to Be in Church
Women	Men
Older Adults, 50 and Up	Younger Adults, 18 to 29

I believe women and older adults flock to church because it speaks to their hearts. It's built around their values. But men and young adults skip church because many congregations ignore or vilify their values.

What do I mean? Studies show that men and young adults tend to be *challenge oriented*. Some of their key values are adventure, risk, daring, independence, change, conflict, variety, pleasure, and reward. Individuals in these groups are more likely to seek thrills, take chances, and accept dares. They want to be known as bold, adventurous, even *dangerous* among their peers.

On the other hand, studies demonstrate that women and older adults tend to be *security oriented*. Some of their key values are safety, stability, harmony, cooperation, predictability, protection, comfort, responsibility, support, and tradition. Individuals in these groups are more likely to play it safe, seek security, and avoid risk. They don't mind being known as reliable, practical, and friendly among their peers.

Of course, there are exceptions to these generalizations. There are teens who play it safe and seniors who go bungee jumping. There are practical young men and dangerous middle-aged women. But if these four populations were polled and their values were plotted on a graph, the distributions would look something like four balloons, with the larger ends of the balloons representing the majority of the respondents, and the smaller ends of the balloons representing the minority:

Security Oriented:

Safety
Stability
Harmony
Predictability
Protection
Comfort
Nurture
Duty
Support
Preservation

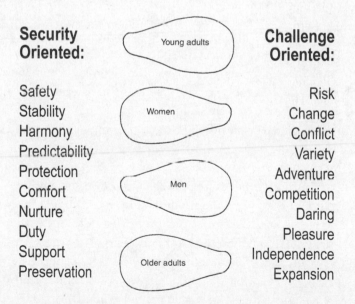

Young adults

Women

Men

Older adults

Challenge Oriented:

Risk
Change
Conflict
Variety
Adventure
Competition
Daring
Pleasure
Independence
Expansion

(*Author's note:* This graphic is not meant as an exact scientific illustration of what these populations value. However, it does portray traits that have been observed in decades of studies and opinion polls.)

Take a good look at the values on the left and right sides of the graphic. Which values is a worshipper most likely to encounter on Sunday morning? Does today's church offer a secure environment or a challenging environment? The answer is clear. In a world of constant change, the church is an anchor of stability, predictability, and tradition. In a dangerous and risky world, the church is a sanctuary of safety and protection. In a world of conflict, the church is a place of peace, harmony, and comfort. Judy is looking for an anchor, a sanctuary from her unpredictable, harried life. Greg is not. She wants security. He wants challenge.

Men and young people are B.O.R.E.D.: busyness, obligation, ritual, education, and duty are the pillars of modern church life. Cynthia Woolever and Deborah Bruce surveyed U.S. worshippers and found "a large percentage say that they attend as a way to fulfill an obligation."[4] *I owe, I owe, so off to church I go.* Men are rarely motivated by guilt, duty, or obligation.

Our congregations can't gain any traction with men and young adults because their adventurous spirits abhor the safety of the modern church. Again, we're not talking about what's preached and taught. The pastor may be offering stirring sermons, but the actual Christian life lived by most churchgoers is about as challenging as finger painting and as exciting as a bologna sandwich.

Of course, there are young adults and men who love church just as it is. (They show up on the graphic.) There are significant minorities of young adults and men who are security oriented. That's why you find so many nice, safe, predictable guys in church. The modern church tends to attract any person—man or woman, young or old—who is security oriented. Meanwhile it repels any person who is challenge oriented. (I offer more specific evidence in chapter 9, "The Gap of Personality.")

When it comes to men, the modern church is dangling the wrong bait. There just aren't as many security-oriented men as there are challenge-oriented ones. So the church catches fewer men.

Did Jesus intend for His church to become a place of security, free of risk, challenge, and adventure? Did Christ come to tame men or to set them free? Is Jesus looking for docile men or wild men? John Eldredge notes, "I think most men in the church believe God put them on the earth to be a good boy."[5] Be safe. Uphold tradition. Keep your promises. Be nice.

Now try this on: *be dangerous*. What if that were our message to men? If churchgoing held the prospect of risk, adventure, and daring, you'd have an abundance of men, teenagers, and young adults signing up. That's precisely what we find in the persecuted church today. It was also the situation in the early church when Christians were routinely stoned, beaten, or fed to hungry lions. When it's dangerous to be a Christian, men are more likely to count themselves in.

But today's church is all about safety. What's our top prayer request? "God, keep us safe. Keep our kids safe. Watch over us and protect us." God's job is to keep our well-ordered lives flowing smoothly.

If we want to shed our reputation as a place for little old ladies of both sexes, we must recapture the challenge of following Jesus. The Christian life is not about becoming a nicer person. It's a quest. When men see other men living the adventure, they'll want in. When young adults see church as the place to find abundant life (the challenging life), they will come back.

There are wise churches that are taking risks, dreaming big, and bringing a measure of adventure back to the Christian life. These churches are built on values that men can relate to. They set high standards and ask much of their members. Their people are encouraged to rock the boat, challenge one another, and take risks. In short, these churches have guts. The biblical translation of the word *guts* is "faith." Read any book on church growth: the congregations that are reaching the unchurched are sticking their necks out and accomplishing great things. *Men are drawn to churches (and Christians) with guts.*

CHALLENGE: THE KEY TO REACHING WOMEN?

Women are also leaving the church. Barna Research reports that women's church attendance declined 20 percent from 1991 to 2000, and their volunteerism in local churches declined 21 percent during that period. Women between the ages of eighteen and thirty-four were the generation least likely to participate in church.[6] It's not hard to understand why. As women storm the formerly male-dominated worlds of business, sports, and higher education, they are becoming more comfortable with the masculine values they encounter. Today's young women seek adventure and challenges every bit as daunting as those sought by men. Setting the thermostat of the church away from security and toward challenge may be the key to reaching the next generation of women as well.

What can you do? Take an honest look at the thermostat in your church. Are you taking risks as a body? Are your members challenging each other or comforting each other? How about you personally: Do you walk with God for adventure or security? Do you pray for God's will or God's protection? Do you embrace change or try to stop it? If you want to see men (and young adults) back in church, begin moving the thermostat away from security and toward challenge. When church leaders push the body toward the unknown, do not stand in their way. Instead, hang on and enjoy the ride!

4

THE MASCULINE SPIRIT AND THE FEMININE SPIRIT

POP QUIZ. EXAMINE THESE TWO SETS OF VALUES. WHICH ONE best characterizes Jesus Christ and His true followers?

LEFT SET	RIGHT SET
Competence	Love
Power	Communication
Efficiency	Beauty
Achievement	Relationships
Skills	Support
Proving oneself	Help
Results	Nurturing
Accomplishment	Feelings
Objects	Sharing
Technology	Relating
Goal oriented	Harmony
Self-sufficiency	Community
Success	Loving cooperation
Competition	Personal expression

Over the years I have shown this chart to hundreds of people: men and women, Christians and non-Christians. More than 95 percent of the time, people choose the Right Set as the best representation of true Christian values. You probably did too.

I culled these lists from chapter 1 of the best seller *Men Are from Mars, Women Are from Venus*. The Left Set includes the values of Mars, while the Right Set includes the values of Venus. What's clear from this exercise is that when most people think of Christ and His followers, they think of feminine values. People think of Jesus as having the values that come naturally to a woman. Thus, true disciples of Jesus should adopt values that are commonly found in women while rejecting those most often found in men.

Dr. Woody Davis of TEAMinistries studied this issue more formally. Davis "conducted a series of focus groups to identify the primary themes of the Christian faith. The ten most mentioned responses all came from American culture's feminine set, including such themes as support, nurture, humility and dependence."[1] There's widespread agreement among the religious and the irreligious that to be a Christian is to embrace feminine values.

Tell me, when did feminine gifts become synonymous with Christian goodness? Early Christians were known for risk taking, power, aggression, and heroic sacrifice. But somewhere in church history, somebody monkeyed with the definition of a Christian! Today, a *good Christian* is known mostly for meekness, sensitivity, passivity, and sweetness. This standard of Christian behavior is very tough on men (even those who are sold out to Jesus) while it's easier for women to achieve. Men have gotten this message: *you're flawed the way God made you. You need an extreme makeover.*

And we wonder why men hate going to church.

CHURCH: ISN'T IT A MEN'S CLUB?

For years the experts have told us the church is a men's club. Feminists condemn the church as hierarchical and male dominated. Academics view the church as too patriarchal. Reformers complain that the language of the Bible and hymns is sexist and excludes women. Liberals accuse certain churches of oppressing women by refusing to allow them to become pastors or elders. The media have a field day anytime the word *submission* is uttered by a church leader.

Perhaps you've heard the story of the blind men who tried to describe an elephant. Each man based his description on the part he happened to touch. In the same way, the church can be seen as either male or female dominated. If you look at the relatively thin stratum of professional clergy, then the church *is* male dominated. But if you look at lay leadership, lay participation, and ideal Christian values, Christianity is female dominated. The church is a peculiar organization, led by males, but dominated by women and their values. Dr. Leon Podles says it well: "Modern churches are women's clubs with a few male officers."[2]

One time my wife baked a chocolate cake and set it on the counter with a note next to it: "Dig In!" Chocolate and I have a special relationship, so I quickly grabbed a knife and cut into the rich brown frosting. To my horror, I found a white cake lurking beneath. The church is like that cake. It looks male dominated on the surface, but inside it's feminine in every way. Men like Greg and Cliff plunged their knives into the cake, found no chocolate, and withdrew.

To be truly healthy, a church must be marble cake. You know, white and chocolate mixed throughout the batter. Every congregation needs a generous helping of both *the feminine spirit* and *the masculine spirit*. You see this balance in the churches that are growing today. A masculine concern for quality, effectiveness, and achievement pervades everything they do. Yet they are supportive, nurturing, and tender with people.

THE FEMININE SPIRIT AND THE MASCULINE SPIRIT

What do I mean by feminine spirit and masculine spirit? Here's an example: the world of sports is steeped in the masculine spirit. The core values of sports are competition, achievement, and victory. On the other hand, elementary education is steeped in the feminine spirit. Its core values are harmony, cooperation, and nurture.

The feminine spirit is a wonderful thing. A healthy church has to have it. But most churches today are out of balance, brimming with the feminine spirit while short on the masculine spirit. Men sense this and withdraw.

When the masculine spirit shows up in church, Christians and non-Christians roundly condemn it. People who speak the truth too boldly are stifled because they might hurt someone's feelings. Leaders who make bold moves are accused of being power hungry. Efforts to make the church more efficient or effective are tabled in the name of harmony. Churches that set specific goals and measure achievement are looked down upon for being too focused on numbers. And how many times have you heard this chestnut: "the church is run too much like a business"?

Again, to be absolutely clear about two things: first, the return of the masculine spirit does not mean male domination. Nor is it an angry, finger-pointing, pulpit-pounding Christianity. No, there is a life-giving side to the masculine spirit that is missing in the church today. Congregations need masculine strength, nobility, and resolve. Second, the answer is *not* the triumph of the masculine spirit over the feminine. A church must have both. A shortage of one or the other leads to abuse.

TOO MUCH MASCULINE SPIRIT OR FEMININE SPIRIT LEADS TO SPIRITUAL ABUSE

A church with too much masculine spirit succumbs to legalism. It's all about performance—what you do for God. There's often a pastor who rules the congregation with an iron fist. There are silly rules, frustrating rituals, and simplistic black-and-white answers that don't work in the real world. It's about fear, not grace. Salvation is a free gift, but everything else must be earned.

A legalistic church can foster horrific abuse. I have a friend who was being physically and verbally abused by her husband. She went to the elders of her church for help. These men read her Scripture and accused her of "being under the influence of a spirit of rebelliousness." They told her to "go home and submit to your husband." They did not rebuke the man; he continued to enjoy his position within the church.

Since too much masculine spirit has the potential to create this kind of abuse, one might think the solution is to reject the masculine in favor of a feminine spirit. Yet this leads to another kind of abuse I call *Velvet*

Coffin Christianity: show up on Sunday, participate in comforting rituals, listen to a pabulum sermon of familiar truths; then go home and forget all about your faith until next Sunday. Velvet Coffin Christianity is rampant in America today. After Cynthia Woolever and Deborah Bruce surveyed more than one million churchgoers, they reported that "half of all worshippers say they are not growing in their faith."[3] I suspect the true figure is 75 to 80 percent; after all, would you admit to a pollster that you were not growing in your faith?

Legalism makes the headlines, but Velvet Coffin Christianity is the real cancer in the church today. Its key characteristic is comfort. Everyone is so nice to each other. And we choose a church based on how comfortable it makes us feel. I wish I had a dollar for every conversation I've heard like this one:

CORRINE: Why did you choose First Church, Mary?

MARY: I'm so comfortable here. Everyone is so nice to me and the kids. The pastor is so nice.

Men gag on this kind of religion. It's angel food cake, soft, spongy, and unsatisfying. It does not reflect the wildness of Jesus. Everywhere Christ went, He created uproar and discomfort. He made it a point to insult people (Matt. 23:13–39). He even called His best friend "Satan" (Mark 8:33). (That was a horrendous insult, akin to calling a Holocaust survivor "Hitler.") Although He comforted the needy, an encounter with Jesus was often an uncomfortable experience, especially for religious people.

Is Velvet Coffin Christianity really abuse? Yes, just as legalism is abuse. People don't see it as such because it's not sensational or salacious. It doesn't make good gossip. It feels so nice. But it's abuse nonetheless. Churches are comforting Christians to death, because the feminine spirit has taken over and the masculine spirit has withdrawn. In time, so do men.

THE PROBLEM WITH TOO MUCH FEMININE SPIRIT

Men like Cliff and Greg resist church because it has a feminine spirit. From the moment they walk into the building, it doesn't feel right to them. They don't know why, but their spirits cry: *You're out of place! Get away!* It's that same uncomfortable feeling a man gets when his wife tricks him into visiting the women's apparel department at Sears.

> WOMAN: Honey, hold my purse while I try on these blouses. You can sit on this little stool.

Guys, you know what I'm talking about. You've sat on that stool: a hard metal plate covered with a tattered velvet cushion. You've looked around at the racks of brassieres, blouses, skirts, and the mannequin having a bad hair day. The women's apparel department is an environment with a feminine spirit. It is designed by women, for women. You do not belong there. What's worse, if you gaze into the distance, you can see a place with a masculine spirit—the power tools department—but because you're holding a purse, you can't get there!

The church's feminine spirit causes a lot of men to believe deep in their hearts that Christianity is not for them. Dr. Woody Davis asked one hundred men why they didn't go to church. Their number one response: "Church is for women, children, and wimps." Author and pastor Gordon Dalbey notes, "The current lack of male participation in our churches seems clear testimony that men will not be tamed by a program based exclusively upon feminine virtues."[4] Men will gladly be tamed by an organization with a masculine spirit, however. The military, sports teams, and even street gangs have no problem attracting enthusiastic men. These organizations feel right to men. Church does not.

WHAT YOU CAN DO

How do we get the masculine spirit back in our churches? You've just taken the first step: realizing the so-called male dominance in the church is only frosting deep. I said it in chapter 1, and I'll say it again: *too often it's not what the leadership imposes but what the laity demands that causes the church to repel men.* If your vision of church is a place of comfort, safety, and loving affirmation, realize that your vision may be keeping men away. Pray and ask God to give you a bigger vision of what it means to follow Jesus—a vision that welcomes the risky, unpredictable, masculine spirit.

5

ADJUSTING
THE THERMOSTAT

As we learned earlier, every church has a spiritual thermostat. Where it is set will determine whether that body attracts or repels men. Here are six common settings found in today's congregations:

Challenge

Confrontation   **Comfort**

Conformity   **Ceremony**

Control

The three settings atop the thermostat represent the methods of Jesus. Christ *confronted* the religious, and He *comforted* the needy. But He *challenged* everyone else. Challenge was the Master's default setting. That was why men loved Jesus: men love to be challenged. But Jesus hated the bottom three settings—and so do men. These were favorites of Pharisees.

If a church wants to reach men, its bread and butter must be challenging people to follow Christ. Challenge is men's love language. Should churches comfort people and confront them as the need arises? Absolutely, but these cannot be the modus operandi. A church too focused on comforting or confronting will repel men. Churches focused on ceremony, control, or conformity will do even worse attracting males. Let's go around the dial for a description of each setting.

THERMOSTAT SET ON COMFORT

Rick Warren calls these *family reunion churches,* and he estimates about 80 percent of America's congregations fall into this category.[1] The greatest commandment in comforting churches is *be nice.* The pastor's job is to keep the peace. Keep 'em happy and in the pews. We please God by getting along with each other, living a decent life, and being a family of God. Although you won't hear this preached, it's the reality in hundreds of thousands of American congregations.

A church based on comfort focuses inward on the family that meets within the walls of the church. The pastor can preach a challenging sermon, but not too challenging, or people will become uncomfortable. Barna Research found that only half of America's churchgoers frequently leave the worship service feeling challenged to change.[2] And most Christians would never think of challenging each other. That would be rude! Members talk about getting out into the world and making a difference, but few actually do it.

Men have a hard time in comforting churches because they feel smothered. It's Velvet Coffin Christianity. Everything is so easy. So sweet. So nice. Nothing great is asked of men, so that is what they give— nothing.

THERMOSTAT SET ON CEREMONY

Push the thermostat past comfort, and you find ceremony, an extreme form of comfort. We please God by performing certain rituals. Familiar sacraments, prayers, and traditions are the keys to a successful worship service. The true (yet unspoken) purpose of church is not to change the world; it is to preserve tradition.

Rituals and tradition are deeply meaningful to some men, especially those who grew up in high churches. But most liturgical churches do a pitiful job reaching unchurched men, who are drawn to the practical rather than the mystical. As Chip MacGregor puts it, "Men want reality, not more ritual."[3]

Even nonliturgical churches can become ceremonial. I heard of a Baptist pastor who was nearly fired when he failed to offer an altar call after his Wednesday night message. Never mind that everyone in the small crowd was already a Christian. Any church can become fixated on its particular ceremonies.

THERMOSTAT SET ON CONTROL

The polar opposite of challenge is control. Churches exert two kinds of control:

Feminine control. These churches control their people through guilt. Men who grew up in church often level this complaint. "They were constantly sending me on a guilt trip," said Jerry. "After every service I felt beat up, like I was wicked and evil."

Masculine control. The pastor or his inner circle controls everything. There are rules, rules, and more rules. Words such as *authority* and *submission* are tossed about. It is a toxic environment for men because they despise being controlled.

THERMOSTAT SET ON CONFORMITY

Conformity is a form of control, though not quite so invasive. In conformity churches everyone is expected to do the same things, read the same version of the Bible, practice the same spiritual disciplines, hold the same political beliefs, and on and on.

Rod Cooper asks, "Have you ever played Nintendo? That's a conformity environment if there ever was one. There are certain rules and you had better follow them. If you don't, you're immediately punished. You may lose points; you may lose a 'life.' Lose enough lives and you're done—game over. The Pharisees would have loved it!"[4] Men will not thrive in a Nintendo church environment, full of pitfalls, gotchas, and other traps. Christ came to liberate men, not crush them.

THERMOSTAT SET ON CONFRONTATION

Now we're getting close. Jesus used confrontation a lot. But some churches go beyond Jesus' example and hammer their parishioners with a weekly broadsheet of sins they need to avoid. Right doctrine and theology are of paramount importance—our church is right; everyone else is going to hell. It's us versus a world of sinners.

There are times when confrontation is good and necessary. But confrontation should be done one-on-one or in a small group of close friends, not from the pulpit. And it must be done in love, by people who really know the one being confronted. Rod Cooper points out that "a man doesn't mind being confronted with the truth when he knows that those who confront him will be with him when he has to face reality and make painful changes. Confrontation without commitment leads to destruction."[5]

THERMOSTAT SET ON CHALLENGE

Nestled between confrontation and comfort is the sweet spot for men. A church that challenges its members without overconfronting or over-comforting will attract guys. But this is rare.

What are the marks of a challenging church? It casts a specific vision of greatness before its people. Ministry is constantly pushed outward into the world. Challenging churches are constantly raising up leaders, to foster a culture of person-to-person challenge. It's a little bit comforting and a little bit confronting.

How is it comforting? A challenging church is loving with people, providing consolation during times of sorrow. It stresses God's grace, not His anger. It does not coerce people or make them feel guilty, but always invites people to join the adventure.

How is it confronting? Teaching is direct and to the point. Leaders set high standards and ask much of the congregation. Christians are expected to live exemplary lives, but teachers do not nag people or focus too much on specific sins, depending instead on the Holy Spirit to convict and correct.

Make things too comfortable for a man, and he'll lose interest. Try to control a man, and he'll rebel. Overconfront him, and he'll resent you as a nag. But challenge him the way Jesus challenged the disciples, and he will grow. A church that challenges its members is a church where men can thrive.

CHALLENGE: NOT JUST FROM PASTORS

Of course, pastors must offer challenging sermons, but this is not enough. If we are serious about reaching men, laypeople must foster a culture of person-to-person challenge. Two Scriptures come to mind:

> As iron sharpens iron, so one man sharpens another. (Prov. 27:17 NIV)

> Let us consider how we may spur one another on toward love and good deeds. (Heb. 10:24 NIV)

Challenge can't come just from the pulpit. A properly set thermostat requires Christians to challenge each other. But this is rare in church today. Gallup found that less than a third of churchgoers strongly agreed with this statement: "In the last six months, someone in my congregation has talked to me about the progress of my spiritual growth."[6] No, Christians mostly comfort each other with small talk.

Why are we so reluctant to challenge each other, as the Bible prescribes? It's considered rude. Let's say a man you barely knew approached you at church and said, "Do you have any unconfessed sin in your life?" You'd probably be offended, and rightly so. It's none of his business. But let's say you heard the same question from a trusted friend who'd agreed to hold you accountable. Such probing is not offensive; it's the key to spiritual growth!

How do we create a culture of challenge in the pews? How do we create rich relationships where people feel free to challenge each other? It's time to rediscover *discipleship*.

Discipleship is probably the most misunderstood word in the church today. Here's a simple definition: *discipleship is people leading each other to maturity in Christ*. As the Bible says, it's one person sharpening another.

It's a band of brothers spurring each other on toward love and good deeds. It is the model left to us by Jesus.

THE MODERN CHURCH HAS ABANDONED THE DISCIPLESHIP MODEL

Today's evangelical church has discarded the *discipleship model* in favor of an *academic model*. Instead of discipling people, we teach them. We put people in classrooms and present them with Bible knowledge. We offer a weekly lecture (sermon) from an educated person with a seminary degree. As for laymen, the more you know, the more accurate your doctrine, the more God is pleased. Christianity is something that happens inside your mind.

Why is this academic approach to faith so discouraging to men? Simple. Men are less comfortable in a classroom. Figures from the U.S. Department of Education indicate that women are more likely than men to go to college and earn 57 percent of all the BA degrees and 58 percent of the master's degrees.[7] Boys drop out of high school at a rate 30 percent higher than that of girls.[8] Girls outnumber boys 124 to 100 in advanced placement courses.[9] Ninety percent of the expulsions from British grammar schools are boys.[10]

We cannot expect men to come to maturity in Christ in a classroom environment. Although reading, study, sermons, and classes can help, these academic exercises cannot penetrate to the hidden places in a man's heart. But discipleship can, because it's teaching by example. Christ didn't hand out a study guide; He demonstrated a life pleasing to God. His example, even more than His words, produced eleven men who shook the world. That is why a man who has sat in church for thirty years without much life change will be suddenly transformed after going on a mission trip. *Men are changed by what they experience, not necessarily by what they are told.*

Discipleship in the local church takes many forms. It may be a small group with a regular meeting time, or a one-to-one between believers over coffee at Denny's. The common denominator: it's not one smart person imparting knowledge to the masses; it's one follower helping another. Or it's a band of believers sharing their lives and following

Jesus *as a team.* These are the ancient ways of propagating the Christian faith. Less efficient, but more effective.

We think that any small gathering of Christians is an example of discipleship. Not so. Genuine discipleship takes place only when the members of the group are *spurring one another on.* A spur in the flank hurts! When iron sharpens iron, sparks fly! They must know each other deeply, trust each other implicitly, and be willing to speak the truth even when it hurts.

Men learn by example. We can preach and teach until we are hoarse, but men will not mature in Christ until we rediscover discipleship. We cannot simply graft discipleship onto our existing model of church; we must build the new church upon it.

At the conclusion of the gospel of Matthew, Jesus gave His followers three responsibilities: "Go therefore and make disciples of all the nations, baptizing them in the name of the Father and of the Son and of the Holy Spirit, teaching them to observe all things that I have commanded you" (28:19–20). Our orders are simple: (1) make disciples, (2) baptize them, and (3) teach them to obey Christ's commands. Today's church has reversed this process. We teach a lot of people, baptize some, but produce very few genuine disciples. What can you do?

First, be discipled. Come under the guidance of another more mature Christian (of your gender) and ask him or her to disciple you for a short time. Ask for mentoring in a specific area.

If there are already discipleship groups in your church where folks truly challenge each other, get involved. If there aren't any, start one. I recommend single-gender groups (for reasons I'll explain in Part 5). For a list of helpful books on the subject, please visit my Web site, www.churchformen.com.

A number of America's most dynamic churches are discipleship based. Every member is expected to be a part of a discipleship group, and participation runs 70 to 90 percent. Seek out these churches, and observe their model. A church so involved in true discipleship can't help having its thermostat set on challenge.

6

MEN: WHO NEEDS 'EM?

CHURCH INVOLVEMENT IS GOOD FOR MEN. BUT SINCE WHEN do men do what's good for them? Men regard churchgoing like a prostate exam; it's something that can save their lives, but it's so unpleasant and invasive, they put it off. Others see the worship service as their weekly dose of religion, a bitter elixir one must swallow to remain healthy, but not something to look forward to.

So men avoid church—and suffer for it. Men are more likely than women to be arrested, die violently, commit and be victims of crimes, go to jail, and be addicted. They also die more often on the job, have more heart attacks, commit suicide in greater numbers, and live shorter lives than women. I could go on.

If men want to avoid these pathologies, they should go to church. A study by the Heritage Foundation found that churchgoers are more likely to be married and express a higher level of satisfaction with life. Church involvement is the most important predictor of marital stability and happiness. It moves people out of poverty. It's also correlated with less depression, more self-esteem, and greater family and marital happiness.[1] Religious participation leads men to become more engaged husbands and fathers.[2] Teens with religious fathers are more likely to say that they enjoy spending time with their dads and that they admire them.[3]

Obviously, men need the church. But does the church need men?

Honestly, men don't play a large role in the spiritual life of the church. They don't volunteer or contribute much. If every man (except the pastor) left on a weekend retreat, the church's ministries would probably chug along with women covering a few empty slots. But imagine the chaos if every woman took Sunday off!

Heck, maybe the church *would* be better off without men! Men are always making messes and getting people upset. They are not as outwardly caring or as biblically literate as women. Some men become power hungry, controlling, or even abusive. And there are always a couple of men who criticize the pastor's every move or think they could do a better job in the pulpit. So why not leave the church to women? Why even try to get men back?

Because the church *needs* men. After studying religion in America for more than fifty years, George Gallup concludes, "Women may be the backbone of a congregation, but the presence of a significant number of men is often a clear indicator of spiritual health."[4] Jack Hayford notes that "if the church is to reach its maximum potential, men must find their places in God's economy."[5] Women alone cannot constitute the body of Christ.

But men have gotten the message that the church does not need them. How did this happen? First, let's look at the way most churches deploy their volunteers. Here is a typical local church's job board:

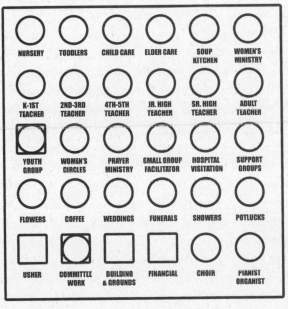

Generally speaking, men's gifts and abilities do not match the ministry needs of the typical American congregation. Men are square pegs, trying to fit into a sea of round holes.

You may be thinking, *What do you mean round holes? Men are welcome in every one of those positions!* It's a question not of welcome, but of expertise. Most jobs in the church require verbal and relational skills that men may not possess. They demand proficiency with children, music, teaching, hospitality, or cooking, areas where women typically have more experience. A woman is so much more valuable in church than a man because her natural gifts and life experiences enable her to fill so many slots.

Here's an example: Scott and Nancy are visiting the statistically average eighty-four-member congregation. After the service Pastor Mark practically jumps over a pew to greet Nancy because she's a potential nursery worker, Sunday school teacher, singer, cook, hospital visitor, prayer team member, or wedding and funeral coordinator. He largely ignores Scott because he's a potential . . . usher. Somewhere in church history the masculine roles were discarded (or assigned to professional clergy), while roles for laywomen multiplied. Women are urgently needed, but men are just accessories, like hood ornaments on cars. Nice, but not necessary.

Men want to serve in an area where they have experience and skill. Steve Sonderman says: "For many guys a huge roadblock to their serving in the church is their fear that they won't do the job right. Men fear failure."[6] This contributes to men's legendary passivity in church. Thad has gone to church for fifteen years but has never volunteered. Why? "There's nothing that really interests me," he says.

Because men don't usually possess the soft skills needed for spiritual work, they tend to gravitate toward practical ministries: building, finance, usher, and committee work. But these square holes are not the core work of the church and may even be regarded as necessary evils that are less important than the round holes. Tell me, what's more vital to God's kingdom: the financial team or the prayer team? Which is the truly *spiritual* work of the church? The job board is another subtle way we tell laymen they are a cut below laywomen.

Church-based social service is often a poor fit for men. Human services such as hospital visitation, soup kitchens, and care for the sick have been the responsibility of women for centuries. Ceremonial events such as weddings and funerals have also been the domain of women. Men often feel uncomfortable, unskilled, or even emasculated in these roles.

Meanwhile, men feel that the church does not need their natural gifts unless they happen to be exceptionally verbal, sensitive, or musical. Russell Rainey asked a number of men why they didn't go to church. A common response: "There's nothing for me to do." Nothing to do? Are they crazy? Aren't churches always scrambling for volunteers? Yet men say there's nothing for them to do! How can they possibly believe this? Rainey continues, "When you ask them, 'Why don't you do something in the church?' they'll say, 'Well, I'm not a preacher, and I've been an usher.'" These men believe the local church offers only two gender-appropriate roles. And it's a big jump from usher to preacher!

Men are not spiritually lazy, as some have suggested. Men want to serve God. The problem is, the modern church does not need men's gifts, or holds them in contempt, equating them with sin! What if Mary had viewed the gifts of the wise men this way?

WISE MAN: Greetings! We bring you gifts from the East.

MARY: Wonderful. (unwraps gifts) What are they?

WISE MAN: Gold, frankincense, and myrrh.

MARY: Phew! I'll take the gold, but you can keep this smelly stuff.

This is how the church treats men. We love men's gold, but we have no use for their *smelly stuff.* Competition? Goal orientation? Performance? Power? These things stink up the church! I challenge you to answer this question: How might a man use these kinds of gifts in your congregation? Your brain probably hurts just thinking about it.

Because the church does not need men's gifts, they feel rejected. George Barna interviewed Al Perkins, a nominal churchgoer:

When you reject the things I stand for—excellence, strategic thinking, progress, efficiency, vision, controlled risks, bottom-line performance— you reject me. I used to take it personally, but I've minimized the anger by making my church involvement less of a priority.[7]

John Gray warns, "Not to be needed is slow death for a man."[8] You crush a man's spirit when you reject his gifts. So how can we make men feel needed again?

- *Tell them!* In *The Lord of the Rings,* Frodo stumbled many times on his journey to Mordor, but the words of Lady Galadriel kept him going: "This task was appointed to you, and if you do not find a way, no one will." Men need to hear a similar message when they come to church: "We need you desperately. God has a sacred role just for you, and if you do not do your part, all is lost." Think of the men in your congregation. Do they know how important they are? Has anyone ever told them? Have the women of your church ever hosted a dinner for the men to let them know how *needed* they are?

- *Jettison the job board approach to ministry.* The job board keeps Christians of both genders from using their gifts. Less than half of America's churchgoers strongly agree with the statement: "In my congregation, I regularly have the opportunity to do what I do best."[9]

- *Fit the role to the person, not vice versa.* Al Winseman recommends, "Instead of creating roles and then finding people to fit those roles, congregation leaders should start with the person and then define the role."[10] Deploying people in their areas of giftedness changes lives.

- *Expand ministry into areas where men have expertise.* I will offer some specific ideas in chapter 22, "Ministry and the Masculine Spirit."

- *Take an inventory of your gifts; then think of creative ways to deploy them for God's kingdom.* Encourage others to do the same. Refuse to take a job you feel unqualified or uncalled to perform, no matter how worthy the cause or urgent the need.

MINISTRY TO MEN IS OFTEN THE LOWEST PRIORITY

The church and the *Titanic* have something in common: it's women and children first. The great majority of ministry in Protestant churches is focused on children, next on women, and then, if there are any resources left, on men.

I have a confession to make: I used to believe in the children-first approach. It's so logical. If a young person receives Christ, she has her whole life ahead of her to influence the world. Statistics show young people are easier to convert than adults. At least two studies reported that most born-again adults received Christ during their teenage years.[11] Barna Research found most Americans decide what they believe by the time they are thirteen, and those beliefs change little in adulthood.[12]

Raising children in the faith (particularly the children of church-goers) is now the de facto purpose of many a congregation. In the typical Protestant church, more than 40 percent of the people ministered to during the week are children.[13] This is an almost unbelievable figure, given that married couples with children are the minority profile in church today, and a majority of churchgoers have no children at home.[14]

It's important to reach young people with the good news, but today's kids-first church is a radical departure from Christianity's historical mission. Keep in mind that neither Sunday school nor youth ministry even existed two centuries ago. In those days kids were loved, but they weren't the focus of church. Today they are. In many a church the nursery, Sunday school, and the youth group are the three largest ministries (after the worship service) in terms of volunteers deployed. What's the biggest outreach of the year in nearly every evangelical church? Vacation Bible school.

Instead of trying to reach adults with the gospel, today's church has adopted what I call *the McDonald's approach:* reach the children in order to reach the parents. Renee Evans writes, "Churches can take a lesson from the fast-food giant: If you make an impact on kids, you can reach their parents. McDonald's makes 40% of its sales on Happy Meals."[15]

The McDonald's approach feels right to a woman because it lavishes ministry resources on her top priority: her children and grandchildren.

And it works. Focusing on children *can* create transfer growth. My years as a church elder confirmed that women will switch churches based on the quality of the children's programs.

But this is one more way men get the message that church is not for them. If church is all about children, a man will tend to see it as his wife's responsibility, not his. We have millions of men like Frank. "I go to church because my kids need moral instruction," he says. "There are lots of bad influences out there, and they need the lessons the church provides." But Frank is utterly passive in church—simply attending services and nothing more—because he sees it as something for his children, not for him.

Our feverish focus on children may also be driving teens away from an enduring commitment to Christ. Many studies have shown a sharp drop-off in church attendance as soon as kids leave the nest. Perhaps we've done such a good job of linking church with childhood that teens, wanting to be grown-up, toss Christianity into the same dumpster as LEGOs and Barbie dolls. This is especially true for boys. Does it have to be this way? I believe much of this apostasy could be avoided if only young people saw their fathers following Jesus. As the father goes, so goes the family.

In most churches, women's ministry is the church's next priority. One day I was browsing a catalog of ministry offerings at a large church. This congregation offered *eight pages* of ministry to and for women: women's Bible studies, women's prayer circles, women's retreats, women's teas, MOPS groups, women's support groups, on and on. The men's ministry page—excuse me, *half page*—offered two options: a monthly men's breakfast and an annual retreat. This church had two full-time ministers to women, but no minister to men. Why the huge disparity? Probably because women sign up for things and men don't. Nevertheless, this eight-to-one ratio of ministry offerings sends a powerful message to guys: *church is for women, not for you.*

JESUS' APPROACH TO MINISTRY

What's wrong with the women-and-children-first focus of today's church? After all, men aren't very interested. Why should Christians knock themselves out to minister to men? Simple. Because Jesus did. Jesus did not focus His ministry on children, or women for that matter. Jesus' approach was *men first.*

I know I lost a lot of you with that last sentence. Some of you may have thrown the book across the room. Before World War III breaks out, let me say that Jesus loved women and children. He welcomed women and children. He blessed women and children. He made it clear that they were equal in every way to men—*perhaps even greater than men* ("whoever humbles himself as this little child is the greatest in the kingdom of heaven" [Matt. 18:4]). Women were among His most faithful followers; children were among His greatest joys.

But Jesus did not focus His ministry on women and children. Nor did He command us to. His example is clear: if we want to change the world, we must focus on men. Not to the exclusion of women and children—however, the spiritual development of men must become our top priority.

How have we missed this?

Perhaps you're thinking, *Well, that was the first century. The Jewish culture of Jesus' day was male centered. This would have made discipling of women and children unacceptable.* Makes sense until you consider that Jesus broke just about every relational taboo of His day. Remember the stir He caused by dining with sinners? How shocked the disciples were to find Him speaking to a Samaritan woman? How surprised the crowds were to see Him touching a leper? Challenging the prevailing culture was His specialty!

If Christ had intended women and children to be the primary focus of the church, He would have set up a women's circle and a Sunday school. Instead, He focused like a laser on a ragtag band of twelve men. I think He did this for two reasons. First, Jesus knew that men play an indispensable role in His body. When men are absent or anemic, the body withers. Second, I suppose Jesus knew His message would resonate with women. It was obviously more feminine than the ruthlessly masculine legalism of the Pharisees. Patrick Arnold writes:

> Christianity was and is distinctive among Western religions in its high valuation of feminine religious qualities. Its worship centers around the

domestic motif of the Eucharistic meal, and its morality encourages meekness, humility and even a certain passivity. The irony in all this is that, though the early Christians focused on the newness of the feminine gifts, they displayed thoroughly masculine qualities in promoting their new doctrine! Masculinity is assumed in early Christianity and shoots through the whole New Testament like an electric charge: Jesus' bold confrontations with the Pharisees, Peter's courageous leadership of the new sect, Paul's aggressive missionary strategy, and so on. Most of the first generation was martyred for its beliefs—hardly a mark of the meek and mild! And though one is hard put to find a New Testament text urging Christians to the masculine values of aggressiveness, independence, bravery, or resistance to injustice, these are precisely the qualities these people displayed in the face of Jewish and Roman oppressiveness.[16]

Arnold has brought one of Christianity's great paradoxes into clear focus: while Christian values tend to be perceived as feminine, they must be lived out in an aggressive, masculine fashion.

This is why the church needs men. Men's natural gifts are just that, gifts to the church. They are not sins in need of repentance. God didn't foul up when He made guys. He made men the way they are because we need what they've got. Just as a flu shot causes momentary pain but promotes long-term health, the exercise of masculine gifts may cause a congregation to be momentarily less nurturing, tender, and supportive. However, over the long term, men's "go for it" spirit promotes health in many different ways.

HOW MEN'S GIFTS PROMOTE CHURCH HEALTH

Men's Expansionist Outlook Promotes Church Health

Men make things happen. Men expand the church and its influence in the world. Richard Rohr and Joseph Martos write:

> When male energy is absent, creation does not happen, either in the human soul or in the world. Nurturance happens, support and love perhaps, but not that new "creation out of nothing" that is the unique prerogative associated with the masculine side of God.[17]

Men's Orientation Toward Risk Promotes Church Health

Men are hard-wired for risk taking. The number one killer of fifteen-to twenty-four-year-old males is accidents.[18] Men pay higher insurance premiums than women do.[19] Female investors hold less risky investment portfolios than their male counterparts and generally take fewer chances with their money.[20] Both men and women gamble, but men are more likely to bet the farm on one roll of the dice.

Jesus made it clear that risk taking is necessary to please God. In the parable of the talents (Matt. 25:14–26), the master praises two servants who invested their assets and produced more, but he curses the servant who played it safe. He who avoids all risk is, in the words of Jesus, "wicked and lazy" (v. 26). My wife, Gina, says, "Women *want* safety, but we *need* risk. We need men to lead us to greater adventure."

Men's Focus on the Outside World Promotes Church Health

The masculine spirit is naturally directed outward. Men are always building things, creating things, and subduing the earth. A man may not feel complete until he has left his mark on the world. The dark side of this tendency is that men get wrapped up in their careers and neglect their families. They scar the earth and fail to build relationships.

But men's outward focus is a gift to the church. Without a masculine spirit the church turns inward. It begins to minister primarily to *the family in here* instead of *the world out there.* Today most churches do little outreach, preferring to wait for the world to come to them. Few give more than a tiny percentage of their budgets to world missions.

Men's Concern with the Rules Promotes Church Health

Women tend to exalt relationships over rules. Men tend to exalt rules over relationships. Isn't this legalism? Didn't Jesus value people over the rules? Of course, but He made it quite clear that rules have their place. Christ said, "Don't suppose that I came to do away with the Law and the Prophets. I did not come to do away with them, but to give them their full meaning" (Matt. 5:17 CEV). He warned those who would abandon the rules, "If you reject even the least important command in the Law and teach others to do the same, you will be the least important person in the kingdom of heaven" (Matt. 5:19 CEV).

Without rules heresy creeps into the church. Several mainline denominations are debating whether to abandon scriptural commands so everyone can feel loved and accepted. This is a battle between the masculine
spirit and the feminine spirit, written large.

Men's Pragmatism Brings Innovation to the Church

Men are always trying to improve things. They're tinkerers. They
like to open the hood and adjust things to get maximum performance.
A generation ago men like Rick Warren and Bill Hybels asked, "How
can we do church better?" They opened the hood and tinkered with the
mechanics of the worship service. The results are Saddleback and
Willow Creek, two of the most dynamic churches in the world. Two
churches that have scads of committed men.

Men Bring Strength to the Church

Edwin Louis Cole said, "You can derive spirituality from women in
the church, but you get strength from the men."[21] Not a very politically
correct statement, but what does your experience tell you? Doesn't the
presence of spiritually alive men bring strength to the body? Gordon
Dalbey notes, "A unique and truly awesome power arises when men
gather together: the power which God gives especially to men collectively, to get His work done in the world."[22]

Men Bring Money to the Church

A straight-shooting pastor once told me, "When she comes to church
and he doesn't, you get the tithe off the grocery money. When they
come together, you get the tithe off the paycheck." A Gallup study found
that people who are actively engaged in their local church give three
times as much as those who are disengaged.[23] Conceivably, a church
could triple its contributions just by engaging men.

Godly Men Attract Women

Twenty-eight-year-old Sabrina from Australia says, "There's something sexy about a man who's following after God." Bruce Barton points
out, "Women are not drawn by weakness. The sallow-faced, thin-lipped,
so-called spiritual type of man may awaken maternal instinct, stirring

an emotion which is half regard, half pity."[24] Without dynamic, life-giving men, a church will eventually lose its women as well, especially the younger ones.

Men Bring Their Families to Church

Here's an oft-quoted statistic in men's ministry circles: when a mother comes to faith in Christ, the rest of her family follows 17 percent of the time. But when a father comes to faith in Christ, the rest of the family follows 93 percent of the time.[25] I've seen it time and again. When a man encounters Christ, his family follows.

There's a beautiful picture of this in Acts 16. Paul and Silas shared the gospel with their jailer. The man was instantly changed. He immediately took the apostles to his house, where they shared Christ with his family. Before the night was through, the entire household was baptized and following Jesus. In the Bible, fathers lead their children to God, not the other way around.

Curtis Burnam, a twenty-year veteran of youth ministry, identifies a clear relationship between a dad's participation in church and his children's participation in youth group. "Kids who are taken to church by mom but not dad are harder to keep in church," he says. "They tend to drop out at higher rates when they reach adolescence. They are also harder to engage when they do come to youth group. This is true for girls as well as boys."

IF CHRISTIANITY IS TO SURVIVE, WE NEED MEN!

Christianity is still growing worldwide, but it is losing ground to two aggressive competitors: secularism and Islam. At the risk of sounding alarmist, I believe the church has at most 250 years before it is totally overrun by this duo—unless we reengage men.

Secularism is the de facto religion in much of Europe today. Rationalism, materialism, anarchy, and radical environmentalism are a few of its common guises. It's on the rise in America as well. The Graduate Center of the City University of New York found the number of adults who say they subscribe to *no religion* doubled during the 1990s. The survey "detected a wide and possibly growing swath of secularism among Americans."[26] The number of unchurched Americans (who don't attend services except for holidays or weddings/funerals) nearly doubled between 1991 and 2004.[27]

Islam is the world's fastest-growing religion, and what do you know? It's also enormously popular with men. Since 1950 the number of Christians in the world has doubled, but the number of Muslims has more than tripled.[28] In the heavily Christian United Kingdom there are approximately 1 million practicing Christians and about 750,000 practicing Muslims.[29] British Muslims live their faith, while most Christians do not. During the last three decades, Islam has emerged as the second religion of Europe after Christianity.[30] It's not just growth via immigration: observers report an influx of white faces worshipping among the brown faces.[31] The tepid European church is accomplishing what the Moors could not: delivering Europe to Islam.

Islam is growing in the U.S. as well, and it has made its strongest inroads in the African-American community. More than 90 percent of the converts to Islam in the United States are African-American men, such as Suleiman Azia. He grew up in a Baptist church in Tennessee, but turned to Islam as an adult. His chief reason: his church was attended mostly by women. "In Islam I found a stronger ideal of brotherhood and moral discipline—and of manhood," Azia says.[32]

Why are secularism and Islam on the rise? I believe it is their ability to capture the hearts of men. *In spiritual matters kids tend to follow their fathers.* Throughout human history, men have been the religious leaders of society. A Christianity without significant masculine presence will atrophy and die. If something doesn't change, I fear that our great-great-grandchildren will grow up either godless or going to a mosque.

John Eldredge reminds us, "Christianity isn't a religion about going to Sunday school, potluck suppers, being nice, holding car washes, sending our secondhand clothes off to Mexico—as good as those things might be. This is a world at war. Something large and immensely dangerous is unfolding all around us."[33] Now, if you were the evil one, trying to defeat the church, what would your strategy be? Sideline the most aggressive, bold, risk-taking warriors. Make them feel unwanted, unneeded, and uncomfortable. Hide the battle beneath a veil of comforting religion.

Men have no idea how vital Christ is to the future of mankind. Nor do they realize how needed they are. Without men and their warrior spirit in the church, *all is lost*. Our job is to lift the veil of religion and call men to the battle. But not yet. Before we can call men, the church must recover its ancient, masculine voice. You will play a key role. Are you ready?

PART 2

THE THREE GENDER GAPS

There are actually three gender gaps plaguing the church today. The three gaps form an unholy trinity that is keeping men away from Christ, and sapping the life of men who do show up on Sunday.

The gap of presence. Women attend church in greater numbers than men. This is true all over the world, in nearly every branch of Christianity.

The gap of participation. Women are more serious about their faith. They are much more likely than men to participate in the life of the church beyond Sunday morning worship services. They are also more likely to practice Christian disciplines such as prayer, discipleship, and evangelism.

The gap of personality. Entire personality types are largely missing from the church. These types show up frequently in the Bible but are no-shows in today's congregations. The absence of these personalities makes it harder to attract men to our churches.

7

THE GAP OF PRESENCE

The Gap of Presence   The Gap of Participation   The Gap of Personality

THE TYPICAL AMERICAN CHURCHGOER IS A WOMAN. THE U.S.
Congregational Life Survey pegged her as a fifty-year-old, married, well-educated, employed female.[1] An ABC News/Beliefnet poll found that a worshipper is most likely an older, black female who lives in the South.[2] Figures from Census 2000 and a study by Barna Research estimate a weekly gender gap of more than 13 million in America's churches:[3]

Adult women in church	48,660,177
Adult men in church	35,348,028
Gap size	13,312,149

The U.S. Congregational Life Survey concurs: "While the U.S. population is split fairly evenly between men and women, there are more women (61%) than men (39%) in the pews. This difference is found in every age category, so the fact that women live longer than men does not explain the gender difference in religious participation."[4]

Today 20 to 25 percent of America's married, churchgoing women regularly attend without their husbands.[5] After Thom S. Rainer studied two thousand American congregations, he noted, "Most churches indicated that their members included a significant number of churched wives who were married to unchurched husbands." He told the story of a woman named Carol, who loves her Sunday school class because "every woman in the class is in the same boat I'm in. We're all married, but our husbands don't attend church."[6]

To my knowledge, there is no Christian sect or denomination in America that attracts more men than women. Various surveys have indicated anywhere from 3 to 9 percent of America's churches have more men, but in five years of research I never found such a church.[7] Rod Stark, a sociologist of religion, speculates that churches on military bases or Metropolitan Community Churches (a heavily gay denomination) might attract more men. (If you know of a church that consistently draws more men than women, please post me a message at www.churchformen.com.)

WHAT KINDS OF CHURCHES HAVE THE BIGGEST GAPS?

This section highlights some results from the National Congregations Study (NCS) of 1998. The NCS shows us what kinds of churches suffer the worst gender disparity.

To conform to the findings of the NCS, any congregation with at least 12 percent more women than men will be considered *gender gapped*. So for our purposes, a gapped congregation looks like this:

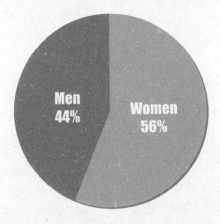

GENDER-GAPPED CHURCHES BY DENOMINATION

Percentage of congregations reporting at least a 12% gap

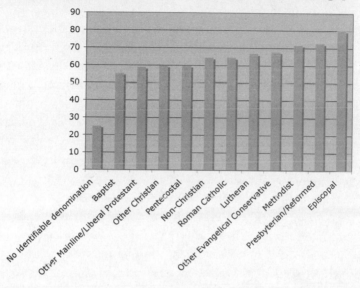

Clearly, nondenominational churches are the least likely to report a gender gap. Just 25 percent of these independent congregations report a large surplus of women. Among the major denominations, Baptists are least likely to report a gap. (Before you Baptists start celebrating, note that more than half of your congregations report a substantial gender gap.) Other Protestant, Pentecostal, and Catholic churches are more likely to be gapped, and the liberal mainline churches are the most likely to be gapped. An astounding 80 percent of Episcopal churches report a noticeable gender gap!

These numbers suggest the gender gap and church decline go hand in hand. Mainline denominations such as Lutheran, Presbyterian, Methodist, Church of Christ, and Episcopal have been hemorrhaging members for decades, and they are also very likely to be short on men. On the other hand, nondenominational churches are growing by leaps and bounds—and are much less likely to report a gap.

These figures also point to the denominational loyalty of women. Men are absenting themselves from all kinds of churches, but seem particularly disenchanted with the established denominations. In many cases faithful women are keeping the doors of these traditional churches open, but with scant male participation they seem unable to reverse the fortunes of their congregations.

The Catholic Church is having a particularly hard time attracting men. An ABC News/Beliefnet poll found that just 26 percent of U.S. Catholic men attend Mass on a weekly basis, compared to 49 percent of Catholic women.[8] This poll was taken *before* the worst allegations of sexual abuse by priests came to light.

But no one has it tougher than the traditionally black denominations. A staggering 92 percent of African-American churches in America reported a gender gap, the highest of any faith group.[9] Observers such as Edward Thompson and Jawanza Kunjufu confirm that 75 to 90 percent of the adults in the typical African-American congregation are women.[10] Contrast this to black Muslims, who are overwhelmingly male.[11] The African-American community faces the prospect of separate religions for each gender: Christianity for women, Islam for men.

Which faith groups in the U.S. have a reverse gender gap? Surveys indicate that atheists, freethinkers (a form of atheism), agnostics, Muslims, Buddhists, Jews, and *no religion* attract more men than women.[12] Food for thought.

GENDER-GAPPED CHURCHES BY YEAR OF FOUNDING

Younger churches seem somewhat more successful in attracting and retaining men. This suggests that as a church ages, it loses its men and is unable to attract more.

What causes this? Think of the needs of a young church. Start-up congregations need men's gifts. Risks must be taken. Plans must be made. Buildings must be built. Men love this stuff. They have a lot to offer a young church. But as a congregation ages, it begins to value feminine gifts such as nurturing, stability, and close-knit community. Philip Yancey notes, "I have watched a pattern time and again: a church starts off with high ideals, generates a flurry of activity, and then gradually tempers its vision, settling for something far less than ideal."[13] Women stay loyal because of the relationships they've developed, but the less relational men fall away. Men need vision—not just relation-ships—to stay motivated in church.

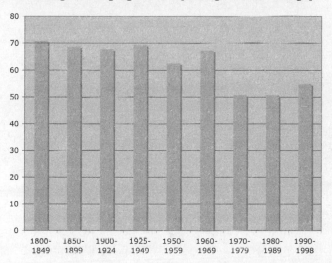

Percentage of congregations reporting at least a 12% gap

GENDER-GAPPED CHURCHES BY CONGREGATION SIZE

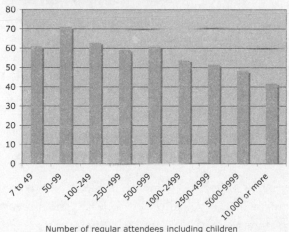

Percentage of persons in congregations reporting at least a 12% gap

Number of regular attendees including children

The typical U.S. Protestant church draws eighty-four attendees on a Sunday.[14] This is exactly the size of church most likely to report a gender gap. But as a church gets larger, the likelihood of a gap decreases.[15] This brings up a chicken-or-egg question: Do men attend because the church is large, or does the church grow large because men attend? Let's examine both sides of this question.

CHICKEN: MEN PREFER LARGE CHURCHES BECAUSE THEY ARE LARGE

Men love the quality offered by large churches. They are often led by a gifted pastor who's a talented speaker. The music is superb. The presentation is slick and polished. Men are not embarrassed to invite their friends, because they know everything will be done with taste and professionalism. Large churches have a buzz of success about them that men find attractive.

Men see their values emphasized in big churches. These congregations speak the language of risk, productivity, and growth. They become known in the community. Big churches measure effectiveness, celebrate achievement, and are constantly launching new projects and initiatives. A large church's greatest weakness—difficulty creating warmth and intimacy—is actually a plus for a lot of men.

Some cynics have suggested that men are drawn to large churches because they can hide out, simply attending Sunday worship while avoiding the pressure to get involved that might hound them in a smaller church. Others suggest that men like the anonymity of a large church. The most cynical suggest men use large churches as a business networking opportunity (hundreds of potential clients versus a handful in a typical congregation).

EGG: THE CHURCH GROWS LARGE BECAUSE OF THE PRESENCE OF SO MANY MEN

This theory suggests churches grow when they have a core of strong, committed men who are true followers of Jesus. The presence of spiritually alive men buoys the entire congregation.

Does this seem surprising to you? Christ established this pattern. He poured His life into twelve men for three years. These men drew other men. Three thousand men became followers of Jesus at Pentecost— changed not only by what they heard *but also by what they saw*: a small group of men empowered by the Holy Spirit. This is how the church grew in New Testament times, and it is no different today. Men come to Christ, and by extension, to church, when they see other men living under the influence of God's Spirit. This brings us to one of the key points in this book:

Men don't follow programs; they follow men. A woman may choose a church because of the programs it offers, but a man is looking for another man he can follow. Throughout their lives, men are transformed through encounters with inspiring men. Every successful man will tell you of a father, an uncle, a teacher, a coach, or a sergeant who made the difference in his life. The movies men love often feature an inspirational coach, commander, or teacher. Men are dying for a leader. Every man, regardless of his age, needs another man to look up to and say in his heart, *I want to be like him.*

This is why a dynamic pastor can turn a church around. Bold leadership attracts men. But even more attractive than a dynamic pastor is the sight of men in the pews who are true followers of Christ. Their mere presence in a worship service adds a crackling excitement that cannot be manufactured.

Spiritually alive men are vital to the health of a church. I've spoken to men who drive for miles to attend such churches, passing dozens of other churches along the way. Furthermore, women seem to love worshipping in the presence of transformed men. It's hard to close the gender gap in these churches, because even as men pour in, women gush in faster!

This is not to minimize the importance of godly women. Their presence is essential to church health as well. But transformed men are so precious *because they are so rare!* Every church has upright Christian women, but seeing a spiritually alive man is so unusual that people take notice. Saint Irenaeus said, "The Glory of God is a man fully alive!" When the men are unengaged, passive, or absent, the church declines. But when there's a core of spiritually alive men, the church thrives!

Have large, young, nondenominational churches found the secret to closing the gender gap? No, because these congregations still draw many more women than men. There is no branch of Western Christianity that's even close to conquering its gender gap.

THE GENDER GAP: NOT JUST AN AMERICAN PHENOMENON

The gender gap exists all over the world. Although some evidence suggests that Eastern and Greek Orthodox churches in Europe and Asia do not suffer a gender gap, every other branch of Christianity does. No variant of Catholic or Protestant church is immune. Research finds a pattern of male absence going back at least a century in the churches of England, Wales, Spain, Germany, and France. Asian, Australian, and African churches also attract more women than men on a typical weekend.[16] The gender gap now threatens to stall the explosive growth of evangelical/Pentecostal churches in Latin America. Joshua Georgen of Latin America Mission notes, "Following Jesus Christ isn't usually seen as the most macho thing for a man to profess. As a result, throughout Mexico many mothers take their children to church services alone, while their husbands remain at home." The lack of male involvement creates a vicious circle: most church leadership positions go to "well-meaning and seemingly more responsible Mexican women." But Mexico's *machista* culture makes it difficult for men to be subject to women, further eroding male participation. "Hence, the lack of male involvement has created a church in Mexico with a leadership and workforce highly skilled in reaching women and children."[17]

IS THE NUMBERS GAP A MODERN PHENOMENON?

Most people assume that the gender gap is something new. Men used to be more religious, right? Wrong. Men have been underrepresented in the church for at least seven hundred years, according to Dr. Leon Podles. Men began to withdraw from church life during the thirteenth century when a new bridal mysticism began to sweep the church. A call to weakness and passivity replaced the church's historic emphasis on struggle and self-sacrifice. The Virgin Mary took center stage. Mother church took care of everything spiritual. Medieval men simply attended Mass, took the sacraments, and paid their tithes and indulgences.

Religious men might have settled the New World, but their holy zeal did not always guarantee their presence in the pews. New England churches whose rolls go back to the 1600s show the majority of their members were always women.[18]

The gender gap became a yawning chasm in the 1800s. The great evangelist Charles Finney wrote in the 1830s: "Women composed the great majority of members in all churches." Fredric Dan Huntington, an Episcopal rector, wrote in 1856 that the church was "composed chiefly of females and aged men."[19] Even in the post Civil War Bible Belt, one observer wrote, "The altars of our churches are pitiably devoid of young men," and "There has scarce been a religious young man here in years."[20]

WHERE DID ALL THE MEN GO?

The shortage of men was partly due to new working conditions brought on by the industrial revolution. Men were working longer hours at factories and mines, some of which operated on Sundays. Others had to leave town to find work, spending long stretches away from home and their familiar parishes. Women, children, and aged men were the only ones left in church.

Clergymen, finding the pews filled with women, began to tailor their messages to them. The vengeful God of the Calvinists was supplanted with a warm, comforting Jesus who matched the sensibilities of the predominantly female congregation. One of the era's favorite hymns began, "Jesus, Lover of My Soul, Let Me to Thy Bosom Fly."[21] This romantic view of Jesus was popular with women whose husbands had little time for them. But men were repulsed by Christ as lover and had no desire to fly to His bosom.

During the Victorian era, men and women were consigned to strict gender roles, but pastors were something in between, a special class of men who were allowed to exercise feminine gifts. Pastors moved in feminine circles; preaching to women, counseling women, drinking tea and eating cakes with women. The image of the thin, weak, sissy pastor was common in literature of the day. Ann Douglas writes, "It seems highly likely that, in a period when religion was more and more the province of women, many of the young men drawn to the church were seen to be deeply attached and even similar to the women they knew best, namely their mothers."[22] Victorian women adored these effeminate, sensitive, caring men, but their husbands were not impressed. They steered clear of church as a result.

As the twentieth century dawned, women and pastors worked against male pleasures such as drinking, gambling, cursing, and whoring. Their political alliance reached its zenith in 1919 with the passage of the Eighteenth Amendment, making alcohol illegal in America. For many men that was the last straw. Surveys taken in the 1920s found a 60–40 gender gap,[23] similar to the one we find in today's church.

Then, the unexpected. After the privations of the Great Depression and World War II, prosperity returned to America. And men returned to church. The 1950s and 1960s were something of a golden era for church attendance. Americans filled the pews in historically large numbers. It's no coincidence that male involvement was also at a record high. Church growth expert Lyle Schaller's 1952 survey found adult attendance in America's mainline churches was 53 percent female, 47 percent male, mirroring the U.S. population.[24] Men went to church, and the church grew.

The 1950s and 1960s were the heyday of the so-called *builder* generation. Church buildings popped up like mushrooms after a rain. But once the paint dried, men began to get bored. There was nothing for them to do. The church of the 1960s knew nothing of discipleship and offered men no way to exercise their masculine gifts. So they began to drift. They either left the church or became spectators. Spectators became critics. Pastors bore the brunt of this criticism. The tension between men and pastors returned. Men became uninterested in church; pastors became uninterested in men.

The 1950s and 1960s were an anomaly. Men have been less interested in the Christian faith for centuries. Men have had the pulpit; women have had the pews. But even this is changing. Mainline Protestant seminaries now admit about as many women as men, and overall, more than a third of divinity students are women, a number that has been steadily rising

since the 1970s.[25] If current trends continue, women will eventually dominate the clergy, just as they have every other aspect of church life in
America. Dr. Podles predicts, "The Protestant clergy will be a characteristically female occupation, like nursing, within a generation."[26] *Newsweek*
columnist Kenneth Woodward thinks this may not be such a good idea:

> On any given Sunday, in Protestant as well as Catholic churches, there
> are always more women than men. More women than men study for
> the ministry in the major divinity schools. Most Christians do not get
> their formation in the faith from men but from women: Mom, the
> Sunday school teacher or the nun who prepares the kids for their first
> communion. As I see it, the last bastion of male presence in the church
> is the altar and the pulpit. I would hate to see the priesthood turn into
> an essentially female calling.[27]

The New Testament had its own builder generation. The Bible
records the stories of dynamic men who sacrificed everything to see
the kingdom of God built up. Their focus was not physical buildings,
but building the church into a force for positive change in the world.
The early church grew like mad, and if there was any gender gap, it
seemed to be a surplus of men rather than women, although the Bible
is not clear on this.

Nevertheless, both men and women played prominent roles in the ori-
gins of Christianity. It was a shared stage. Today men still have the lead
roles, but the supporting cast is almost totally female. That's the subject
of the next chapter.

8

THE GAP OF PARTICIPATION

The Gap of Presence · The Gap of Participation · The Gap of Personality

HOWARD HENDRICKS OF DALLAS THEOLOGICAL SEMINARY sees two kinds of people in the church: the *pillars* and the *caterpillars*. The *pillars* uphold the church with their prayers, their work, and their donations. They build the kingdom of God by the sweat of their brows. The *caterpillars* crawl in on Sunday morning, sing a few songs, listen to a sermon, and crawl out again, not to be seen for a week.

If your church is typical, most of the pillars who uphold it are female. Women are much more likely than men to devote themselves to Christianity beyond simple church attendance. Researcher George Barna found women are

- 100% more likely to be involved in discipleship.
- 57% more likely to participate in adult Sunday school.
- 56% more likely to hold a leadership position at a church (not including the role of pastor).
- 54% more likely to participate in a small group.
- 46% more likely to disciple others.
- 39% more likely to have a devotional time or quiet time.
- 33% more likely to volunteer for a church.

- 29% more likely to read the Bible.
- 29% more likely to attend church.
- 29% more likely to share faith with others.
- 23% more likely to donate to a church.
- 16% more likely to pray.[1]

Women put more faith in their religion, according to a study by the Gallup organization. American women agreed far more often than men when given these statements about their spiritual lives:[2]

	M	W
Religion is very important in my life.	48	68
I'm a member of a church or synagogue.	59	69
Religion can answer today's problems.	59	72
When making decisions, I pay attention to God.	40	56
When making decisions, I pay attention to my own views.	54	37

In addition, 38 percent of men described themselves as *spiritual but not religious* compared with just 28 percent of women, suggesting "traditional religious institutions may be somewhat less equipped to fulfill the spiritual needs of men."[3] This is further evidence that men are interested in God, but uninterested in Christianity as it's currently practiced.

The Gallup organization's Congregational Engagement Index measures the commitment of individuals to their particular faith community. Not surprisingly, 28 percent of women are fully *engaged* in the life of their church versus 21 percent of men. *Actively disengaged* members are the opposite: 24 percent of men are actively disengaged versus just 16 percent of women.[4]

The most interesting finding was that women are *more* scriptural in their beliefs than men. Barna concludes:

The survey data show that nearly half of the nation's women have beliefs which classify them as born again (46%), compared to just about one-third of men (36%). In other words, there are between 11 million and 13 million more born again women than there are born again men in the country.

Women are also more likely to share their faith with another person and to provide spiritual mentoring to others. Women are doing the legwork of evangelism today and fulfilling the Great Commission while men sit on the sidelines. Barna sums up his findings: "Women are the backbone of the Christian congregations in America."[5]

DENOMINATIONAL AND PARACHURCH ORGANIZATIONS ATTRACT MORE WOMEN

Women's organizations within churches are much stronger than their men's counterparts. Almost every Southern Baptist congregation has a WMU (Woman's Missionary Union). There is no equivalent Baptist men's organization that even comes close in size or influence. Same with the Presbyterian Women, who are active in practically every congregation in the United States. Although there is a Presbyterian Men's organization, few churches can muster enough guys to join. Nationally, the United Methodist Women outnumber the United Methodist Men 875,000 to 248,000.[6]

Bible Study Fellowship (BSF) International is the world's premier parachurch Bible study program. It offers three to five times more classes for women. Here are numbers from five states in different parts of the country:[7]

State	Women's Classes	Men's Classes
Texas	84	26
Massachusetts	3	0
Illinois	26	5
Washington	39	13
South Carolina	8	3

BSF's gender gap also shows up in different regions of the world:

Nation/Continent	Women's Classes	Men's Classes
Canada	11	3
Europe	17	2
Africa	18	11
South America	5	2
Australia	40	5
Asia	24	7

WOMEN ARE THE GREATEST PARTICIPANTS IN CHRISTIAN CULTURE AND COMMERCE

Women are more likely than men to shop at a Christian bookstore, watch a Christian TV station, or listen to Christian music. Christian retailers and media executives know this. They market and sell their products accordingly.

In every Christian bookstore in America the women's section is bigger than the men's section—usually three to four times bigger. Savvy booksellers know women buy about 75 percent of Christian products, so they work hard to create an atmosphere of femininity. The moment a man walks into a religious store he knows he's out of his element. Susan Faludi describes her visit to a Christian bookstore this way:

> The "men's" section was consigned to a back shelf . . . [It was] hopelessly outnumbered and outflanked by the pink devotional pamphlets and rose-adorned spiritual guides that lined the other shelves, frilly Bible covers and lambs-and-chicks crib ruffles that jammed the cabinets, flower-festooned jewelry and smiley-faced Jesus figurines that blanketed the display cases, out-of-focus portraits of serene homemakers sipping tea and sniffing flowers that covered the walls, and uplifting sugary music that emanated from floral jewel boxes, windup infant mobiles, and music-box-bearing stuffed animals, generating a cacophonous cross talk of treacle.[8]

A look at the Christian Booksellers Association (CBA) top one hundred Christian books shows "six titles directed to the special needs of men and 21 titles to the special needs of women. This latter category, which ranges from *Hugs for Mom* to *Bad Girls of the Bible,* reflects the fact that most buyers of CBA books are women."[9] In fact, the CBA magazine does not have a men's interest category. When Pat Morley, one of America's leading men's ministers, approached CBA about starting one, he was turned down.[10]

Not only do women read most of the Christian books; they write most of them as well. Although many of the blockbuster titles are still written by men, there are far more women writing for the church market. I recently attended a Christian writers' conference that attracted sixty-five women and five men. I felt as if I'd stumbled into the studio audience of the *Oprah* show.

Women are more likely to listen to a Christian radio station. Radio listeners in general are an exact replica of the population: 51.7 percent female, 48.3 percent male. But Christian AC radio (the format playing on most contemporary Christian music stations today) draws an audience that's 63 percent female and 37 percent male. Christian stations garner, on average, 21 percent more women listeners than mainstream stations.[11]

K-Love, America's largest syndicated Christian music radio service, with affiliates in 189 cities and towns,[12] targets its programming at eighteen- to forty-five-year-old women. The K-Love disc jockeys have created a mythical average listener, whom they call Kathy. She is a mother in her midthirties with two kids, a minivan, and a mortgage. Kathy is very busy, driving her kids to soccer practice, piano lessons, and youth group. As she drives, she listens to K-Love. Kathy's name comes up frequently during staff meetings, and the DJs make sure their on-air antics won't upset or offend her sensibilities.

Finally, women are more likely to watch Christian television than men. Barna Research found that women are the primary users of all forms of Christian media. The older the woman, the more likely she is to watch.[13]

THE GAP OF PARTICIPATION IS REAL
...AND COULD BE GETTING WORSE

Has your church experienced difficulty getting enough volunteers to run its various ministries? You are not alone. Nationwide, churches are struggling to find volunteers. Women used to have lots of time to volunteer, but with so many working (or home-schooling or taxi driving their kids) there's not much energy left for church work. George Barna sounds this note of caution:

> While women represent the lion's share of Christians and the majority of participants in religious activities, many women appear to be burning out from their intense levels of involvement. Maybe most telling has been a 22% slip in church attendance since 1991 (55% to 45%). There has also been a 21% decline in the percentage of women who volunteer to help a church (29% in 1991 and 24% in 2000). Women's monumental effort to support the work of the Christian church may be running on fumes.[14]

This may be the hidden tragedy of the gender gap: without men shouldering their share of the ministry load, women are feeling trapped, overworked, and underappreciated. Some are actually leaving the church because of these feelings.

Women cannot and should not be the pack mules of modern Christianity. Men need to take their rightful place in the church. But as we've seen, many men don't feel they *have* a rightful place in today's church. Changing that perception is the first step to bridging the gap of participation.

9

THE GAP OF PERSONALITY

The Gap of Presence

The Gap of Participation

The Gap of Personality

NOW WE BEGIN OUR EXPLORATION OF THE THIRD GAP, *THE GAP of personality*. This gap is harder to understand because it's tougher to quantify. Classifying people by their church attendance or participation habits is easier because noses can be counted. Personality types are harder to pin down.

Nevertheless, certain types of people rarely involve themselves in a local church. I call this *the gap of personality*. Although individual congregations may have a great diversity of personality types, the church in general is short on certain types of people, while it yields a bumper crop of other types. Think of the gap of personality as a triangle with three sides. We are going to explore these sides one at a time. Side one is known as *the passivity side*.

THE PASSIVITY SIDE OF THE TRIANGLE

Churchgoers are more likely to have passive personalities than the population in general, according to Dr. Mels Carbonnel, who has administered personality tests to thousands of Christians over the past twenty years. While about 62 percent of Americans have passive personalities, about 85 percent of the Christians whom Carbonnel has tested fall into the passive category.[1]

What are the implications of this imbalance? Any institution so heavily tilted toward passive personalities will itself become passive. It will tend to value tradition and stability over innovation and growth. Anyone who's served in leadership in a local church knows this is true.

In most churches passivity is a highly developed art. Tradition is revered. Change and innovation move at a glacial pace. Even the slightest change at church can make people very upset. For example, two Christian monks got into a bloody fistfight when a chair was moved from one spot to another.[2] In another tragic case a fifty-three-year-old parishioner put arsenic in the coffee at a Lutheran church, killing one man and sickening fifteen others. He was upset over talk of a merger with another congregation.[3] Every pastor can tell you stories of members who've become hysterical over minor changes to a worship service. You might say that today's church is full of *passivity activists* whose greatest energies are devoted to fighting change.

What's even more disturbing about this finding is that many of the people tested by Dr. Carbonnel are Christian leaders, such as pastors, teachers, and elders! In the secular world people with active personalities gravitate toward leadership positions. But in the church it is usually the passive who lead. A leadership crisis is hobbling the church, and a lack of bold, visionary leadership is driving men away from churches.

George Barna uncovered similar results.

"We recently interviewed more than 2400 Protestant pastors and discovered that 92% of them said they are leaders. Then we gave them the definition that we use of leadership and saw the proportion drop to less than two-thirds," Barna continued. "When we then asked if they felt that God had given them one of the spiritual gifts that relates to leading people, such as leadership, apostleship or even administration, the proportion plummeted to less than one out of four. Finally, we asked them to dictate to us the vision that they are leading people toward—that is, the very heartbeat of their ministry—we wound up in the single digits."[4]

Barna discovered that today's church is led by wonderful, loving people who are not gifted in the area of leadership. Most paid leaders in America's churches today are either teachers or musicians who may have never been trained in leadership, nor do they possess a vision for leading a congregation. It's not just paid staff. Christian leaders at every level tend to have passive personalities.

Churches led by people with passive personalities drive men away for at least two reasons:

1. Passive-led churches are very busy, but no one stops to consider whether all this busyness is achieving anything. Men would rather join the Rotary Club—at least it accomplishes something.

2. Passive-led churches are not moving toward a compelling vision—and according to Proverbs, "Where there is no vision, the people perish" (29:18 KJV).

Men want to devote themselves to something that's effective, not something that's going to make them busy. Many women will put up with passive leadership out of loyalty, but most men will not. Men are achievement oriented and have little tolerance for a team that always plays defense and never plays offense.

THE LOW M SIDE OF THE TRIANGLE

Studies show that men who are interested in Christianity have a less masculine outlook on life than other men. I call this tendency *low M*. The church has a reputation for attracting gentle, sensitive, bookish guys who are less masculine than average.

Is there any truth to this? Dr. Leon Podles cites a study by psychologists Lewis M. Terman and Catharine Cox Miles. The pair presented a set of questions to men and women. They studied how each gender answered the questions; those responses that were most often chosen by women were deemed *feminine*, and those most often chosen by men were deemed *masculine*.

Men who expressed an interest in art or religion were more likely to answer *like a woman* than other men. In other words, the answers of artistic and religious men looked more like the answers given by women. The researchers wrote, "Interest in religion or art is a mark of definitely greater femininity than lack of interest in these matters." They continued, "Most masculine of all are the men who have little or no interest in religion." Podles observes, "Very masculine men showed little interest in religion, very feminine men great interest . . . young men, athletic men, and uneducated men tended to be more consistently masculine than old men, sedentary men, and educated men."

Now here's a surprise: the pattern held with women too. Women who had highly feminine scores were also especially religious, while women who had more masculine scores were neutral or averse to religion.[5]

This study seems to indicate that anyone, man or woman, who has a very masculine outlook (high M) on life tends to shy away from the church. Isn't this true in your experience? Think of the macho men you know. Think of the driven, career-oriented women you know. Are they in church on Sunday? Even if they do attend, do they seem particularly devoted, or is their true allegiance elsewhere?

On the other hand, those who have a less masculine outlook (low M), be they men or women, tend to flock to the church. This may explain why so many gay men are drawn to church, while lesbians avoid it. A study published in the *Journal for the Scientific Study of Religion* found that "gay men were significantly more active in religious organizations [as a percentage] when compared to heterosexual men." The author notes that gay men are similar to female heterosexuals in their religiosity and attend church "without having to be dragged to services by female partners—as is the case for heterosexual men." Yet "lesbians and female bisexuals have very low rates of religious activity."[6]

Why do so many effeminate and gay men attend church? Maybe because the church is one of the few institutions in society where there's no pressure to act like a man. In fact, men are encouraged not to. Where else in our society can a man express his feminine side and be applauded for it?

Furthermore, as men get older and more sedentary, they tend to develop a more feminine outlook on life, focusing on security rather than risk taking. These are precisely the men the church is still somewhat successful in attracting. Mostly absent in church are young, athletic, and uneducated men, who possess a more masculine outlook on life.

CHURCH: NATURAL HABITAT OF THE SOFT MALE

The lack of machismo among churchgoing men has not gone unnoticed. The average churchman is what writer John Bly calls *the soft male*. He is a tamed man. Mr. Rogers is his mascot. The stallions hang out in bars; the geldings hang out in church. Gordon Dalbey writes,

> "The greatest disappointment in my lifetime of ministry," a friend and fellow pastor in his late 50's once declared to me, "has been that I just never seem to be able to draw men into the church." He paused and sighed, confused and frustrated. "Sure, I've gotten males—but frankly, they've been mostly quiet and withdrawn guys with strong, dominant wives. I wish I could get some real men in my church!"[7]

Susan Faludi, after observing men at a Promise Keepers rally, put it this way:

> If they were plotting the overthrow of a feminist world, they showed no signs of it. Mostly they seemed intent on being mannerly and tidy. In an era when the sports spectators who were the bleachers' usual clientele left the stadiums littered and vandalized, the Promise Keepers were careful to throw away all their trash. They obediently took notes during the speeches and displayed at all times their Promise Keepers ID bracelets, which looked exactly like the identification bands worn by hospital patients . . . They were willfully docile, as though, if they just obeyed long enough, they would at last get their reward.[8]

We're clean. We're courteous. We're conscientious. Above all, we're nice. What our Sunday school teachers told us years ago is still true today: we are God's little lambs.

Successful Christian living is defined not by the bold actions we take, but by the foolish actions we avoid. It's not the goals we accomplish, but the sins we escape that make us good Christian men. We are supposed to be weak, humble, and sweet. Real men visit our churches, look around at the soft males sitting in the soft pews, and beat a path to the exit. Real men do not want to be safe—*they want to be dangerous.*

Real men have no place in the church today. Frankly, we don't want them. We say we do, but if a number of real men showed up, we wouldn't know what to do with them. I call these perpetual church avoiders *the missing men.*

THE MISSING MEN SIDE OF THE TRIANGLE

Many types of men are absent from the church today, but these three subscts of high M men seem particularly alienated: risk takers, fun lovers, and dangerous men.

Risk Takers

There was a time when being a Christian could be hazardous to your health. In the first century emperor Nero employed Christians as human torches. Thousands of early Christians perished on crosses or in the jaws of ravenous beasts.

Although there are still many risk takers in the persecuted church, our comfortable Western churches attract relatively few. There's a shortage of high-achieving men who possess a risk-taking mentality. Adventurer types are largely absent from churches today. Entrepreneurs are under-represented.

So how can a church attract risk takers? By taking risks! Pursue outrageous, God-given visions. Develop ministries that are dangerous. Send people on foreign mission adventures. Tell the stories of men who have jeopardized everything for Christ. Start with the stories of the martyrs. Scores die every day for Christ, yet their stories are rarely told in Western churches. The Web site www.persecution.org tells the stories of modern-day martyrs. Visit this site regularly. It will deepen your faith.

We need risk takers in the church today. Without risk takers church-governing boards have a tendency to play it safe because they are composed of cautious people. After years of safe, practical decisions, a church begins to decline. Men leave. *A growing church is a risk-taking church.*

Fun Lovers

Fun-loving people are underrepresented in church today. It's little wonder why. Church services aren't much fun. They're usually very serious affairs. A daring pastor might tell a joke at the beginning of the sermon, but he'll get complaints if he tells two jokes. Laymen who try to liven up the service with humorous announcements or silly skits might draw a stern rebuke or an angry letter from a longtime member.

If you're a party type, you may end up on the church fellowship committee. *Fellowship* is a term invented by Christians who fear the word *fun.* The fellowship committee is a grudging admission from the powers within the church that there is a time and a place for fun, just as long as it doesn't break out spontaneously, especially during a worship service! The fellowship team is an ingenious mechanism that controls the joy and celebration, allowing them to burst forth only at theologically acceptable times and in preapproved locations.

Fun-loving people may detect joy bubbling somewhere beneath the surface of the church, but because it rarely breaks forth, they fall away. They seek out a more lively church that doesn't take itself so seriously, or they opt for a party lifestyle. This lifestyle requires staying up late on Saturday night, so many fun lovers just skip church. After all, in most people's experience the dullest party is more fun than the hippest church service.

John Piper describes the worship service as "The Feast of Christian Hedonism."[9] The Westminster Shorter Catechism begins, "Man's chief end is to glorify God, and *enjoy* him forever" (emphasis mine). We're supposed to enjoy God. Isn't it possible we're also supposed to enjoy church? We need fun-loving people in church to help us recapture the joy of worship. Only then will we recapture men (more in chapter 20, "Worship and the Masculine Spirit").

Dangerous Men

This is a catch-all category for a third kind of man who doesn't go to church. How many ex-cons go to your church? How many

Harleys roar into the parking lot Sunday morning? How about mud-covered pickup trucks? How many tattoos are visible during the worship service?

The dangerous man is another kind of risk taker: he's adopted a lifestyle and a persona that tell the world he's someone you don't want to mess with. But not every dangerous man is a biker or an ex-con. Any man who projects an image of toughness falls into this category. Construction workers, diesel mechanics, sailors, welders, and the like are dangerous men. Just the kind of men Jesus hung out with.

When a dangerous man shows up in church, he often feels judged. Lee Strobel quotes one such man: "I thought people were going to whisper behind my back, 'Look! It's one of them. It's one of those hell-bound pagans! Quick, hide the valuables! Protect the women!'"[10] Some preachers spend a lot of pulpit time predicting doom for worldly people. Such preaching makes dangerous men feel unwelcome.

Men who like dangerous things or who work in dangerous jobs may feel out of place in church. Loggers, oilfield workers, military men, and hunters are openly vilified in some liberal churches. On the other hand, men who have dangerous habits such as smoking and drinking are shunned in some conservative churches.

We need dangerous men in the church. Jesus attracted dangerous men. These social outcasts were His biggest fans. It's a sure sign of church health when dangerous men start showing up on Sunday. But they won't stay unless we stop condemning them and learn to speak their language: the language of risk.

WHY THESE THREE GAPS ARE SO ALIENATING TO MEN

The numbers gap. It's a vicious circle: there are fewer men in church, so fewer men attend. Men look around the sanctuary for other men they can relate to. If the sanctuary is full of women, children, and wimps, a man's gut tells him this is not a place for him. He may drop out, leaving one less man for the next guy to relate to.

The participation gap. Men who try participating beyond Sunday morning find ministries dominated by women and their values. They

feel incompetent and drop out. Low male participation keeps other
men from volunteering, and so on.

The personality gap. Men are looking for strong, risk-taking leaders to
show them the way. They are looking for healthy role models for their
sons. Men need wise spiritual fathers who will tell it to them straight.
They are not finding them in church, so they look elsewhere.

With God's help, we can close the three gaps. But every churchgoer
must do a better job of understanding men. Join me now for a journey
through a man's subconscious mind, the field upon which these battles
will be waged.

PART 3

Understanding Men and Masculinity

Men find the church too feminine for their liking. So what? Can't men just get over all this macho stuff? No, they can't. You might as well ask a woman to get over her maternal instincts. The fact is, men's bodies, brains, histories, and cultures make it nearly impossible for them to flourish in today's church environment.

We assume that when a man becomes a Christian, God will change him, and he'll start liking church. Too often this is not the case. During the 1990s Promise Keepers led thousands of men to faith in Christ, yet male church attendance actually declined slightly during that decade.[1] What happened? Men encountered Christ in a rather masculine environment, but returned home to a rather feminine church. The PK rally felt right, but church did not.

Dan Schaffer asked a roomful of Christian guys, "Is the church a masculine or a feminine place?" They immediately voiced loudly, "It is a feminine place." Then he asked how this affects the way they respond in church. They said it made them hesitant, timid, and restrained. Schaffer realized that men would never give themselves fully unless they could practice their faith in a way that felt comfortable to them.[2]

Men's passivity in church springs not so much from *laziness* as from *uneasiness*.

So what do men want? That's what the next four chapters are about. As we gain a better understanding of men's needs and expectations, it will become clear why men hate going to church and what individual Christians can do to turn things around.

10

WHAT BIOLOGY
TEACHES US ABOUT MEN

MEN'S BRAINS ARE DIFFERENT FROM WOMEN'S BRAINS; SO SAY scientists. Men also have different levels of certain hormones than women. These biochemical dissimilarities cause the genders to behave differently on the job, at home, and in school. But the differences are particularly striking in church.

When husband and wife walk into church, he is at an immediate disadvantage. His brain is wired in such a way that he simply cannot understand or relate to a lot of what goes on Sunday morning. It's not that he is unwilling to try. The hormones coursing through his body make it hard to sit still. His brain will not allow him to respond the same way his wife does. The more involved he tries to become, the more frustrated he may feel.

Meanwhile, she's perfectly comfortable in church. Her brain comprehends and appreciates everything that is happening. She easily processes information as it is dispensed from the pulpit. Her hormones help her react appropriately in every situation.

She flutters through the church like a butterfly—he crawls around like a slug. She glibly shares her feelings—he's tongue-tied. What's the difference? For the answer, let's look inside their bodies.

HORMONAL DIFFERENCES BETWEEN MEN AND WOMEN

Men have much more testosterone than women do. Testosterone is the hormone that, more than any other, makes a man a man. Testosterone makes men aggressive and more apt to take risks, causes their legendary interest in sex, and sparks their drive for independence. It's associated with dominance, physicality, and high self-esteem—in both men and women.

Men are not able to check their testosterone at the church door; they bring it with them into the sanctuary. Testosterone makes it hard for men to sit still. Boys are four to nine times more likely to be diagnosed with hyperactivity than girls. A survey found one-third of U.S. boys are considered excessively hyperactive or "hyperdistractable."[1] Harvard researchers reported that men's testosterone levels are higher in the morning, lower later in the day,[2] suggesting Sunday morning might be the worst time to ask men to sit still for a class or a lengthy sermon. One man said, "Men can't sit still that long. It's why they want to be ushers—at least they get to move around."

Thom and Joani Schultz wanted to know why children learn so little in Sunday school. They interviewed grade-school-age kids and found their least favorite thing about Sunday school is *sitting in chairs.*[3] The classroom format, with its emphasis on *sit still, be quiet, read, memorize, and verbalize,* ensures that boys will not do as well as girls. In Sunday school the girls usually win, and the boys usually lose. The more testosterone in the boy, the more likely he is to lose. From an early age we send boys (particularly masculine boys) this message: *you just can't cut it in church.*

How can we help men?

- *Friendly, physical competition for men and boys.* Many churches avoid all forms of competition because it creates winners and losers. Even some youth groups are doing away with competition—fun and games are being replaced with singing and a sermonette—church lite. Boys need friendly competition to motivate them. A more active worship environment with friendly competition would help men and boys.

- *Reinvent Sunday school.* What boy wants to go to school on Sunday? There is an alternative to the classroom model—our church calls it *Summit Kids.* Instead of teaching lessons in classrooms, our grade-school kids meet in a gym for a highly kinetic worship and teaching experience. The kids play games, sing silly songs, run around, and learn about Jesus. Both boys and girls love it. My nine-year-old Victoria can't wait for *Summit Kids* each week. "It's funner than Sunday school," she says. "And I learn a lot more about God."

- *Intermission.* If your worship service is longer than sixty minutes, consider inserting an intermission as a weekly feature. A number of churches are adding intermissions, and they're finding it not only helps the men; it's giving everyone a chance to get better connected than the thirty-second turn-and-greet time.

- *Physical activity.* Give men opportunities to be physically active. Men can't spend hours sitting still in a conference room. Next time you're planning a conference or retreat, be sure to include lots of physical movement and activity. Go beyond standing and sitting for singing. Let men move around. They'll love you for it.

WOMEN HAVE MORE SEROTONIN

While men have more testosterone, women generally have more serotonin, a specialized hormone known as a neurotransmitter. It calms people down. So women are naturally more self-controlled, less aggressive, and less prone to violence than men.

Women get angry, but serotonin allows them to handle conflict differently from the way men do. Two men will get mad, have a fight, then shake hands and be friends again. All is forgiven. Not women. Serotonin lets women suppress their anger, allowing it to smolder while they plot their revenge. Men get mad; women get even.

Now think of how conflict and anger play out in church. When two church members get crossways, do they settle it like men? Have you ever heard an elder say to a deacon, "Henry, let's step outside and settle things, *mano a mano*"? Of course not. Most Christians would view a fistfight among believers as terribly unchristian behavior. Even a sharp public exchange of words is considered a horrible failure, something to be avoided at all costs.

But conflict always comes, and how does the church handle it 99 percent of the time? The feminine way, allowing it to simmer just below the surface. The battling parties are polite in public but vicious in private. Church battles routinely feature backstabbing, gossip mongering, and revenge. All this takes place in secret, and only church insiders know the details. Publicly, everyone grits his teeth and pretends things are just fine. Eventually, one warring party leaves the church, or in extreme cases the church splits.

Men can't handle this. When a man gets drawn into a church conflict, he's out of his league. His brain tells him to fight it out, clear the air, and move on. But that's not how things work in most churches. So men fall away. There are legions of men who have given up on church because of the hypocrisy that arises when the church handles conflict in the feminine way.

Churches can do a lot for men in this area:

- Deal with conflict decisively, and don't allow it to fester.
  Speak the truth, even if it hurts. It's often better to lance the
  boil and let the healing begin.

- Not all conflict should be handled in secret, especially conflict
  that affects the whole body. Encourage both sides to bring
  their differences into the open whenever possible.

- Some youth pastors might allow boys to settle their
  differences through competition or a controlled fight of
  some sort, such as an arm-wrestling match. A boy must learn
  to be a gracious winner as well as a good loser. What better
  venue for these lessons than church?

If these suggestions seem odd to you, consider how Christ dealt with conflict. He was not diplomatic. He was so brazenly open in His clashes with the Pharisees that He even embarrassed His disciples. He dealt with situations decisively and moved on. When the church learns to deal decisively with conflict (as Christ did), men will be spared injury.

DIFFERENCES IN THE BRAINS OF MEN AND WOMEN

Scientists have found the brains of men and women differ in a number of ways. Two are especially relevant for our discussion:

1. *Men have a larger amygdala.* No, amygdala is not the princess in *Star Wars.* It is a tiny feature at the base of the brain in the middle of the hypothalamus. Dr. James Dobson writes:

> The amygdala never forgets a fearful moment, which is why traumatized people often find it so difficult to get over their hair-raising experiences . . . the amygdala can respond only to what is in its memory bank. It does not think or reason. It emits an "irrational" chemical and electrical response that may save your life in an emergency—but it can also precipitate violence and make matters much worse.[4]

Men have a larger amygdala than women. This explains why they have a greater fight-or-flight impulse, and why men are prone to flashbacks when they encounter a situation that resembles a threatening one. In the 1970s you'd hear stories of Vietnam veterans who experienced flashbacks when they saw bamboo, for example. Male Holocaust survivors who return to long-shuttered Nazi concentration camps are sometimes overcome with a desire to flee. Blame these reactions on the amygdala—it doesn't reason; it simply responds.

Men who had negative boyhood church experiences may panic at the sight of candles, stained glass, or hymnals, because these sights put them right back into that painful situation, even decades later. When a man says he's uncomfortable in church because of what happened twenty-five years ago, he's probably telling the truth. He can't *just get over it.* His brain may be working against him.

Fortunately, there is great diversity in the church today. A man may be able to find a church whose worship style, building, and trappings are very different from the church he grew up in. Perhaps this is one reason why large, nondenominational churches founded since 1970 have the smallest gender gaps. Modern megachurches often jettison the symbols of childhood religion. A nontraditional approach to worship can help men who were traumatized as boys.

2. Men have a smaller corpus callosum. The corpus callosum (CC) connects the right and left sides of the brain. It's a bundle of fibers that routes traffic between the brain's two hemispheres. Think of it as one of those complex freeway interchanges, with cars speeding along slender ramps, moving toward their destinations. The CC in women's brains is much larger, enabling more traffic to pass from one hemisphere to the other. A typical man's CC is like a two-lane highway, but a woman's CC is like a superhighway interchange, with double and triple lanes on each ramp. These superior connections allow women to outperform men at several tasks that are common in church today.

Women Are Often Better Readers

Reading is a relatively complex task that draws on both sides of the brain at once. To read well, you need a big corpus callosum. Advantage: women. This may explain why males are diagnosed with reading disorders such as dyslexia at four times the rate of females.[5] Fifty-five percent of women read literary works for pleasure; just 37 percent of men do so.[6]

Sunday services are often full of reading. Some men have a hard time keeping up during responsive readings, unison readings, and liturgical readings. Singing unfamiliar songs can be tough on some guys because it requires reading and singing at the same time.

Children are often asked to read aloud in Sunday school. This well-meaning effort to increase class participation can be horrifying to boys who have trouble reading. They often miss the entire lesson because they're praying that they won't be called on. Reading aloud is particularly tough in churches that use the King James Bible.

Reading is regularly upheld as one of the pillars of the faith. Evangelical pastors frequently admonish their parishioners to *get into the Word* or read their Bibles every day. Sound advice, but it's problematic for men who have trouble reading.

How can we make things easier on boys and men?

- Christian educators should find other ways to involve their students besides reading aloud.

- Some churches are getting away from unison readings and hymns with complex or archaic lyrics.

- Pastors and teachers should remind their flocks that the Bible is now available on tape and CD. Computer programs can now read the Bible to you.

- Many churches are using easier-to-read modern Bible translations. This helps men.

A WOMAN'S BRAIN POSSESSES MORE VERBAL RESOURCES

The regions of a female's brain that are devoted to language are larger than their equivalents in the male. Girls outperform boys by huge margins on tests of verbal fluency.[7] Studies reveal that women use more of their brains during speech, which makes them much better at expressing themselves verbally. Other studies show that a typical woman speaks 20,000 to 25,000 words a day, while a typical man speaks just 7,000 to 10,000.[8]

Women love to talk. If you doubt this, hang around after the church service. Who's standing around and talking? Mostly women. Women are comfortable in the world of words; men are comfortable in the world of objects. That's why she's talking, while he's in the car fiddling with the radio. Kevin Leman says, "If you've always wondered why your husband is less than enthusiastic about going to an evening Bible study . . . his reluctance probably doesn't have anything to do with his lack of interest in spiritual things; it's just as likely that he's tired of talking and wants to spend a quiet evening at home."[9]

Brain differences play out in the entertainment men and women choose. Women buy romance novels; men buy pornographic magazines. She's stimulated by words; he's stimulated by images. Women watch TV shows where people talk about their problems; men watch sports and crime shows where words are secondary to the action.

Elvis Presley put it this way: "A little less conversation, a little more action, please." Yet today's church has become an almost entirely verbal experience. Christianity is big on *verbal learning* and small on *active learning*. Start with adult classes. Most are led by a teacher who lectures the class or leads a discussion. He may write words on a chalkboard or pass out a study guide covered with words. Some teachers play videos, but guess what? Most are just videotaped talking heads. Once the lesson is completed, the class might break into small groups for *sharing*, which involves more talking. If the teacher assigns any homework, it inevitably involves reading, typically Bible reading, which the teacher refers to as *the Word*.

Once class is over, it's on to church. Church services are a deluge of verbal communication. There's visiting to be done before and after the service. There are words in the bulletin, words in the hymnal, announcements in the bulletin, liturgies, prayers, and readings.

The centerpiece of most Protestant services is the sermon—a nonstop torrent of words. Here's what I want to know: *Just who decided that the lecture-style sermon was the best way to teach people about Jesus?* According to many studies, a long, uninterrupted monologue is the *least* effective way to teach people anything![10] What are we thinking? We have the most important message in the world, yet we use the least effective method to spread it! And who has the hardest time learning from a lecture? Men.

Sermons put men in an impossible situation: they must remain alert as a flood of words rushes forth from the pastor's mouth. Men must not only comprehend those words but also, using the other side of the brain, respond emotionally to the pastor's appeal. Very few men are physiologically capable of this feat. Their brains are simply not wired this way. Men find sermons boring not so much because of their *content*, but because of their *format*.

Are there alternatives to the long, monologue sermon? Yes, and these models are proving effective with men. We'll learn more in chapter 19, "Teaching and the Masculine Spirit."

Men simply fail to grasp much of what is taught in church today because their brains are not suited to its highly verbal teaching style. When the church returns to the visual, hands-on style favored by Jesus, men, young people, and women will all respond. Women are blessed in that they understand verbal, visual, and hands-on communication styles. If this is the case, why not use the styles everyone can understand instead of sticking with the verbal style that only women seem able to grasp?

MEN AND WOMEN REALLY ARE DIFFERENT

The church is one of the few institutions that refused to buy into that great lie of the 1970s and 1980s: there's no difference between men and women. We Christians always recognized the differences between the sexes, even in the face of public ridicule. How ironic that we refuse to accommodate these differences! Yes, we believe men and women are different, but we minister to them in exactly the same manner. We expect them to act the same, to process information the same, and to like the same things.

Christianity doesn't change a man's physiology and body chemistry. It's time for Christians to take a hard look at how we do things. Small changes will make men much happier in our churches.

11

WHAT THE SOCIAL SCIENCES TEACH US ABOUT MEN

WE NOW TURN TO THE SOCIAL SCIENCES—SPECIFICALLY psychology and anthropology—to learn more about men and their deepest needs.

WHAT PSYCHOLOGY TEACHES US ABOUT MEN

Boys grow up in a feminine world. A boy spends his first nine months inside a woman's body, and after he is born, a multitude of women— his mom, babysitters, nursery and day care workers, and schoolteach- ers—care for him. At some point, however, a boy must make a break from the feminine and begin to define himself as something different from the mother from whose body he sprang. Psychologists call this *separation/individuation*. A boy must reject his mother and her feminine ways, and take his place in society as a man. A male who fails to sepa- rate psychologically from his mother faces a lifetime of gender confu- sion, abuse, or dysfunction. (Think Norman Bates in the film *Psycho.*)

A common term for this separation is *cutting the apron strings.* Jesus cut Mary's apron strings a number of times in Scripture. At the age of twelve He remained behind with the men in the temple while his family returned to Nazareth. As an adult, when His mother asked Him to turn water into wine, He initially refused her request. Jesus loved His mother, He respected His mother, but He was not controlled by His mother. He made it clear: He was under the control of His heavenly Father.

As a young man reaches adolescence, he begins looking for apron strings to cut, and church is an obvious one. Most men are introduced to Christianity by women: nuns, nursery workers, Sunday school teachers, and of course, moms. Protestant Sunday schools always have more female teachers. A study of thirty-six Catholic parishes by Notre Dame University found that 80 percent of catechism sponsors were women.[1] A boy may attend church his entire life and never have a male teacher.

Studies show Mom is more likely than Dad to model religious practices such as saying grace at meals, Scripture memorization, and bedtime prayers. She may lead family devotions, while Dad is passive or gets up and leaves the room. Mom is also more likely than Dad to read the Bible, and she spends more time at church.[2]

So very early, boys associate the faith with women. Working in the church is something women do, while men occupy themselves elsewhere. Many men never return to church because of its strong association with women. In fact, a young man may get the impression that the only way to be devoted to God is to become a clergyman—not a popular career aspiration for teenage boys.

If you are a mother raising a son without a churchgoing husband, here's my advice: identify a male spiritual mentor for your son. Ideally, he will be a married man about your husband's age. You want to find a man who is genuinely walking with Christ, and one who knows how to challenge young men. Your son needs such a role model early, beginning in first or second grade. Ask the mentor to get to know your son and to single him out for attention whenever he sees him at church. Give him permission to challenge your son. If you have no husband, ask the mentor to take your boy to father-son events.

Why is a mentor so important? Boys follow men, not religions. *If your son never gets to know a man who is walking with Christ, chances are very slim he will ever walk with Christ.* Let me be blunt: if there is not a spiritual mentor in your church, you may want to find another church.

Men Fear Psychic Regression

Sigmund Freud, the father of modern psychology, said men have an intense fear of something called *psychic regression,* the return to a second infancy in order to evade reality. Society considers men who regress, or run back to their mommies, as failed men. For example, a woman can go home to Mother, but a man cannot.

The feminine spirit of the church is so scary to a man because of the fear of regression. It's not that the world of women is strange and alien; the problem is, it's comfortable and familiar! The church and its feminine spirit remind a man of his childhood and simpler times. Psychologically, it is a warm, comforting womb. Even men who are interested in God end up rejecting the church because of its strong subconscious association with childhood. Churchgoing is a subconscious step toward Mom, toward childhood, toward regression.

When Stressed, Women Run to Community, But Men Isolate Themselves

Men and women even react differently to stress. University of Pennsylvania psychologists found that females *tend or befriend* when under stress, while males *fight or flee*. In other words, a stressed-out woman looks to others to help her through the challenges of life, but a man usually wants to handle his problems by himself.[3] To a woman, church involvement is a stress reliever. Church is a place where she can get support and talk about her problems. But a stressed-out man will flee from others and retreat to his cave to work out problems.

WHAT ANTHROPOLOGY TEACHES US ABOUT MEN

Anthropology, the study of human beings, can give us insight into men's discomfort with church. Many Christians mistrust anthropology because its best-known tenet is the theory of evolution. Relax, we're not going there. Instead, we are focusing on cultural anthropology, which has much to say about male and female roles, why these roles were established, and how they play out in society—and the church—today.

Men Were the Hunters, Women the Gatherers

When the study of anthropology took off in the nineteenth century, there were still a number of undisturbed hunter/gatherer societies left on earth. Anthropologists rushed to study these peoples before they were contaminated by modern society. They discovered male and female work behavior was amazingly consistent everywhere in the world:

Everywhere men hunt large land and water fauna, trap small animals and birds, hunt birds, build boats, and work with wood, stone, bone, horn and shell. Everywhere women gather fuel and food, fetch water, prepare drinks and vegetable foods, and cook. Most of women's activities are performed close to the home and involve monotonous tasks that require no concentration and can easily be interrupted and resumed. Male activities may require long absences from home and travel over great distances, not possible for women burdened with children. Male tasks may be dangerous, because men do not bear or rear children, and may be more highly valued in order to motivate the expendable male to perform them.[4]

Social scientists use this hunter/gatherer model to explain a variety of human behaviors that persist today. Men love the outdoors, including hunting and fishing. Men derive joy from catching their own food, even though it's often cheaper and easier to buy it at the supermarket. Centuries of gathering may be one reason women love to shop and seem to excel at repetitive work, such as assembly line and clerical jobs.

Some scientists believe men developed superior three-dimensional spatial perception from all those centuries of finding their way back to camp. Others say women developed the verbal centers of the brain more than men did because they were free to talk all they wanted in camp. Men on the hunt had to be silent and became experts at non-verbal communication. Gatherer-women seem better able to keep lots of small details in their heads. I marvel at my wife's ability to keep so many balls in the air. Hunter-men seem more likely to develop tunnel vision and focus on a single target.

These differences play out not only in our relationships; they appear in church settings as well. So is church easier for hunters or gatherers? Let's look at the evidence.

Men Tend to Be Project Oriented

Because men focused all their energy on hunting, they tended to become *project* oriented. Their lives consisted of planning for the hunt, going on the hunt, celebrating the hunt, and resting from the hunt. *Plan; work; celebrate; rest.* This is a man's natural cycle. It is the reason why guys usually prefer to work on a project, complete it, then move on to the next one. (It also explains why men feel entitled to veg out in front of the TV after a hard day at work. It's their rest time.)

The gatherer's camp-based life was more predictable. Women improved their lives by creating systems that made their lives easier. They became *program* oriented. A program is a clever method of organizing people and resources to meet ongoing needs. For example, by organizing the younger girls to watch the babies, mothers could travel farther from the camp in search of better roots and berries.

So, is today's church *project* oriented or *program* oriented? Probably 90 percent of the volunteer hours donated to local churches are tied to ongoing programs: educational programs, worship programs, child care programs, benevolence programs, and outreach programs. The larger the church, the more programs it offers.

Men may be frightened to involve themselves in church programs for several reasons:

• Programs do not provide the plan-work-celebrate-rest cycle
  that men crave. They are ongoing, and can become
  monotonous.

• Programs sometimes have fuzzy goals. Some church
  programs continue even after they have outlived their
  usefulness. Men may not understand why a program remains
  in existence.

• Programs usually offer no exit point. Men draw the
  conclusion that God's work is never done. It's an ongoing
  commitment that never ends.

A church that wants to involve men will offer more project-based ministry opportunities. These are one-time or short-term events such as a foreign mission trip, a community service day, or a Habitat home-raising. Projects have a clear objective and an exit point. They're exciting to men. They also involve the four elements of male engagement: plan, work, celebrate, and rest.

Men Tend to Be Outdoor Oriented

The hunter's domain was the outdoors. Even today men feel more alive when they're outside. Meanwhile the gatherer's domain was the indoors—the safety and security of hearth and home. In most cases women are still more indoor oriented than men. My wife subscribes to *Better Homes and Gardens*. I subscribe to *Backpacker.*

So where does 99 percent of Christian worship take place? Indoors. Christian classes? Indoors. Seminary training? Indoors. Even in good weather we rarely think of moving ministry outside. Most churches offer just one outdoor worship service per year: Easter sunrise service. (Have you noticed that a lot of men attend this service?)

Men who say, "I feel closer to God out in the woods," are not lying. Men do not expect to meet God at church because it takes place indoors. For men, God lives outside. He's the God of the sky, the burning bush, the pillar of fire, and the mighty wind. The greatest moments in Jesus' ministry came while He was outdoors.

Ever wonder why some churches still hold tent revivals? Why would they go to all the trouble to erect a tent with a comfortable church building sitting right next door? Why does Billy Graham prefer open-air stadiums for his crusades, despite the risk of inclement weather? Saddleback Church experienced some of its most explosive growth while meeting in a tent. Robert Schuller started his ministry at a drive-in theater and built the world-famous Crystal Cathedral to let the outdoors in. Why were Promise Keepers stadium rallies so effective at reaching men? Why do so many young men accept Christ at lakeside summer camps? *Men have an easier time finding God outdoors.*

If you want to reach men, move as much of your church's ministry as possible outdoors. Open the windows of your sanctuary, and let the light in. Bring in plants and greenery. When in doubt, move it out! It's one small way you can say to men, "We care about you."

Men Were the Warriors

Besides hunting, men had a very important secondary job: waging war against rival bands. Warfare is still imprinted on the male psyche. Men love to watch war movies and read war novels. They play war games on computers. Polls show men always support military action more than women.

Liberal churches infuriate men in this arena:

- Some churches are consistently opposed to war, no matter how justified. The pope, the National Council of Churches, and many large denominations offer automatic opposition to all military action, which the press reports as the *Christian* point of view on war.

- Some churches are removing all military imagery from teaching materials and music. For instance, "The Battle Hymn of the Republic" would be unacceptable in many churches today.

- As for spiritual warfare, Satan has disappeared in many churches, even though 68 percent of Americans believe in his existence.[5] These churches have eliminated the enemy. There's no one to fight against, so men lose interest.

Liberals may hate all the war in the Old Testament, but it's there for a reason: battle stories speak to men's hearts. Douglas Wilson reminds us, "The Christian faith is in no way pacifistic. The peace that will be ushered in by our great Prince will be a peace purchased with blood. As our Lord sacrificed Himself in this war, so must His followers learn to do."[6]

Men must realize they are playing for keeps. They are in a battle against a real adversary who wants to destroy them. Men need to fight an evil one, not just evil as a concept. This is why there's always a bad guy in the movies. Without a real threat from a real enemy, men don't want to fight. That was the lesson of Vietnam.

Men Were Called to Self-Sacrifice

Throughout history, men have known that one day they might have to sacrifice themselves for the good of the tribe. Men have always been the expendable sex, so self-sacrifice is burned onto the psyche of men. Have you noticed how many books and movies feature a hero who lays down his life for the good of others? Last week I watched two films: the superb *Braveheart* and the silly *Space Cowboys*. Both featured a character who sacrificed himself so others could have life.

In Christianity we have such a figure, Christ Himself. When we tell the story of His sacrifice, we speak to the hearts of men. But we rarely hold out the possibility of death to His followers. Have you ever been warned in church that, as a Christian, your life may someday be required of you? That you are walking a path that may lead to your death? As I mentioned earlier, dozens of people die daily for Christ, but their sacrifice is rarely acknowledged in our churches. It would be too disturbing to the children.

Deep in his heart, every man has a desire to expend himself for a great cause. Paul said, "I want to suffer and die as he did, so that somehow I also may be raised to life" (Phil. 3:10–11 CEV). When Jesus predicted His death, Thomas and Peter immediately offered their lives as well (John 11:16; 13:37). Men are drawn to religions where self-sacrifice is a real possibility. If you doubt this, look at what's happening in Islam.

Religion Has Traditionally Been the Domain of Men

Anthropologist Ernestine Friedl found that in most preliterate societies, men were the keepers of religion. This "includes the idea that men are responsible for controlling sacred or spiritual aspects of the universe and women the profane or secular aspects."[7] Think about this. For thousands of years in societies the world over, men have taken the lead in religious life. Men have had the sacred role of passing faith to the next generation. But modern Christians have rewritten this ancient equation: women are now the keepers of the faith, transmitting religion to the next generation, while men focus on the secular aspects of life.

This is bad news for Christianity. As I said earlier, when it comes to spiritual matters, society has always followed the lead of men. Today's men are focused on the secular, so civilization is gradually turning its attention that way as well. Unless Christianity reengages men, its influence will continue to wane.

12

MEN SEEK GREATNESS

IT WAS THE BOTTOM OF THE NINTH INNING. THE LITTLE
League Pirates were down by 2. The city championship was at stake. But
with the bases loaded, there was still hope. Little Billy Simmons, not
quite five feet tall, stepped into the batter's box, shivering with fear. It was
a lot of pressure on a twelve-year-old catcher. When the first pitch hung
over the plate, Billy swung hard. The white orb soared high into the air,
clearing the outfield fence by a car length. Home run. Pirates win 6-4.

The Pirates' dugout emptied, and Billy's teammates mobbed him at
the plate. It was truly the greatest moment of young Billy's life. But
then something strange happened. Billy's dad came tearing out of the
stands and began yelling, "Hey! Why are you cheering for him? I taught
him everything he knows! I was the one who taught him how to swing
a bat. I got up early and drove him to practice. The credit for that
homer belongs to me . . . *me!*"

What would we think of such a father? Strange? Yes. Insecure? You
bet. A jealousy problem? Absolutely!

Yet this is exactly how many Christians perceive our heavenly Father!
We see Him as this insecure man in the sky who gets cranky if His kids
receive so much as an ounce of recognition for their accomplishments.
Most fathers are thrilled when their children achieve great things, but not
our heavenly Father. We have this crazy notion that He's threatened
by His children's success. When a Christian receives praise, he'd better
deflect it to God—or else God will come marching out of the stands to
take revenge!

There are certain churchgoers—I call them *the humility police*—who
see it as their job to humble anyone who might get praise or credit. The
humility police hurt men, because men, who are created in God's image,

98

aspire to do great things, just as God does. The humility police make sure this doesn't happen—at least not in church.

President Woodrow Wilson said, "Men are in love with power and greatness." Men constantly fantasize about it—the movies they watch, the video games they play, and the books they read always feature a powerful hero who does great things. Every man wants to be a hero, to become a great man. Boys do not dream of sitting in a cubicle; they dream of slaying the dragon, rescuing the princess, and absconding with the treasure. My boyhood fantasy was to catch the winning pass in the Super Bowl. I can't tell you how many times I stretched out my arms and fell across my bed, hauling in that game winner as the crowd went wild in the stands.

Not only do men want to be great, but *they want to be recognized as being great*. An athlete who wins a championship wears a ring the rest of his life. A fellow who gets the high score on a video game calls his friends over to look at the screen. Businessmen work hard not just for money, but also for the recognition that accompanies their achievements. (The number one reason people quit their jobs is not a lack of money—it's a lack of recognition.)[1] A man who attracts a good-looking woman shows her off as a symbol of his greatness. Guys, let's say you got a date with Miss America. Wouldn't it feel great to walk down the street with a statuesque beauty on your arm, and the more guys who saw you, the better?

What does all this mean? If you want to capture the heart of a man—especially a younger man—you have to offer him a shot at greatness. Men will not invest themselves wholeheartedly in any endeavor that does not offer this possibility.

But most people do not see the local church as a place to achieve greatness. It's a place to worship God. To be inspired. To see friends. To be in community. To help others. To live a moral, upright life. The idea of church as a springboard to greatness in life, especially heroic greatness, is completely foreign to most people. Let's say a pollster asked one hundred men, "What's the best place for a man to achieve greatness in life?" Would even one man mention church? Or what if you asked, "How does one become a great man?" I suspect less than one in ten would mention Christianity.

Furthermore, there are plenty of churchgoers who will make sure you don't achieve greatness. Attempt the extraordinary in your local church, and you'll run into a buzz saw of opposition, led by the humility police.

Men gravitate toward venues where they can achieve some measure of greatness. Sports, business, hobbies, video games, gangs, love affairs. All these offer the possibility of triumph and achievement. I'll say it again: *most men will not fully invest themselves in anything that does not offer a shot at greatness.*

IS IT A SIN TO SEEK GREATNESS?

The Lord promised greatness to two Old Testament patriarchs: Abraham and David. What did the Lord say to Abraham? "I will bless you and make your name great" (Gen. 12:2). How about David? "Now I will make your name great, like the names of the greatest men of the earth" (2 Sam. 7:9 NIV). In both instances He promised these men a great name. A name that would go down in history. Like any good father, *God wants His children to grow up into great men and women.* He doesn't seem offended if others recognize this greatness.

What was Jesus' attitude when two of His disciples sought greatness? Mark 10:35–37 (CEV) tells us:

> James and John, the sons of Zebedee, came up to Jesus and asked, "Teacher, will you do us a favor?" Jesus asked them what they wanted, and they answered, "When you come into your glory, please let one of us sit at your right side and the other at your left."

James and John were doing what men do: seeking greatness and recognition. They wanted the best seats in God's kingdom. Notice what happened next:

> When the ten other disciples heard this, they were angry with James and John. (v. 41)

Two men seek greatness, and right away 83 percent of the church is spitting mad! (This was the first recorded meeting of the humility police.) Jesus called the Twelve together. I can imagine what Judas was muttering under his breath: "Boy, are they going to get it. I bet Jesus rips their heads off!" Christ had already reprimanded the two knuckleheads for suggesting that He call fire from heaven and destroy a town that had not welcomed them. But to everyone's surprise, Jesus did not rebuke the brothers. Instead, He showed them the way to greatness:

> If you want to be great, you must be the servant of all the others. And if you want to be first, you must be everyone's slave. The Son of Man did not come to be a slave master, but a slave who will give his life to rescue many people. (vv. 43–45)

Those first six words are remarkable: "If you want to be great." In other words, it's okay to seek greatness. The desire to be a great man is not sin; it is virtue. Instead of opposing James and John's lust for greatness (as the ten disciples did), Jesus directed it. *The way up is down, boys.* In John 14, Jesus made a remarkable prediction: the disciples will do even *greater* things than He did! These are not the words of a jealous, insecure Savior.

Notice Jesus also said, "*If* you want to be great." The path of greatness is not one every person will tread. In fact, few do. But the possibility of greatness must be set before men, for a certain kind of man will not follow without it. James and John were nicknamed "sons of thunder." I suppose that would make them the aggressive type. (Exactly the kind of men who'd be missing in today's church.)

Like Jesus, we must give men a vision of true greatness, then set them loose to achieve it. Allow men to shine and to receive recognition when they are servants and slaves. Men must know it's okay to reach for greatness as long as it's done the way Jesus prescribed—not through self-promotion, but through self-sacrifice. And we must admire men when they achieve this greatness. Listen to the words of Pastor Robert Lewis, one of America's foremost ministers to men:

> Robert Bly said, "If you're not being admired by other men, you're being hurt." That struck a chord with me. As I talk with men about their struggles, I realize many men are languishing because nobody is recognizing the noble things in their life. Men need male cheerleaders. If no

one cheers for nobility, men are going to collapse back into a dumbed-down masculinity that follows the cheers of the world—obsessive careerism, selfish pursuits, and ignoble deeds. We try to cheer men on—for the right things.[2]

The world offers men the possibility of greatness. The world cheers for men. Too often the local church does not. What a tragedy! It is no sin to recognize men for the good they do. It's not about exalting individuals; it's about celebrating what God is doing in people's lives.

Ever since Abraham, men have wanted to become great. Is this so bad? What if the church, instead of opposing men in this dream, actively partnered with them? What if the church focused on raising up men of wisdom, character, and strength? *What if your church were in the business of turning out great men?*

THE DIFFERENCE BETWEEN GREATNESS AND GLORY

If this talk of greatness is giving you heartburn, or you're afraid it will create a church full of raving egotists, let me define *greatness* for you. Greatness is not glory, which clearly belongs to God. Think of greatness as reflected glory: just as the moon reflects the light of the sun, a man who achieves something for God's kingdom is simply reflecting God's glory to the world. When we follow the example of Jesus, we reflect His glory to all.

We Christians must stop treating the pursuit of greatness as an affliction. Let men reach for greatness within the local church, and the entire body will be revitalized. Applaud your men. Set them up as examples. (Remember the words of Paul: "Follow me as I follow Christ.") And don't worry about someone getting the glory. God's a big boy; He can take care of Himself. If some hypocrite is serving out of impure motives, God knows. Remember the words of Jesus repeated three times in Matthew 6, "I tell you the truth, they have received their reward in full" (NIV). It's not our job to be the humility police.

Why do men seek greatness? Why are achievement, success, and manliness nearly universal obsessions with men? That's the subject of the next chapter.

13

The Pursuit of Manhood: His Greatest Quest

Why do men act so macho? Why do they avoid anything associated with femininity? Why do so many men cultivate a dangerous image instead of a warm, friendly one? Why do certain men strut their manliness like a peacock displays its plumage?

This is not a recent development. Masculinity has been of paramount importance to men for thousands of years. But it's also been important to society. Without masculinity there would be no civilization as we know it.

Masculinity: Key to Survival of the Human Race

Every society needs people to do the dangerous jobs. Throughout human history, someone has had to fight the battles, travel long distances without the comforts of home, and hunt down dangerous animals. Today we need people to work in mines, fight in wars, and rush into burning buildings. We need people to catch the bad guys and rescue lost children.

Men have always done the dangerous jobs, and they still do them. Today 94 percent of occupational deaths occur to men.[1] Men also do a disproportionate share of dying for their country. If any civilization is to survive and prosper, it needs men who will *act like men* when the need arises.

But how do you convince men to sacrifice themselves? How do you keep a man from deserting the battle when he's scared out of his mind, from running away when an animal tries to kill him, or from sneaking back to camp when food is running low or he's freezing cold? The answer is *masculinity*.

WHAT IS MASCULINITY?

Masculinity is an informal code imposed on all the men of the tribe. In order to be accepted as a man, one must stand up to danger, bear up under suffering, and sacrifice oneself for the good of others. This code of conduct helps a man overcome his natural instincts (fear, hunger, loneliness, etc.), so he will do what's best for the tribe, not for himself. Masculine traits such as bravery, stoicism, and self-sacrifice don't come naturally to a man: they are drawn from this cultural well.

If a man fails to be brave, stoic, or self-sacrificing, he's branded a coward. He becomes an outcast. He suffers total rejection. This may seem cruel, but remember, the survival of the tribe depended on men who would fulfill their roles. And this transmitted a powerful lesson to the boys: *be a man, or you will be rejected.* The masculine code is alive today, especially in time of war. Soldiers still get scared, but relatively few desert. They stay and fight, not out of the fear of court-martial but out of the fear of shame that would follow them the rest of their lives.

From this perspective, men are preoccupied with machismo because society demands that they be masculine. When a young man does risky things, he's just practicing for the day when he may be called to risk everything to save his family or his country. The masculine code forces men to be manly in peacetime, to ensure their bravery in wartime.

But here's the rub: masculinity isn't something you switch on and off. If a man is going to stand tough in the face of danger, he needs to practice being tough every day. Just as an Olympic sprinter practices day after day, year after year for a race that's over in a few seconds, a man practices masculinity every day so when the time comes to be strong, he's ready.

Manhood is something a man earns. One deed at a time, a task at a time, an interaction at a time. Anthropologist David Gilmore puts it this way:

> Real manhood differs from simple anatomical maleness, that it is not a natural condition that comes about spontaneously through biological maturation but rather is a precarious or artificial state that boys must win against powerful odds.[2]

Manhood is something you earn. One coin at a time.

How Men Earn Their Masculinity

Here's a helpful word picture: every man has within himself a *masculinity bank*. Each time he succeeds in a manly endeavor, a few coins drop into his bank: ka-ching, ka-ching. For most men, the bank can never be filled. A man will spend his entire lifetime gathering masculinity coins, although his pursuit of coins may become less consuming as he ages. Men don't know they have a masculinity bank; they just know it's important to do things that are *manly* in the eyes of their peers.

Not all men are macho, so different men fill their banks differently. For example, Rob the corporate executive proves his masculinity by having a corner office, complete with an attractive young secretary. This would mean nothing to Louis the artist, who measures his masculinity by winning awards for his exceptional paintings. But artistic skill means nothing to Tom the police officer, who proves his masculinity by being the best marksman on the force. However, Kenneth the college professor has never touched a gun. He proves his masculinity by seeing how many female students he can coax into bed with him.

Is there a positive side to all this manhood proving? Of course. It produces bravery, heroism, generosity, self-sacrifice, and innovation. Every day men prove their worth by working hard, sacrificing for their families, and serving their communities. I'm not a particularly macho fellow, but a few years ago I took up home remodeling. I enjoy slicing boards and driving nails, partly because it feels manlier to me than sitting at a computer all day (my regular job). My desire to fill my masculinity bank results in a nicer home for my family. When a project is finished, I invite my friends over, who praise me for my carpentry skills (ka-ching, ka-ching). Even writers and artists like me have a masculinity bank to fill, and we must find clever ways to prove our manhood because we lack a macho persona and profession.

Masculinity banks experience withdrawals as well. If a man fails in manly endeavors, he loses a few coins. If he does something that his peers regard as *womanly*, it's like pulling the stopper out of the bank and dropping coins down a sewer. For instance, if word gets around that a man wears lacy underwear, that pretty much cleans out his masculinity bank in a matter of seconds.

Since men work so hard to fill their masculinity banks, they are naturally reluctant to give up their coins. Men avoid anything that might drain their banks. This explains why womanly behavior is so damaging to a man. Why being called a "girlie man" or hearing "you're such a woman" is a stinging insult to a man.

Churchgoing:
A Good Way to Deplete Your Masculinity Bank

Because many men regard churchgoing as womanly behavior, it costs a fellow a few coins every time he enters the sanctuary. It costs him more if word gets around at work that he *loves Jesus*. Imagine this scene one Wednesday night after a long, hot day on the construction site:

BILL: Hey, where you guys going after work?

DEAN: I'm going out for a beer.

JEREMY: I've got tickets to the Dodgers game.

BILL: How about you, Sam?

SAM: Ummm . . . I'm going to church.

Can you hear the masculinity coins spilling out of Sam's bank? In the eyes of Sam's peer group, going to a bar or a ball game is masculine behavior. Going to church is not. Here's the popular image of *real men* vs. *church men:*

Real Men . . .	Church Men . . .
live a wild life.	live a restrained life.
enjoy sexual conquest and sexual variety.	experience sexual deprivation or monotony.
look at women.	look at their Bibles.
drink beer.	drink grape juice.
go to parties.	go to potlucks.
drive cool cars.	drive the church van.

light cigarettes.	light candles.
hang out with babes in bars.	hang out with babies in the nursery.

Never mind that most of these stereotypes are exaggerations; the reputation is persistent and powerful. In short, a lot of men are reluctant to go to church because of the reputation that would follow. They are not afraid of God; they are afraid of emasculation.

There is an exception. If a man goes to church for purely cultural reasons but there's clearly no commitment to Christ, the loss of coins is minor. I call this *the Mafia Exception*. For instance, Mafia thugs can attend Mass, but their masculinity remains intact, because it's obvious they're not really religious. And there are millions of guys who employ a Mafia strategy: they attend church but are careful to remain unaffected by what they hear. These men attend services to keep their women happy or to preserve cultural tradition. But the gospel bounces off their souls like bullets off Superman's chest. These clever men have found a way to intersect with the church without losing their masculinity. I suspect many of these men realize they are hypocrites, but they don't care: their manhood is intact.

CHURCH: A WOMAN'S DESTINATION

Anyplace women hang out is a woman's destination in the minds of men. Shopping malls, quilting bees, cosmetic counters, flower shops, kitchens, and churches have this reputation. As I said before, a man who spends any more time than is absolutely necessary in these precincts is calling his manhood into question.

I went to a sportsman's show and polled ninety-five guys on the question of women's destinations. Thirty-two percent of the men thought church was a woman's destination, while only 12 percent thought it was a man's destination. Sunday school was even more lopsided: 51 percent thought it was a woman's destination, while just 3 percent thought it was a man's destination.[3]

A man will go to a woman's destination, but he will not tarry there.

For example, on occasion my wife has sent me to the fabric store to pick up some sewing notions. I'm like Flash Gordon: in and out before anyone can see me. A man can walk into a flower shop, purchase something for his wife, and leave without shame. But to stand around, smelling the lovely bouquets and commenting on the beautiful arrangements, is masculine suicide!

Men deal with church as they would any other women's thing: they choose not to go, or they go with reluctance, projecting an air of disinterest or mild hostility during the entire service. Once the service is over, they scoot out the door as fast as they can. It's okay in some men's minds to attend church as long as they're not seen enjoying it! (This is the Mafia strategy in practice.)

Millions of men who *do* attend church never speak of it in public—especially among other men. Churchgoing men are embarrassed—not because of Christ, but because churchgoing implies that a man is feminine. Saying, "I like to go to church," is akin to saying, "I like to go to baby showers." It's something men keep quiet about.

Priests Abstain from Manly Behavior

Men have a natural hunger to create something: to build a business, a family, a career. Yet the Catholic Church, America's largest denomination, is led by men who create none of these things. Catholics venerate men who turn their backs on typical manly behavior. Jesuit Patrick Arnold writes,

> "Real (spiritual) Men" must abandon most of the values and enterprises nearest to men's hearts—competition, fighting, sexual expressiveness, generativity, economic productivity, adventure, autonomy—in favor of a eunuch's existence. The eunuch motif is even present in the premier model held up to married Christian men: Joseph the husband of Mary, usually presented as an old man, sexless and frozen ideal. It is little wonder that so many men get a strong unconscious message that involvement with Christian spirituality requires a kind of emasculation. It seems to them that the men best suited for Christian life are odd and asexual, nerds, or very old and "out of gas."[4]

How Money and Manhood Go Together

Ever wonder why men think churches ask for money too much? Men need money to prove their masculinity—a trophy home, a fishing boat, a titanium driver—the trappings of manhood are expensive. American society looks down on men who lack money. Men are expected to provide, and surrendering that 10 percent makes it that much harder to meet society's expectations. Men may also feel the church is talking out of both sides of its mouth: on the one hand, we're supposed to give generously, but on the other hand, we're not supposed to worry about money or work long hours.

Men hate shelling out money for something that benefits them not a whit. For example, my friend Reed was forced to pay child support for kids he rarely saw. He loved his kids, but he resented the financial burden. However, Reed's resentment eased when his ex-wife allowed him to become more involved in the children's lives. In the same way, when men understand their church's mission and become fully engaged, their resentment disappears—and their giving increases.[5]

Women Can Be Manly, but Men Cannot Be Womanly

Many women don't understand a man's need to prove his masculinity, because they have no similar need to prove their femininity. In fact, if a woman does something that society considers unwomanly, she experiences not shame, but a delicious sense of rebellion. Today's women cross over easily into men's roles and do so with delight. Women who take on traditionally male roles are held up as models. *But men are absolutely prohibited from crossing over into women's roles.*

This begins early in life. A young girl who copies boys in her mannerisms and dress is lovingly referred to as a *tomboy*. This is a celebrated stage of female development. However, there is no equivalent *tomgirl* stage for boys. Instead, an effete boy is called a sissy—if he's lucky. Any trace of femininity in young men is suspicious. How might our society react to a ten-year-old boy who plays with dolls, wears dresses, plans tea parties, and applies lipstick?

The one-way barrier continues throughout adolescence and adult-hood. Girls play varsity sports, but boys rarely take ballet. Women are clawing their way into male-only schools, but few men attempt the reverse (at least they never call a press conference to announce it). Many women are taking *men's jobs,* but few men are taking *women's jobs.* For example, 29 percent of the lawyers in America are women, but less than 2 percent of kindergarten and pre-K teachers are men.[6] (I must apologize for the political incorrectness of this discussion, but it's the way things are.)

Men are deeply embarrassed to appear feminine in public. When my wife says to me, "Hold my purse for a minute," I'm mortified. I don't want to be seen in public holding a purse. But when I say to my wife, "Hold my hammer for a minute," she feels no shame. In fact, women are intensely curious about men's stuff and are anxious to learn all they can. Women now make about half the purchases at America's home improvement megastores.[7] Our local Home Depot features Do-It-Herself Workshops on Monday nights. I can just hear the conversation between Sheila and her girlfriends at lunch the next day:

> SHEILA: Hey, girls, guess what I did last night? I went to Home Depot and learned how to work a band saw!
>
> SHEILA'S FRIENDS: Oooooh, that's cool!

Now, picture this conversation between Chuck and his buddies:

> CHUCK: Hey, guys, guess what I did last night? I went to Michaels Craft Store and learned how to make decorative pillow shams!
>
> CHUCK'S FRIENDS: (*Stunned silence*)

The media enforce gender roles. In film, when a woman poses as a man, she's noble. *Shakespeare in Love, Mulan,* and *Yentl* come to mind. But when a man takes on a feminine role, he's a joke! *Mrs. Doubtfire, Tootsie,* and *Mr. Mom* are laughingstocks. In *Meet the Parents* a handsome, muscular male nurse has his manhood questioned simply because he's not a doctor.

Can you see why it's so hard for men to go to church? If a man (or his friends) sees church as a woman's thing, then it's something he just can't do. It's emasculating. Women pay no similar price. It does not "efemulate" a woman to go to church. *The myth of the male-dominated church only makes it more attractive to women—it's another gender barrier that women are courageously crossing.*

This brings up two very important questions: Did Christ intend for men to give up their masculinity to follow Him? Is giving up one's manhood part of the cost of following Jesus Christ? No, and no again! Christ did not come to make men more feminine; He came to restore them to real manhood. There is no indication from Scripture that emasculation is a requirement of the Christian walk. Men must give up many things to follow Jesus. Manhood is not on the list.

But men do not realize this. Millions of men worldwide perceive the church to be feminine, and what they encounter on Sunday morning only confirms their worst fears. How did this happen? We now plunge into the very heart of the book, where we will uncover the dozens of little things that cause men to hate going to church.

PART 4

THE STRAWS THAT BREAK MEN'S HEARTS

Up to this point I've been pretty general in explaining why men resist church. Now we get down to specifics. Perhaps you turned to this section hoping to find a smoking gun, some secret force that is barring men from the riches of life in Christ. Or you may think I'm about to identify some quick, easy method that's guaranteed to get any man to come to church.

Sorry. I wish I could say, "This is it. Here is the barrier that is keeping men from the church." But there is no single barrier. There is no smoking gun. Truth is, there are many different reasons men hate church, because there are many different kinds of men.

Remember the story of the straw that broke the camel's back? For the next three chapters we'll sift through the pile of straws that are squeezing the masculine spirit out of our churches. Individually, these straws are trifles, but together they form a heavy burden that is crushing men's hearts.

Before we dig into this pile of straws, here's my top-ten list of excuses men give for not wanting to go to church:

10. I don't have time.

9. Church just doesn't work for me.

8. It's boring.

7. It's irrelevant to my life.

6. I don't like the pastor.

5. I don't want to talk about it.

4. It's too long.

3. They ask for money too much.

2. It's for wimps.

(drum roll, please)

The number one reason men give for not going to church, that perennial favorite:

1. There are too many hypocrites there.

Do these excuses address the real reasons men don't go to church? Not really. Women face these issues as well but still make church a priority. If you want to get past the excuses to discover the real barriers, you must ask *why: Why do men think it's too long? Why do men find it boring and irrelevant? Why do men think there are too many hypocrites?* And here's the big one: *Why are these attitudes so common in men but rarely found in women?*

14

MEN ARE AFRAID ... VERY AFRAID

MEN AND WOMEN FEAR DIFFERENT THINGS. ACCORDING TO Sam Keen, "Men's fears focus around loss of . . . independence and women's around the loss of significant relationships. We [men] most fear engulfment, anything that threatens to rob us of our power and control. Women most fear abandonment, isolation, loss of love."[1]

If Keen is right, then modern church culture seems likely to frighten men and comfort women. Today's churches place heavy emphasis on giving up power and control—something men need to do, but dread doing. Meanwhile, church involvement means friends and relationships, something women deeply desire. In this way, churchgoing shields a woman from her deepest fear, while it forces a man to encounter his deepest fear.

Now, on top of this deep fear, Christians unwittingly pile other things that make men anxious. A number of common Christian practices can reduce a man to a mouse, emotionally speaking. Rather than face these multiple traumas, men just take a pass on church. In this chapter, I'll identify several things men fear and show you what an individual Christian can do to help the men who show up on Sunday.

MEN FEAR INCOMPETENCE

Men hate to be outshone by women, but it happens all the time in church. Because men are not as studious as women, they often lack the Bible knowledge and Christian vocabulary it takes to shine in an evangelical church. Sarah Sumner writes, "Most men who are bad golfers would rather go play bad golf than go to church. That's how incompetent they feel in the house of God. It would take a miracle for biblically incompetent men to feel excited about gathering with a group of biblically competent women."[2]

Why aren't men becoming competent Christians? As I said earlier, the path to Christ now leads through a classroom. Study. Read. Learn. Attend classes. Acquire knowledge. Perfect your theology. It's a path few men are willing to walk, unless they happen to be the studious type.

MEN ARE AFRAID TO SING IN PUBLIC

If you're going to be a Christian, you'd better like to sing. Christians rarely gather without breaking into song. Yet many men feel incompetent singing aloud unless they have a voice like Pavarotti's. Exhortations such as, "C'mon, Ralph, just make a joyful noise," don't help.

The only place men sing together is a masculine venue. Men will sing the national anthem at a baseball game. Soccer crowds are renowned for male singing (lots of beer helps loosen their tongues). Men in military formation sing in deep cadence. Promise Keepers rallies feature robust singing for three reasons: (1) most of the men are already Christians, (2) they know the songs, and (3) they are in a sports arena with no women around.

Even among churchgoers, singing is more popular with women than men. We polled our fifteen-hundred-member church: while three-quarters of the women chose praise singing as a top priority, only about half the guys chose it.[3]

Robert Lewis has noticed a curious trend in his Arkansas megachurch: praise skippers. These people (mostly men) consistently arrive half an hour late to the worship service. Lewis suspects these fellows are tardy on purpose to miss the singing. There are also a number of men who sneak out as soon as the sermon is over, perhaps for the same reason.

Personally speaking, I love to sing. But I have talked to enough unchurched guys to know that public singing can be a barrier for them. They may not mind a few short songs, but today's contemporary churches feature twenty, thirty, or even forty-five minutes of nonstop praise singing. Verses repeat over and over. And over.

I'm convinced there are a million unchurched men who would attend a worship service this weekend *if they just didn't have to sing*.

Pastor Lewis dropped singing from his Men's Fraternity gatherings and attendance leaped. Some church planter is going to figure this out and reap a rich harvest of men.

MEN FEAR BEING SINGLED OUT AND EMBARRASSED

The conventional wisdom is that visitors to your church expect a friendly greeting and want to be recognized. Rick Warren points out that visitors actually hate all this attention: "Ironically, the way many churches welcome visitors actually makes them feel more uncomfortable than if they'd just been left alone . . . one reason large churches attract so many visitors is because newcomers like being able to hide in a crowd."[4]

I believe men are particularly embarrassed when they are introduced in church because they are naturally less relational or they're worried about who sees them there. It's especially bad for an unchurched husband who's introduced by his holy wife. He may feel she's showing him off, like a trophy.

MEN ARE AFRAID OF THE CHRISTIAN LIFESTYLE

Many non-Christians fear that if they start going to church, they might have to adopt a boring, straitlaced lifestyle, like the one lived by Ned Flanders, a character on the animated sitcom *The Simpsons*. According to a writer in *Christianity Today*:

> Religion informs nearly every aspect of Ned's life, from the doorbell that chimes "A Mighty Fortress is Our God" to his air horn that blares the Hallelujah chorus . . . He belongs to a Bible-study group and keeps notes stuck on his refrigerator with a sign of the fish magnet . . . Ned does not allow the kids to use dice when playing board games because dice are wicked. He is hesitant to buy the children Red Hots candies because there is a lascivious caricature of the devil on the package. The kids' favorite games are Good Samaritan and Clothe the Leper.[5]

A common fear among men is that Christianity will turn them into a nerd or a nut. Wayne Jacobsen notes, "Everyone knows somebody who got excited about God and decided to *live by faith*, which means he stopped working and lived off those who were working. Others have even waited for a word from God before they brushed their teeth."⁶

Other men see Christianity as the end of fun and challenge. Pastor Lee Strobel had this attitude during his years as an atheist:

> I'd think to myself, "Boy, I never want to end up like that." In other words, if Christianity requires a person to become a societal misfit who has no social life except church services and prayer meetings, count me out. [I saw] Christians as being boring, out of touch, and living a "plain vanilla" lifestyle that's devoid of excitement, challenge, or fun.⁷

No man wants to become a Ned Flanders. Fortunately, this barrier often falls away when a man meets Christians who are engaged with the world and enjoying life.

MEN FEAR THEY WILL HAVE TO CHECK THEIR MINDS AT THE DOOR

Well-educated people, and men in particular, have a hard time taking things on faith. They have been taught to believe only what they can measure, identify, and prove with the scientific method. A Gallup study found that young, well-educated males are the group of Americans least likely to be fully spiritually committed.⁸

Many men object to the anti-intellectual, antiquestion atmosphere in some churches. Ed was raised Baptist, but "the last church I went to, I committed the cardinal sin of expressing my opinion and it involved questioning the Bible, or more to the point, my interpretation of it. I was chastised for not having blind faith. Well, it's been twenty-two years, and I haven't had to worry about a confrontation like that again." Other churches have set up modern science as a bogeyman, and they spend as much time trashing scientific theory as they do preaching the gospel.

When educated men *do* try church, they're often faced with a difficult choice. They can attend a mainline church that allows intellectual exploration but offers little in the way of the Spirit. Or they can attend a vibrant evangelical or charismatic church, but they will have to endure frequent indictments of the evils of modern science.

You don't have to abandon biblical orthodoxy to attract men. In fact, theologically conservative churches are growing the fastest. *Well-educated men want a church where God is real, but not one that treats science as an enemy.* They want a church where they can ask questions and challenge the party line. Mainline churches take note: this is one area where you can really make inroads with men. The balancing act is to allow for differences in interpretation without slipping into outright heresy. Proclaim the truth with boldness, but do not make people feel evil or dumb for disagreeing. Conservative churches: let men ask uncomfortable questions, and resist the urge to promote a science versus God sideshow.

MEN FEAR THEIR CHILDREN ARE BEING BRAINWASHED

While most men welcome the moral instruction that the church provides children, some men are openly hostile to it. British pastor Michael Fanstone notes that "many unbelieving husbands have a serious fear that someone will indoctrinate their children—either their mother at home, or others at church."[9] Other fathers fear the church will make their boys weaklings or wimps.

The key here is openness and communication with parents. Teachers, let men know what you're teaching their kids. Invite them to sit in. Show them you have nothing to hide, and their fears will subside.

SINGLE MEN FEEL TARGETED FOR MARRIAGE

The apostle Paul was clear that singleness is a noble status for a Christian, but the modern church didn't get that memo. Many a churchgoer sees singleness as a disease, and baby, we've got the cure! Carol Penner writes, "At times single people may also feel that they are seen only as objects for marriage. This experience may feel like being treated as sick persons needing care until they're well (married). 'How are you? Any special friends we should know about? No? Oh, that's too bad.'"[10]

Single men from ages eighteen to thirty-five are the demographic group least likely to attend church, so when such a man shows up for church, he may feel out of place. Or he may feel like a deer in the gun sights: a target of the many marriage-minded single women of the congregation. My churchgoing, single male friends tell me there's constant, subtle pressure on them to settle down and get married. This may be one reason single men prefer large churches; they are less likely to be hounded about their marital status.

We can help single men by accepting them as they are. Please, resist the urge to play matchmaker.

MEN MAY FEAR THEY MUST BECOME SUPERHUSBANDS

Christian men are supposed to be magnificent husbands. Kevin Leman observes, "Not only are men supposed to attend morning Bible studies, but they're also supposed to get home in time for dinner, spend time alone with each child, date their wives once a week, and earn enough money so that their wives can stay home with their young children. This is a heavy load, and some Christian men start to resent it."[11] Rather than deal with these crushing expectations, a man may just drop out of church.

HUSBANDS MAY BECOME JEALOUS OF CHRIST OR THE CHURCH

Edwin Louis Cole once got a call from an angry husband. "Pastor," he said, "I don't go to your church, but I need to tell you something. My wife has left me for another man. His name is Jesus."

When a woman *falls in love with Jesus,* her husband may panic. Linda Davis writes, "All he knows is that she's in love with someone else, and he is jealous. Instead of remaining the first priority in her life . . . he has suddenly been demoted to number two after God . . . It would be easier for him to understand if she had run off with another man, but she's in love with someone he can't even compete with. He feels helpless."[12] Jeri Odell describes what happened in one household: "When Jill came to Christ, Rob shared that he felt replaced by someone he couldn't see, hear or understand. He admitted to bouts of jealousy and feeling unimportant and unacceptable."[13]

Today's American man typically has just one friend: his wife. When Jesus enters the picture, she's suddenly best friends with someone else. Men feel rejected, so they fight back the only way they know how: by refusing to have anything to do with church. *Take that, Jesus!* It's a normal male response to a rival.

Pastors, Christian teachers, and even Christian books feed this rivalry by inviting women to imagine themselves married to Jesus. One well-known Christian author says to his female readers, "At times, Jesus will be more of a husband to you than the man of flesh that you married. And while your husband may wonderfully meet many of your needs, only the Bridegroom can and will meet all your needs."[14] Another asks her readers to "develop an affair with the one and only Lover who will truly satisfy your innermost desires: Jesus Christ."[15] Another author tells women, "This Someone entered your world and revealed to you that He is your true Husband. Then He dressed you in a wedding gown whiter than the whitest linen. You felt virginal again. And alive! He kissed you with grace and vowed never to leave you or forsake you. And you longed to go and be with Him."[16]

Whew! How is a man supposed to compete with Jesus? He's always patient, kind, loving, and accepting. Not only does He kiss you with grace, but He never needs a breath mint. Jesus never loses His temper, never forgets an anniversary, and never goes out with the boys after work.

Woman readers, if you imagine your relationship with Jesus as a rapturous love affair, I must warn you: you are on dangerous ground for two reasons:

1. You are not the bride of Christ. According to the Bible, there is only one bride of Christ: the church (all believers collectively throughout time and throughout the world). *Individual believers are not brides of Christ.*

2. Your husband will never measure up to your fantasy. He cannot satisfy you if you harbor an image of Christ as your lover or husband.

Whereas some women are in love with Jesus and want to spend all their time at His feet (the Mary syndrome), other women just want to be busy for God (the Martha syndrome). Marthas are in love with the church. That was the situation in my marriage some years ago. Since my wife tells this story better than I do, I'll hand the keyboard to her. Gina, take it away.

GINA: David had just started a business, which required long hours and lots of his attention. Meanwhile I threw myself into church activities with abandon. At one point I was involved in seven ministries. I was so busy in the church that I had no personal life. Correction: church *was* my personal life. It seemed like whenever David wanted to spend time with me, I was busy at church. Naturally, he was jealous.

This went on for years. He was enslaved to his career, and I was enslaved to ministry. Finally, things blew up between us. We went to counseling and found out both of us were having affairs: David with work, I with church. Our story has a happy ending. David learned to cherish me, and I learned to respect him. Now I get my affirmation from my husband, not the choir mistress.

Women, I'm speaking from personal experience: if you are pouring your heart into the church because it gives you affirmation your husband fails to provide, I feel for you. I know what you're going through. But neither church nor Jesus is meant as a substitute husband. As David said earlier, you are on dangerous ground. You are giving your husband a perfect excuse to hate the church: *it gets the time and affection that are rightfully his.* Back to you, David.

MEN FEAR HOMOSEXUALITY IN THE CHURCH

Men are less accepting of homosexuality than women are. Women are more likely to support legalized gay marriage and legal rights for homosexual couples.[17] Men are threatened by homosexuality in a way that women are not. (My liberal readers may be thinking, *Men should just get over their homophobia!* I must remind you, this book is not about how men *should* be.)

We've already seen how churchgoing men are less masculine than average. If a man walks into a church and finds himself surrounded by passive or sensitive men, he may become suspicious. Then there's hand holding. Worshippers are often asked to hold hands with a neighbor. This attempt to model Christian unity can be awkward for men, especially those seated next to other men. (I've been a churchgoer almost thirty years, and I'm still not wild about holding hands with another guy, especially one I barely know.) And certain churches are hug-rich environments. It's one thing for very close friends to embrace, but in some congregations it's customary for relative strangers to enfold. A lot of man-to-man hugging can stir up fears of homosexuality.

The news media are making things worse. When you hear a report about the church these days, it's usually about gays: "Will the church allow gay pastors?" "A denomination appoints the first gay bishop." So the words *church* and *gay* are becoming intertwined in men's minds. Men have long been wary of the church, and these headlines only confirm their fears.

Society never regarded pastors as the manliest of men. Now the Catholic priesthood, the nation's most visible pastoral group, is said to be more than 50 percent homosexual.[18] The upcoming generation of Catholic priests may be up to 70 percent gay.[19] This was a quiet little secret for years, but with the controversy over abusive priests, clergy sexual practice is front-page news. Protestant ministers tend to be painted with the same brush since non-Christians often fail to make the distinction between Catholic and Protestant clergymen.

Whether you favor gay rights or not, it's easy to see the corrosive effect that all of this attention to gay issues is having on men's church participation. Not surprisingly, the denomination at the forefront of the gay rights movement, the Episcopal Church, is the one with the worst gender gap. Catholic churches also have a difficult time attracting men, and recent sex scandals may make things worse. A report from the U.S. Conference of Catholic Bishops admits that four out of five abuse victims were teenage boys, and "the crisis was characterized by homosexual behavior."[20] We've given fathers the perfect excuse to abandon Christianity: they are shielding their sons from possible sexual abuse.

Other Fears in the Area of Sex

Since the Victorian era, the church has been associated with extreme prudery when it comes to sexual matters. The image of Christians is: they don't talk about sex, they don't like sex, and they probably don't get much sex. Today's unchurched men regard biblical prohibitions against premarital sex as outdated, and the celibacy rules for priests seem just plain bizarre.

There's no way to be delicate about this, so I'll just say it. Some men are reluctant to go to church because it says to the world, "I'm not getting much sex." A churchgoing single guy says to the world, "I'm celibate." In some circles a single man who's voluntarily celibate is believed to be sexually impotent or gay.

This is a huge subconscious hurdle for a lot of men. Even men who aren't sleeping around are loath to put a sign on their heads that says, "I've been sexually tamed." Church affiliation implies that you are not performing as a man. Plus Christian men mustn't engage in locker room boasting, a primary form of male communication.

The point of this argument is not to say the church should loosen its moral stands to attract more men. I'm merely noting another aspect of the subconscious battle that rages in men's minds: *church threatens their ability to fill the masculinity bank.*

MEN ARE AFRAID OF HEAVEN

Let's end this chapter on a lighter note. Popular notions of heaven strike fear into men's hearts. What man wants to spend eternity wearing a white robe, floating on clouds, plucking a harp? Men fear heaven because it sounds so dull. No challenge. No uncertainty. No fun. In heaven there's nothing to do.

Excuse me, there is one thing to do: sing. As a youngster, John Ortberg sang in the youth choir under the direction of Mrs. Olson. He said, "When she became frustrated with the boys, she'd clap her hands and say, 'You children better start singing, because when we get to heaven, that's what we'll be doing.' For an 11-year-old boy, the thought of ten billion years under the enthusiastic direction of Mrs. Olson was not my idea of eternal bliss."[21]

An eternity singing in the choir. Contrast this with Mormon heaven, where faithful men spend eternity making celestial babies. Or consider Muslim heaven, where martyrs enjoy the everlasting ministrations of seventy-two virgins. Guys, which sounds better to you: eternal singing or eternal sex? Is it any wonder why Mormonism and Islam are growing so rapidly, and are so popular with males?

Men, regarding heaven, there's hope in the parable of the talents. Remember the words of the Master: "Well done, good and faithful servant; you were faithful over a few things, I will make you ruler over many things. Enter into the joy of your lord" (Matt. 25:21). This passage implies, at least, there will be something to do in heaven besides singing. As a man, let me tell you, that's really good news!

15

THE CHURCH IS OUT OF TOUCH

A LOT OF GUYS FIND THE CHURCH HOPELESSLY OUT OF TOUCH with the real world—irrelevant to their everyday lives, stuck in the past, hypocritical, and self-serving. In this chapter we'll examine these objections in detail and see what we can do to battle these perceptions.

THE CHURCH IS HOPELESSLY OUT OF DATE; MEN ARE PUZZLED BY ITS OLD-FASHIONED WAYS

If a man from the 1870s were suddenly transported to modern America, he'd find a different world. The ways that people relate, communicate, travel, and do business have completely changed. But if he visited the statistically average church of eighty-four people, he'd feel right at home. He'd sing familiar hymns,[1] sit in familiar pews, hear a familiar sermon from a pastor wearing a familiar robe. Truth is, a lot of churches (and Christians) are frozen in time. Why is this?

In chapter 9 we saw that 85 percent of churchgoers have change-resistant, passive personalities. George Barna found that most people form their religious identities by the time they're thirteen years old.[2] For many people true worship is what they experienced as children, so you can see why innovation comes painfully slow in the church.

We may love our old-time religion, but unchurched men do not. They are not looking for a trip down memory lane. We forget that most unchurched Americans used to go to church; indeed, many men would prefer to forget their childhood church experiences! By keeping out-of-date traditions alive, we may be unintentionally driving men away.

Are traditions always a barrier to men? Not when they understand them. My suggestion: examine your traditions and emphasize the ones

126

that are most meaningful to men. If a tradition has lost all meaning, discard it or update it for a modern audience.

MEN REALIZE THE CHURCH COULD FUNCTION MORE EFFECTIVELY IF IT EMBRACED MODERN TECHNOLOGY

Men love technology. Men are more likely than women to get excited about gadgets or spend hours with their machines. Men always want the fastest computer, the biggest engine, the smallest cell phone, the most powerful firearm.

But many churches are wary of technology, and adopt it at a glacial pace. Some churches still don't have e-mail or a fax machine, and at least 18 percent of churches don't even have a telephone answering machine.[3] Thanks to the Veggie Tales cartoons, many churches have replaced their filmstrips with TVs and VCRs. But the march to deploy technology often stops at the door of the sanctuary.

Some church members regard technology in the sanctuary as blasphemous. They believe that the sanctuary is holy ground and that bringing in modern technology defiles it. "It would ruin the sacred feeling of the service," commented one longtime church attendee. "Jesus didn't need a computer," said an older man I know. "I don't want to see PowerPoint on Sunday," declared one woman. "It reminds me too much of work."

Why is it important to embrace new technologies in church? George Barna reports that among those under fifty, "Information conveyed through the use of technology often has a higher degree of believability than does information coming directly out of a speaker's mouth."[4] Younger men will believe what they see on a screen more readily than what they hear from a live person.

Churches that want to reach men are using the Internet. Men want information before they commit to something, and a user-friendly Web site allows visitors to check out a church from a safe distance. Many of these sites offer sermon downloads (text, audio, and streaming video), places for members to connect, contact information, activity calendars, and extensive information on ministry offerings. Even small churches can post directions, activity calendars, and sermon audio on the Web.

A few churches have jumped headlong into the technology pool. One church in Dallas has installed a wireless computer interface in the sanctuary, so congregants can follow the sermon outline on their portable computers. St. Luke Lutheran Church in Haslett, Michigan, gives parents a restaurant-style personal pager when they check their little ones into the nursery. More pastors are using modern media to illustrate their messages. One Seattle church features a custom-produced video each week, around which the pastor builds his sermon. Other pastors use clips from popular movies to illustrate their messages.

Your church doesn't necessarily need to put a computer in every pew, but it shouldn't run from technology either. Technology is neither good nor evil; it is merely a tool that can help men (and women) understand the gospel. Bringing technology into the church does not defile it. A church that uses the latest technology to teach and encourage will be sending a strong message to men and young adults: *we speak your language.*

MEN RESPECT EXCELLENCE AND QUALITY; THEY HAVE LITTLE PATIENCE FOR MEDIOCRITY

When men think of church, *excellence* and *quality* are often the last two words that come to mind. In fact, church has a reputation for mediocrity in the minds of many men. When Pastor Rick Warren surveyed hundreds of unchurched Southern California residents, the number one complaint he heard was this: "Church is boring, especially the sermons. The messages don't relate to my life."[5] Not exactly the marks people give to an organization that delivers excellence.

A lack of quality in the worship service causes many men to cringe their way through church. In fact, John Lewis has dubbed this *the cringe factor:*

> He's referring to what happens when a Christian finally gets up enough nerve to invite his unbelieving friend to church, and the Christian quietly cringes through the service because of the off-key singing, out-of-tune piano, bad acoustics, malfunctioning microphones, and disjointed sermon.[6]

Men are turned off by amateurish music, worn-out facilities, and unkempt grounds. Lee Strobel puts it this way:

> I've been at churches where paint was peeling from the walls, sound systems were plagued by distortion, lighting was so dim I could barely see the face of the speaker, musicians read their lyrics instead of having them memorized, and the message sounded as if it were ad-libbed.[7]

Sunday morning is not the time for members to show off their children's musical potential. Walt says, "I've sat through many screeching violin solos and pitiful piano offertories. The mothers in the congregation think these are adorable, but we men do not." Even worse are adults who perform but lack talent. A church that really cares for tone-deaf Tanya will gently direct her away from the choir into an area where she's more gifted.

But few churches have the guts to do this. They just let Tanya sing, because telling her the truth might hurt her feelings. Men who visit the church don't know what a dear soul Tanya is. They just know the music is bad, and they don't come back. By choosing to be nice to Tanya, we don't realize we're closing the door to men.

Have you ever heard the phrase "it's good enough for church"? If we're serious about attracting men, we must banish this phrase forever. Churches that are producing fruit, growing numerically, and reaching men are those that pursue excellence in everything they do. Pastor Bob Russell's Southeast Christian Church has reached tens of thousands for Christ. He asks, "Why have our people been so bold in inviting their friends and so effective in getting them to come? Because they are excited about what they've experienced and are confident that every week the grounds, the nursery, the greeting, the singing, and the preaching will be done with excellence."[8] Eliminate the cringe factor, and men will feel more comfortable inviting their friends.

One last note on this: it is possible for a church to go too far in the pursuit of excellence. For instance, I've visited high churches that feature a professional organist and a paid choir. The quality of performance was impeccable, but the crowd was small, and quite frankly, the

Spirit of God was absent. Once again it's a balancing act: it takes a commitment to quality *and* the power of the Spirit to create the kind of excellence that draws people in.

SERVICES AND/OR SERMONS ARE TOO LONG

Men have shorter attention spans than women do. Anyone who's watched a man with a TV clicker in his hand knows this. Studies show men focus more intently than women, but do so for shorter lengths of time. We've already seen how testosterone makes it harder for men to sit still for a long time. Thanks to television, people are now trained to receive information in six- to eight-minute packages (that's the length of time between commercials).

When Thom and Joani Schultz polled churchgoers about the sermon, they found the following:

- Just 12 percent say they usually remember the message.
- Eighty-seven percent say their minds wander during sermons.
- Thirty-five percent say the sermons are too long.
- Eleven percent of women and five percent of men credit sermons as their primary source of knowledge about God.[9]

Certain ethnic congregations are renowned for their lengthy services. Three-hour worship, featuring a ninety-minute sermon, is fairly common in African-American churches. Jawanza Kunjufu interviewed black men, and every one of them said church services were too long. African-American men know when the preacher asks "for just another minute," he's actually going to take fifteen or twenty.[10] Men are also irritated when church services go late or fail to start on time.

The good news: innovative pastors are rethinking how they teach their people. They know the lecture-style monologue is the least effective way to teach anyone anything. These pastors are reengineering the sermon, and their churches are growing for it. We'll discuss this in chapter 19, "Teaching and the Masculine Spirit."

Local Churches Are Giving Up on Absolutes

The whole concept of moral absolutes is retreating in America's churches, especially in the mainline. Actions that used to be *right or wrong* are now *appropriate or inappropriate,* depending on the situation. Half of Presbyterians agree with this statement: "All the religions are equally good ways of helping a person find ultimate truth."[11] Sin no longer exists; it's been replaced *by poor decisions.* Of course, hell and the devil are completely off the radar screen in many a church, even though polls show the number of Americans who believe in Satan is increasing.[12]

> In de-emphasizing in recent generations a concern with absolutes and ultimates, heaven and hell, and eternity and infinity, modern Christianity has taken a decisive turn toward feminine religion, which is typically interested in the immanent and the incarnational, and finding God in the small things, the everyday, and the mundane . . . As liberal religion stresses increasingly the immanent and "horizontal" dimension of faith to the exclusion of the transcendent and "vertical" reality, it inadvertently ignores the voracious appetite of man for the Great, a Wholly Other, and the Eternal.[13]

The Church Has a Scaredy-Cat Image

For years many evangelical pastors taught their members not only to avoid sin, but also to avoid things that might lead to sin. Good Christians didn't drink, didn't play cards, didn't dance, didn't go to movies, didn't use tobacco, didn't listen to popular music, *and didn't associate with those who did.* This overly cautious, extremely risk-averse posture hurt the church's reputation with men. Although most churches have toned down these teachings in recent years, the reputation lives on.

During the 1970s and 1980s, record-burning ceremonies were common in some church circles. Many a Led Zeppelin, Pink Floyd, and Black Sabbath album met its demise at these events. I remember a Pentecostal church near our house holding a cigarette stomp in which smokers were invited to crush their Marlboros, Camels, and Kools underfoot.

Unchurched men may see these ceremonies as foolish or wasteful. Men think, *Who's afraid of a CD or a pack of cigarettes?*

Most men view records, books, and movies as harmless. They are not frightened by tales of wizards flying around on brooms. Over time, men get the message: *to be a Christian is to be frightened.* Start coming to church, and you, too, will become scared of books, movies, music, beer, cigarettes, and more. Men are reluctant to associate themselves with an institution that's scared all the time.

Don't misunderstand: it's good and proper to shield your family from negative influences. And we must stand up for what's right. But be very careful about public crusades against wickedness. The apostle Paul reminded us where our focus should be: "Keep your minds on whatever is true, pure, right, holy, friendly, and proper. Don't ever stop thinking about what is truly worthwhile and worthy of praise" (Phil. 4:8 CEV). Focusing on good instead of evil is the best way to combat a scaredy-cat reputation.

16

CHECK YOUR MANHOOD AT THE DOOR

NOT EVERY MAN HAS A SPECIFIC REASON FOR HATING TO GO to church. Some just feel a general unease with it. Rod says, "Church just doesn't work for me." Lance is a little more specific: "The style of worship is not compelling to me. It's just the feel of the whole thing. Emotionally, the style doesn't connect with me." Conrad is blunt: "Every Sunday I feel like I'm supposed to check my manhood at the door." Why do men feel manhood and Christianity are incompatible? Here are some specifics:

CHRISTIANS EMPHASIZE CHRIST'S FEMININE CHARACTERISTICS WHILE IGNORING HIS MASCULINE ONES

As we saw in chapter 4, when people think of Christ, they think of His feminine side. How does this happen? The feminization of Jesus begins in Sunday school. Think of the images of Christ you saw as a child. Didn't they suggest a gentle, meek Savior, a well-groomed and tidy man wearing a shining white dress? In these paintings He taps gently on a door, plays with children, or stares lovingly into the eyes of a lamb nestled in His arm. Although these images are comforting, they do little to suggest masculine strength and resolve. Bruce Barton attacked these holy pictures: "They have shown us a frail man, under-muscled with a soft face—a woman's face covered by a beard—and a benign but baffled look."[1] Jesuit priest Patrick Arnold laments Christ's frequent portrayal as *a bearded lady*. Christ has become, as John Eldredge puts it, "Mister Rogers with a beard. Telling me to be like him feels like telling me to go limp and passive. Be nice. Be swell. Be like Mother Teresa."[2]

Christians have so accepted the nonmasculine Jesus that the very idea

133

that He could be sexually tempted touched off a firestorm with the release of the film *The Last Temptation of Christ*. I'm not defending this wretched movie, but the Bible says that Jesus was "tempted in every way, just as we are—yet was without sin" (Heb. 4:15 NIV). Nevertheless, many Christians couldn't imagine Jesus tempted by sex. "He's just not that kind of man," said one woman at the time.

No, He is gentle Jesus, meek and mild. This perception is widely held inside and outside the church. When people are quoted in the media about the character of Jesus, they always stress His sensitivity, inclusivity, and tender compassion. Politicians refer to this Jesus when justifying more government spending. Our songs reflect this view as well: "Jesus, what a wonder You are! You are so gentle, so pure, and so kind."

Apparently, Jesus is so nice He prefers to lose. Kevin Leman tells the story of a mother who caught her two boys arguing over who would get the first pancake. Mom thought she had a golden opportunity to provide a moral lesson, so she said, "If Jesus were sitting here, He would say, 'Let my brother have the first pancake. I can wait.'" The older son turned to his brother and said, "Ryan, you be Jesus."[3]

Liberal churches have re-created Christ as a benevolent Teacher who is always gentle, tender, and accepting. This Christ would never offend anyone, never judge anyone, and of course, never send anyone to hell. If this Christ were a radio station, His slogan would be "all tenderness, all the time."

There are two problems with this view of Jesus: (1) it's not accurate, and (2) no man wants to follow a feminized man. Men are looking for a real man to follow: dynamic, outspoken, bold, sharp-edged. They want a leader who is decisive, tough, and fair. They respect a man who tells it like it is and doesn't mince words, even when it makes them mad. Men most respect a leader who doesn't care what others think of him.

Ironic, isn't it? The Jesus of Scripture was exactly this kind of man. He was fearsome: the Bible says the disciples were "terrified" of Him (Mark 4:41 NIV), and "no one dared ask him any more questions" (Mark 12:34 NIV). He was abrasive: He had no qualms about offending people (Matt. 15:12), and He regularly ridiculed His disciples for their thickheadedness (Matt. 15:16). He was ill mannered: He walked into a dinner party and immediately began insulting His host (Luke 11:37–53).

Truth is, the Jesus of Scripture is more General Patton than Mister Rogers.

Jesus Christ is the most courageous, masculine man ever to walk the earth. But we've turned Him into a wimp. His manliness and toughness are seldom spoken of, and men fall away because of it. Present the Christ of Scripture, and men will be irresistibly drawn to Him.

CHRISTIANS EMPLOY FEMININE THEMES, IMAGERY, AND VOCABULARY

Ninety-five percent of the senior pastors in America are men, but you could not tell it by the sermons they preach. Weakness, humility, relationships, communication, support, and feelings are constantly held up as the ideal values of a Christian. Again, men get the message that Christlikeness is synonymous with Mom-likeness. When was the last time you heard a sermon on competence, efficiency, or achievement? Each of these words describes Jesus, yet He's rarely credited with these attributes.

It's not just pastors: feminine terminology flows freely from the lips of churchgoers. References to sharing, communication, relationships, support, nurturing, feelings, and community are sprinkled throughout the conversation of Christians—both men and women. Gordon MacDonald finds it strange that Christian men use words such as *precious, tender,* and *gentle.* MacDonald admits these are nice words, but not typical masculine conversation.[4] Woody Davis found that Christian men emphasize themes and endorse messages that unchurched people—both men and women—regard as *womanly.* In other words, Christian men talk and think like women, at least in the eyes of the unchurched.[5]

Mainline churches have adopted *inclusive language,* stripping masculine pronouns from hymns, liturgy, and even Scripture, in an effort to make women feel more comfortable in church. It seems to be working: 60 to 75 percent of the adults in our mainline congregations are female. The Father, Son, and Holy Spirit no longer authorize our baptisms; that power now rests with the androgynous Creator, Redeemer, and Sanctifier. Bible translations are expunging masculine references: for example, we are no longer *sons* of God but *children* of God. Interestingly, feminine allusions such as *the bride of Christ* are still widely accepted.

Conservatives use man-repellent terminology as well. For example, in the Baptist universe you have two kinds of people: the *saved* and the *lost*. Men hate to be lost; that's why they don't ask for directions. If you tell a man he's lost, he will instinctively resist you! George Barna notes that a majority of unchurched people resent being referred to as lost.[6] And the only thing worse than being lost is being saved. The term drips with passivity. I've heard many a man ridicule Christianity by crying out, "Hallelujah, I'm saved!" When Hollywood released a movie mocking Christians, they titled it *Saved!*

Although Jesus used the term *saved* a number of times in the Gospels, only twice did He pronounce someone *saved* (Luke 7:50; 19:9). But He called many to *follow Him*. Hear the difference? *Follow* gives a man something to do. It suggests activity instead of passivity. But *being saved* is something that happens to damsels in distress. It's the feminine role. So why not use the descriptor that Jesus preferred? By calling men to follow Jesus, we put Christ's offer in active terms that appeal to everyone— especially men.

Another term from the feminine side is *sharing*. Christians are constantly being asked to share, as in, "Steve, would you please share with us what the Lord has placed on your heart?" Regular men don't talk this way. It sounds too much like kindergarten. Imagine a gang member saying to one of his brothers, "Blade, would you please share with us how you jacked that Mercedes?"

Jesus spoke constantly of the *kingdom of God*. Men are kingdom builders. They think hierarchically. But many churches have replaced the masculine term *kingdom of God* with the more feminine *family of God*. Jesus never uttered this phrase. It never appears in the Bible.[7] But we prefer *family of God* because it resonates with the feminine heart.

The term *relationship* gets a workout in church today. Evangelical churches frequently invite people to enter into a *personal relationship with Jesus Christ*. Does that phrase appear in the Bible? Nope. Nowhere does Scripture invite us to have a relationship with God or Jesus. Yet it has become the most popular way to describe the Christian walk! Why? Because it frames the gospel in terms of a woman's deepest desire—a personal relationship with a man who loves her unconditionally.

Nowadays it's not enough to have a personal relationship with Jesus; many of today's top speakers encourage men to have a *passionate* relationship with Him. These teachers have chosen a very uncomfortable metaphor to describe discipleship! Speaking as a man, the idea of having a passionate relationship with another man is just plain gross. Then we have the ever-popular *intimacy with God*. When men hear the word *intimacy*, the first thing that comes to mind is *sex*. Those dirty-minded guys! But guess what? Whenever the words *passionate* and *intimate* appear in the Bible, they always refer to sex or lust.

When a man loves another man, he uses terms such as *admire, look up to,* and *respect*. Men do not speak of passionate, intimate, or even personal relationships with their leaders or male friends. Can you imagine a couple of bikers having this conversation?

BIKER 1: Hey, Spike, let's go for a ride in the desert so we can develop a passionate relationship.

BIKER 2: Sure, Rocco. I'd like to enjoy some intimacy with you.

It gets worse. More than once, I've been exhorted by a prominent men's minister to *have a love affair with Jesus*. I just saw a new book for Christian men: *Kissing the Face of God*. An ad for the book invites men to "get close enough to reach up and kiss His face!"[8] Time out—this is a *men's* book? Yikes! With the spotlight on homosexuality in the church, why do we increase men's doubts by using the language of romance to describe the Christian walk? Conservative churches may oppose homosexuality, but their imagery is sending another message entirely. The more we describe Christianity as a passionate, intimate, face-kissing relationship, the more nervous men become.

Ministers and teachers, I beg you to be more careful with these terms. Men are very sensitive about their manhood. Using bedroom vocabulary to describe Christianity is not only unbiblical, but it sows doubt in men's subconscious minds. Here's my rule of thumb: when describing the things of God, use terms that would sound right on a construction site. Try words such as *friendship* and *partnership*. Challenge men to *follow* God or *walk* with Christ. See the difference it makes!

One more thing on relationships: men really do need to have a relationship with God. Religion without relationship is bondage! But men are not relationship oriented. *Relationship* is not a term men use in conversation, except when describing a male-female couple. Also, men file their relationships by what they do together; they have fishing buddies, business partners, army friends, and so forth. It's helpful to talk about God in the same active terms. Instead of encouraging men to *have a personal relationship with Jesus,* encourage them to *walk with Christ.* Invite them to *partner with Jesus in changing the world.* Challenge them to *build the kingdom of God.* Now you're talking a language that men can understand.

(One more quibble: Why are Christians always going on *retreats?* What kind of army is always retreating? Why don't we *advance* now and then?)

MUSIC IN THE LOCAL CHURCH FITS THE TASTES AND SENSIBILITIES OF WOMEN AND CHILDREN

Children's songs about Jesus always present His gentle side. I learned this song before I was three years old:

> Away in a manger, no crib for a bed,
> The little Lord Jesus laid down his sweet head.
> The stars in the sky looked down where he lay,
> The little Lord Jesus, asleep on the hay.

Such songs are appropriate for children, but many people carry a picture of sweet, passive, sleeping Jesus their entire lives. Some boys never recover from this image. To balance this impression, the church used to allow aggressive, warlike images of Jesus as well. In 1865 English composer Sabine Baring-Gould wrote this song as a *children's* march:

> Onward, Christian soldiers, marching as to war,
> With the cross of Jesus going on before.
> Christ, the royal Master, leads against the foe;
> Forward into battle, see His banners go!

But by the turn of the twentieth century, hymns had taken a decisive move toward the feminine. In 1913, C. Austin Miles wrote "In the Garden." Notice the difference in tone:

He speaks, and the sound of His voice
Is so sweet the birds hush their singing;
And the melody that He gave to me
Within my heart is ringing.

And He walks with me, and He talks with me,
And He tells me I am His own,
And the joy we share as we tarry there,
None other has ever known.

"Onward, Christian Soldiers" is passé in most congregations, but "In the Garden" is still widely sung. Christ has put down His sword and picked up a daisy. He is no longer a warrior; He is a lover. The very image of Christ taking up arms (as He does in Revelation 19) is simply unacceptable in a lot of churches today.

Praise music has accelerated this trend. Not only are the lyrics of many of these songs quite romantic, but they have the same breathless feel as top forty love songs.[9]

"Hold me close, let your love surround me. Bring me near, draw me to your side."

"I'm desperate for you, I'm lost without you."

"Let my words be few. Jesus I am so in love with you."

"You're altogether lovely . . . altogether wonderful to me."

"Oh Lord, you're beautiful. Your face is all I seek."

"You are beautiful, my sweet, sweet song."

Think of the mental gymnastics that must take place inside a man's subconscious mind as he sings lyrics like these. He's trying to express his love to Jesus, a man who lives today, using words no man would dare say to another, set to music that sounds like the love songs his wife listens to in the car. (By the way, men never call each other *beautiful*, *lovely*, or *wonderful*.)

I think this is why women generally enjoy praise music more than men do. Lyrically and stylistically, praise music resonates with a woman's heart. Men can and do enjoy praise music, but it's an acquired taste.

We can't go back to "Onward, Christian Soldiers." But no one has composed *masculine* praise songs to take its place. Songwriters, please fashion some songs that speak of battle, strength, and victory. Imagine Christ as our Commander, Coach, or Scout, not our Boyfriend. If you need inspiration, look to the Psalms. It's time to balance Christ the Lover with Christ the Warrior again. The men are depending on you.

MEN'S MINISTRY IS NOT VERY MANLY

Tony went to men's small group at his church—once. First, the men sat in a circle and sang praise songs for about ten minutes. Tony was asked to introduce himself and share about his life. Next, he was paired with a stranger and asked to share one of his deepest fears. Then, everyone was asked to share a prayer need or a praise report. The men read from the Bible, taking turns around the circle. Finally, the men stood in a circle and held hands for what seemed like hours, while one by one they bared their souls to God. One man was quietly weeping. The guy next to Tony prayed for ten minutes straight, and his palms were sweaty. Once the meeting was over, Tony didn't stay for cookies. He hasn't been back.

Men's ministry so often falters for this simple reason: *it's actually women's ministry for men.* When Christian men gather, they're expected to relate like women and to enjoy the things women enjoy. Men's ministry is built around the needs and expectations of women—or more precisely, the soft men who show up for men's ministry events. So the men's retreat features singing, hugging, hand holding, and weeping. Men sit in circles and listen, read, or share. We keep our conversations clean, polite, and nonconfrontational.

While there's nothing wrong with men doing these things, *it feels feminine* to a lot of guys. So they stay home. I've heard the same thing whispered about Promise Keepers rallies: certain guys are turned off by the singing, clapping, hugging, and crying that go on there. Fortunately, men's ministry is getting a transfusion of the masculine spirit. More in part 6 of this book.

THE EMOTIVE NATURE OF WORSHIP

Jesus wept. So do Christians. A lot. While there's nothing wrong with emotion, it's hard for American men to be emotional in public. David James writes, "Characteristically, men have been taught to repress most expression of emotion, with the exception of 'classic' male emotions such as lust and anger."[10] Certain churches expect their members to lose control emotionally—expressing the kind of sentiment males are expected to keep inside. It's no coincidence that African-American churches, known for very emotive worship services, are much more popular with women than men.

The answer is not a sterile, emotionless worship. Mr. Spock is not our model. Fortunately, Jesus showed us the balance point. He said that true worshippers would worship Him *in spirit and in truth* (John 4:24). When a church service is all spirit but little truth, men fall away. Same goes for churches that offer truth but no spirit. John Piper writes, "Worship must have heart and head. Worship must engage emotions and thought . . . Strong affections for God rooted in truth are the bone and marrow of biblical worship."[11]

Men are just as emotional as women; they just express themselves differently. So if a church welcomes feminine displays of emotion such as crying, hugging, and hand holding, it's time to welcome masculine displays such as applause, shouts, fist pumping, and high-fives. I'm serious. Men should be allowed to express their love for God in truly masculine ways as long as it is done in good order.

Please, don't gauge a man's commitment to Christ by his tears (or lack of them). I've seen fakes who cry a river at church, but who live sinful lives during the week. Conversely, some men are genuinely broken by God without ever shedding a tear. Sometimes the Holy Spirit works without Kleenex.

PRAYER-AND-SHARE IS TOUGH ON GUYS

Some churches allow folks to stand up and share with the congregation, a so-called *prayer-and-share* time. If your church is typical, the majority of people who speak up will be women. The last time I attended a service with prayer-and-share, nine women and one man offered requests. I believe this is a reflection of a woman's need to talk about her problems, and a man's reluctance to do so.

Prayer-and-share can be an irritant to men. You may have a couple of magpies in your congregation who stand up every week with some trivial thing to pray about: "Please pray for my Aunt Bessie's bunion." You may also have a couple of wannabe preachers who take two or three minutes to *share what God has placed on their hearts*. These are not prayer requests but sermonettes by people who want the spotlight. This grandstanding rankles men. A far better option is to offer one-on-one prayer opportunities at the end of the service since people are more candid when they can pray privately with a layperson or pastor.

THE BEAUTY CONTEST ATMOSPHERE

Some churches have an unwritten dress code. Everyone must show up *dressed for church* or wearing his Sunday best. This is another nod to femininity since women usually care more about their appearance and enjoy getting dolled up more than men do.

Fortunately, church dress codes are passing away. Informal dress is one of the hallmarks of the modern megachurch. One African-American church in St. Louis relaxed its dress code, and in short order its male attendance tripled![12] Men like to dress comfortably, so let them.

One more note on dress: men seem to relate better to informally dressed pastors and priests. A lot of pastors would like to dress down a bit, but their members insist they wear traditional vestments. If you want to attract men, encourage your pastor to dress less formally.

FEMININE HOLINESS IS THE NORM IN CHRISTIANITY

Oftentimes men's holiness is mistaken for sin because it does not look like holiness. Our modern notions of holy behavior were formed during the 1800s, the era when women completely dominated church pews. Victorian women were expected to conduct themselves in a certain way, and we still focus lots of energy on getting Christians of both genders to behave as such. So when a man tries to be godly in a way that feels right to him, others might see his actions as sinful. Douglas Wilson gives us a terrific example:

> Suppose a young girl notices that a friend at school seems somewhat discouraged. She asks if anything is wrong and leaves an encouraging note in her friend's locker. She looks her up after school and offers to pray with her. A teacher who sees all this will naturally thank God for this obvious dedication to love and good works. But that same teacher will not readily make this same assumption when he walks by a boy who is slapping a friend on the back of the head, calling him a fathead—even though the boy was doing this because his friend had asked a non-Christian girl out on a date the night before. His zeal for righteousness is not recognized as such.[13]

Few Christians would recognize a slap on the head or name-calling as godly behavior, yet for a young man ministering to another, such methods are far more effective than notes, cards, or flowers. Bottom line: we often fail to recognize godliness cloaked in the masculine spirit.

The masculine spirit burst forth unexpectedly in my church just yesterday. The pastor was halfway through his sermon when he turned to a man in the crowd who recently began walking with God. He asked, "Ray, has becoming a follower of Jesus changed your life?" In his exuberance, Ray let a mild profanity slip out. After a moment's pause, Ray edited himself, "Sorry, I meant to say *darn* right."

Did Ray sin? Did his spontaneous utterance please or displease God? If the standard for holiness is a Victorian womanliness, Ray committed a sin. Christian ladies don't use naughty words. But God looks at a man's heart. Ray's intent was not to curse, but to bless. He expressed his love for God using the emphatic language of men. It wasn't religious, but it was real.

And the men loved it!

CHURCHES DO NOT ALLOW MEN TO ACT LIKE MEN, AND GET UPSET WHEN THEY DO

There's something ferocious within a man. John Eldredge says men are *wild at heart.* "Aggression is key to the masculine soul," he explains.

"Take that away from a man and what you have left is passivity." But when men bring ferocity into the church, people get upset. Things get unpredictable. Feelings get hurt.

Before he became president of the United States, Teddy Roosevelt was a Sunday school teacher. One day a boy showed up for class with a black eye. He admitted he'd been fighting, on the Sabbath no less. Another boy was pinching his sister, so he took a swing at the scoundrel. The future president told the boy he was proud of him and gave him a dollar. When word of this got 'round the church, Roosevelt was let go.

TR was caught between two scriptural imperatives: *turn the other cheek* and *defend the weak*. One soft, the other tough. He chose to praise the boy for his tough response, but was fired for it, because in most churches the right choice is always the soft one.

When men lead like men, they are censured. I remember asking an entrepreneur in our church to become an elder. He rolled his eyes and said, "No, thanks. I've been an elder." His look said it all. Being a church leader is a frustrating experience, because a man cannot lead like a man. Instead he must be careful, sentimental, and thrifty; make every decision by consensus; talk everything to death. Decisions take months or years to make, and if someone's feelings might be hurt, we don't move forward.

Men are also reluctant to volunteer for ministry positions because they can't act like men. Men are often more physical with kids, and they communicate by giving noogies, wrestling, and teasing their protégés. Men take risks in ministry, which can earn them a rebuke. My friend Randy took the youth group downtown to minister to street people, but got in trouble for giving a ride to a man who had been drinking. Several mothers were incensed. "You're supposed to keep our children safe!" one mother said. "Why can't you just meet at the church and teach the Bible?"

If men are to return to church, we must let them be men. Ferocious, aggressive, risk-taking men. We can no longer expect men to act like proper Victorian ladies. Today's church needs a few more Teddy Roosevelts.

THE STRAWS THAT BREAK MEN'S HEARTS

Nothing in the last three chapters is an absolute soul killer for men. But weighed cumulatively, you have the straws that break men's fellowship with the church.

It's not a sin to focus on Jesus' feminine side, to sing songs that feel feminine, or to dress up for church. On behalf of men, all I ask is equal time for the masculine spirit.

What do men need? Men need permission. Permission to walk with Christ as one man walks with another. Permission to use their masculine gifts to change the world. Permission to awaken the long dormant masculine spirit. How we rekindle that spirit in our congregations is the subject of our next section.

PART 5

RESTORING THE MASCULINE SPIRIT IN THE CHURCH

When I was a kid, my favorite game show was *Let's Make a Deal*. The most dramatic moment came when Monty Hall asked the big question: "Will it be door number one, door number two, or door number three?" That's the question before us:

Keep church the way it is   **Adjust the thermostat**   **Meet men's deepest needs**

Door number one: Keep church the way it is. Meanwhile, we'll continue to pray that God changes men's hearts so they'll come back. But honestly, do you think this is going to happen? Albert Einstein said, "Insanity is doing the same thing over and over again and expecting different results." We are crazy to think that if we just pray hard enough, we can keep doing church as usual, and somehow men will come to their senses and return.

Door number two: Adjust the thermostat. We can take our existing church model and make changes so men will be more comfortable. The next six chapters are packed with ideas on how both laypeople and clergy can make these adjustments.

Door number three: Meet men's deepest needs. Once men are in the building, they won't stay unless we meet their deepest needs. Men must find their sacred role and learn to live the Christian life as a team. The final three chapters offer ways you can help.

If you're really serious about bringing men back to your church, here's my advice: open door number two first, then quickly move toward door number three. But before you open either door, a word of caution: you will run into a hornet's nest of opposition from well-meaning Christians. For the most part worshippers say they are comfortable with church as it is,[1] and anyone (pastor or layperson) who attempts to adjust the thermostat will be accused of abandoning the gospel, dividing the body, and putting performance ahead of people. You may well anger some of your best friends in the congregation. My advice is to pray, pray some more, then pray some more before stepping through either door. Jesus promised His followers persecution; don't be surprised if you experience it at the hands your fellow churchgoers.

My church went through a bold transition about five years ago. A new pastor brought the masculine spirit with him. He set high standards and cast an uncompromising vision. He turned up the heat on passive pew sitters. Hundreds left the church, but God sent hundreds more to take their place. Today our congregation is probably the fastest-growing church in Alaska. It's reaching out and loving the community, and many are coming to faith in Christ and being discipled for the first time. Best of all, there are a *lot* of excited men and young adults in our church. Now here's something you won't believe: my kids, ages sixteen, fourteen, and nine can't wait to go to church. It is the highlight of their week. My sixteen-year-old son is currently an exchange student overseas. I asked him what he misses most about home—his mom's cooking, his bedroom, his friends? "No, Dad," he said. "I miss our church."

Do you want a church like this? If so, open door number two, and see what you can do to awaken the masculine spirit in your congregation.

17

LEADERSHIP AND THE MASCULINE SPIRIT

THERE IS AMAZING AGREEMENT FROM CHURCH EXPERTS ACROSS the theological spectrum: it's time for laypeople to step up and take a greater leadership role in congregations. Gone are the days when the pastor leads and the people follow. If men are to return to Christ, they need strong, godly laymen to help them in their walk.

Unfortunately, the church is experiencing a leadership crisis at every level. Many congregations lack vision, focus, and purpose. Without these things men fall away. But churches with dynamic, gutsy leadership are growing and attracting men. In the area of leadership, our churches desperately need an infusion of the masculine spirit.

Not only do most churches lack leadership, but there is actually a bias against it. Christians tend to see it as a necessary evil rather than a core function of the church. Karl Clauson says, "Leadership is one of the gifts promised in Scripture. But if you say, 'My spiritual gift is leadership,' people look at you kinda funny. Mercy, teaching, giving, those are all acceptable. Leadership is not something Christians are supposed to aspire to."

Christians are uncomfortable with leadership because we're afraid of elevating one person above another. But in the church, leadership is not elevation; it's subjugation! The model in Scripture is the servant leader. Christ flipped the organizational chart.

If you want your church to attract men, you must put a high priority on developing leaders, especially male ones. Men are not looking for theologians, teachers, or facilitators. They are looking for men who will lead them to greatness. For too long we have asked men to follow our teaching, our methods, and our theology. Men do not follow these things. I'll say it again: *men follow men*. Provide men with great male leadership, and they will return.

GREAT LEADERSHIP IS BALANCED: A LESSON FROM THE EARLY CHURCH

Great leadership in the church requires a balance between the masculine spirit and the feminine spirit. The book of Acts records a crucial moment when the early church could have stumbled. Acts 6 (CEV) begins:

> A lot of people were now becoming followers of the Lord. But some of the ones who spoke Greek started complaining about the ones who spoke Aramaic. They complained that the Greek-speaking widows were not given their share when the food supplies were handed out each day. The twelve apostles called the whole group of followers together and said, "We should not give up preaching God's message in order to serve at tables." (vv. 1–2)

Had there been an excess of the masculine spirit, the apostles might have said, "We should not give up preaching God's message in order to serve at tables. We've got to focus! So let's stop feeding the widows. This will give us more time to do the task that Jesus gave us. After all, we've got a world to convert." As a result, you'd have starving widows. Obviously, a bad choice.

Had there been an excess of the feminine spirit, the apostles might have said, "We should not give up preaching God's message in order to serve at tables. However, the widows have become accustomed to having us wait on them, and to stop now would hurt their feelings. Therefore, we will do both. We will preach *and* wait on tables." The apostles would have been distracted from their core responsibility: hearing from God and expanding the church. Eventually, the church would have devolved into a first-century social service agency. Christianity would have died out within a generation or two.

How did the apostles respond to this leadership challenge?

"My friends, choose seven men who are respected and wise and filled with God's Spirit. We will put them in charge of these things. We can spend our time praying and serving God by preaching." This suggestion pleased everyone. (vv. 3–5)

If we want to make the church magnetic to men again, we must follow the example of the apostles. Correction, *we must allow our pastors to follow the example of the apostles.* Here's where you come in.

Christian, allow your pastor to delegate responsibility to godly people in the congregation. Great leadership takes time, but most pastors do not have as much time as they'd like for these important tasks. Why? *Because we expect a lot of them.* We expect them to visit us in our homes, visit us if we're sick, attend every meeting, and be there every time the church door is opened. They are on call twenty-four hours a day. They must also spend time with their families, exercise, study, prepare great sermons, and, oh yes, pray.

We have placed so many demands on our pastors that they have no time to lead us. Most pastors would love to be better leaders, but they simply don't have the time. Oftentimes when ministers try to delegate tasks, the people object. This is especially true in small churches. Like the widows in Acts 6, we've become accustomed to the pastor personally ministering to us. We see him as God's representative on earth. His prayers are more powerful and his insight more keen. His presence lends prestige to a meeting.

God forgive us. We need to get over this.

When we treat our pastors like personal chaplains, expecting them to drop everything and pay attention to us, we distract them from their most important God-given responsibility: leading the church. When pastors are not leading courageously, men leave. Men follow men who are leading them somewhere. But if your pastor is too busy to spend time with God, he will not know how or where the congregation needs to be led. Here are some specific ways you can help your pastor.

- Demand less of your pastor.
- Don't drop in on him. Make an appointment. Respect his time.
- Don't fill his calendar. Instead, make it your goal to relieve him of as many responsibilities as possible so he's free to lead the body courageously.
- Stop thinking of him as the minister. You are the minister; he is your coach.
- Allow him to delegate responsibility to godly people in your congregation.
- Train lay ministers in your congregation to pray with the sick and visit people in their homes. Don't expect the pastor to do this time-consuming ministry alone.
- Don't be disappointed when you receive ministry from a layperson instead of the pastor.
- Don't expect home visitation. Instead, volunteer to do the visitation for him.
- Don't expect him to show up at every meeting. Give him the night off.
- Let him know you want him to be a bold, courageous leader. Encourage him to dream.

What do you get in return? A pastor who has time to pray and seek God. A pastor who has time to dream big and to pursue Christ's vision for the congregation. A pastor who has time to love his family well. Know this: there is nothing more magnetic to men than a pastor who is led by God. Look at what happened after the apostles delegated their table-waiting duties. Acts 6:7 (CEV) tells us that "God's message spread, and many more people in Jerusalem became followers. Even a large number of priests put their faith in the Lord."

The apostles had time to focus on their core responsibility because the early church allowed them to. They were able to *challenge* the world with the gospel, and many men came to Christ because of it. And the widows? They got even better care.

ADOPT THE LEADING PASTOR-TEACHING PASTOR MODEL

God has given people different gifts. Some are great teachers. Others are great leaders. Yet our modern model of church demands that a pastor be good at both, and that's a relatively rare combination. Only 5 percent of senior pastors claim to be gifted in the area of leadership. Most pastors think of themselves as teachers or shepherds, not leaders.[1] Churches are recognizing this and beginning to hire a second pastor who is a talented leader. This pastor tends to the business side of the church, freeing the teaching pastor to focus on ministry of the Word. Sounds like Acts 6, the passage we just read.

The disciples went out two by two. Moses had Aaron. Paul had Barnabas. If your church is serious about reaching men, consider a one-two pastoral combination, as finances allow. You'll probably emerge with stronger leadership and better teaching.

LOOK FOR LEADERS IN CORPORATE AMERICA, NOT NECESSARILY THE SEMINARY

Seminaries teach people to teach. Corporations teach people to lead. Methodist pastor Adam Hamilton has recruited some of his finest staff and lay leaders from the business world: "They will be people who are deeply committed to Christ and exhibit a genuine calling, yet who might never leave corporate America to go to seminary, and who may not have a calling to pulpit ministry, but rather to managing or leading ministries."[2] Pastor James Meeks of Salem Baptist Church in Chicago found his church administrator, Veronica Abney, at IBM.[3] Laymen may respect such leaders all the more because they possess real-world experience.

DEVELOP GREAT LAY LEADERSHIP

Churches need dynamic leaders at every level. The pastor can't do it all, nor should he. A church that wants to reach men will have an intentional system for identifying and training leaders within the congregation. Two years ago my church hired a leadership pastor from corporate America. His only job is to raise up leaders who serve as life coaches to anyone who wants discipleship. Our church now has more than three hundred life coaches who are personally discipling hundreds of young believers. The tales of life change are staggering! Hundreds of women and men are being challenged into a deeper walk with God. None of this would be happening if our church hadn't made leadership development a top priority.

Does this seem like an impossible scenario for your church? You don't need a hotshot corporate executive to begin developing leaders. Try these ideas:

- Identify the leaders in your congregation through personality tests and spiritual gift inventories. Train them well, and let them lead courageously.

- Banish the word *facilitator* from your vocabulary. Men follow leaders, not facilitators. Jesus led, and so must we.

- Support your ministry leaders at every level. Many Christians grew up in a church where the pastor was the only leader, so they submit to pastoral leadership, but rebel against lay leadership. Don't do this.

- Support leadership development and training in your church. It's scriptural, and it's one of the keys to bringing men back.

- Above all, don't shoot at your leaders. Don't sic the humility police on them. Believe the best about their motives.

Men Need Male Leadership

Whenever possible, put men in leadership positions. It's good for your church. Men's natural bent toward risk taking and challenge can change the atmosphere in your church, making it more attractive to men.

You may object to this strategy because it would appear to discriminate against women. Laying aside the biblical assumption of male leadership for a moment, look at the practical side. If men see men in leadership, they think, *This is something I could get involved with. My gifts are needed.* If they see women in leadership, they tend to think the opposite.

The fact is, women will follow a man, but few men will follow a woman unless they are forced. For instance, there are many men who coach women's basketball teams, but it's very rare for a woman to coach a men's team. Men follow female bosses, teachers, and commanding officers only because they can be fired, flunked, or court-martialed. But given a choice, men rarely follow female leadership. One church I know experimented with all-female youth leadership; within six months 75 percent of the boys had disappeared. Pastor Dan Jarrell puts it this way, "When women *lead*, men *leave*." (I know, men are sexist pigs. They shouldn't be this way. But remember, we're talking about men as they are, not as they ought to be.)

Maybe this is one reason the Scriptures presuppose male leadership in the church. Perhaps these commands rise not from first-century sexism but from the realization that both genders respond well to competent male leadership. If you want men to come to your church, give high-profile positions to Spirit-led men. Sounds chauvinistic until you consider that *men* are heavily outnumbered at church. Think of it as an affirmative action program for Christianity's largest minority group.

MEN AND FEMALE LAY LEADERSHIP

Female leadership is a fact of life in the local church. George Barna found that women are 56 percent more likely than men to have held a leadership position (other than pastor) in a local church.[4] Women are more likely than men to head up committees and to organize the various ministries of the church, especially those concerning children, where they have a virtual leadership monopoly.

Since the 1950s and 1960s, a number of denominations have opened their formal leadership posts to women (elder, deacon, etc.). This has sparked debate on the question of female leadership in the church. In one camp are the *egalitarians* who believe that anyone, male or female, should be allowed to assume any position in the church. In the other camp are the *complementarians* who believe that, while men and women are equal, God has assigned them different roles.

I'm no theologian, so I will not presume to speak for God in this matter. However, statistics indicate that denominations that have opened their doors widest to female leadership are generally declining in membership. (Statistics from the Presbyterian Church show a peak in attendance in the mid-1960s, and a gradual decline since then. Other mainline churches have followed a similar pattern. The declines began about the time these churches admitted women to leadership.) While 60 percent of churches with a male senior pastor suffer a gender gap, 80 percent of congregations with a female senior pastor do.[5]

On the other hand, some of the most gifted Christian leaders I've ever met are women. Christian women do a magnificent job of leading in many churches. Women led in the Bible. To say women are never called by God to lead in church or to say they lack the capacity for leadership is quite a stretch. We need great leaders of both genders in the church today.

To women who are in leadership positions, I'd offer this advice:

- Consider men's needs and expectations when making decisions.
- Don't be quick to take leadership away from men. Once a particular area of ministry gets a reputation as female dominated, it's hard to get men involved.
- Don't focus the whole church on the needs of women and children. Make developing men a top priority.
- Lead courageously. You can't lead effectively without angering people. Jesus made people mad all the time.
- Be willing to be tougher. Just as men need to be softer and more nurturing, you may need to be more hard-nosed and goal oriented. God calls all of us—not just men—to transformation.

MEN NEED VISION

The Bible says, "Without a vision, the people perish." Men are the ones perishing spiritually today. Every man longs to live a significant life. Men want to be part of something greater than themselves. Sam Keen writes, "A man finds fulfillment (spiritual and sexual) only when he turns aside from willfulness and surrenders to something beyond self."[6] But men are reluctant to surrender to God because they don't know what He is doing in the world, and they have no idea how they might get in on it.

Jesus had a vision. He called it *the kingdom of God*. It was huge. It involved nothing less than a re-creation of the world, one person at a time. And we are His partners in this task: "This vision was the focus of his entire life. Everything about his life was tied up in this vision. This vision was what kept him focused on his mission. It was the reason he lived and died."[7]

If men don't have a vision of what God is doing in a church, they will not invest themselves. They will see it as a club, not a cause. Christianity becomes either an exercise in moral improvement or pointless busyness. But with vision even menial tasks can become meaningful. Lee Strobel writes glowingly of the people who duplicate audiotapes for his church: "They stand for hours at machines to crank out thousands of tapes, yet they don't see their task as menial or insignificant. They know that God can use those messages in powerful ways, and so they share in the adventure of God touching human lives. That motivates them! They have a mission that really matters."[8]

Here's the problem: we put men to work in the church duplicating tapes, and they think they are duplicating tapes. They are not! They are creating lifeboats that can rescue drowning souls! They are forging swords that can pierce the darkness that binds the captives. Every usher and parking lot attendant, every teacher and team leader must see himself as a link in a chain going back to Christ Himself, a foot soldier in the army that is transforming the world. That's the power of vision, and without it men perish!

Where does vision come from? God! God is calling each believer, each church, to accomplish something great, but few are listening. There are 340,000 churches in America,[9] each one doing just about the same things every other church is doing. What if your church did one thing and did it well? Something unique, specific, detailed, and God-given? Paul told us that Christ's body is made up of many parts, each with a unique function. That unique function is your *purpose*.

MEN NEED PURPOSE

Two women will go out to lunch without an agenda, but two men won't. When Steve asks Lenny out to lunch, he wonders, "What does Steve want?" Before accepting, Lenny will probably ask Steve, "What's up?" or "What's on your mind?" Men won't do anything unless they know the purpose.

The problem is, most guys don't know what the purpose of church is. Really! Guys don't know what church is about! That's because most churches have not agreed on what their purpose is. This is why men love Rick Warren's Purpose-Driven book series. Men are purpose driven. If you can clearly state a unique purpose for your church (and restate it often), the men will be encouraged.

What can you do?

- Try to make church mission statements short and specific. They are often so bland and general, nobody could get excited about them. Al Winseman advises, "The mission statement must be short enough to be easily memorized by every congregation member."[10]

- Once you have your mission or purpose, repeat it frequently to the body, at least once a month. Thom Rainer quotes Eric, a new Christian from Michigan: "I get pumped going to church . . . We're on a mission for God, and we know where we're going."[11]

- Always stress the purpose when announcing events. Here's a bulletin announcement that misses the mark: "The annual men's retreat will be held June 7–8 at Lake Arrowhead. Our speaker will be John Armstrong. Cost is $65. To sign up call Steve Stanley, 555-2398." What's wrong with this announcement? It never states the purpose of the retreat! If you're asking a guy to give up two days of his life, you need to clearly state *what's in it for him.*

- When starting small groups for men, be sure they have a purpose to focus on. Without a purpose the group will dissolve quickly. The purpose can come from the leader, or better yet, challenge the men to pray and discover God's purpose for the group.

- Cancel purposeless meetings. Ron says, "Churches waste so much time in stupid meetings. We spend a lot of time talking about what we should be doing rather than just doing it."[12] If there's no clear purpose for meeting, don't meet. Your men will thank you.

GIVE MEN HIGH STANDARDS: ASK SOMETHING OF THEM

Many people think the church asks too much of its members. In reality, it asks too little. Thom Rainer studied two thousand churches and found that without exception the churches that attracted unchurched people were *high-expectation* churches. He stated, "People have no desire to be a part of something that makes no difference, that expects little. And, frankly, many churches have dumbed down church membership to the point that it has no meaning at all." He quoted a man named Sam who came to Christ thanks to a high-expectation church: "I may not have realized it at the time, but I was looking for a church that expected something of me."[13]

Research from Dr. Chris Bader of Baylor University supports this idea: "Groups that are growing in membership are the ones that require more of their members."[14] Rick Warren built Saddleback Church on this philosophy: "Ask confidently for a big commitment. Jesus always asked for commitment clearly and confidently. He was not at all reluctant to ask men and women to drop everything and follow him." Warren adds, "People do not resent being asked for a great commitment if there is a great purpose behind it."[15]

We are afraid to ask men for a great commitment, so they think we're after their wallets, not their hearts. We plug them into the ministry machine, but forget to show them how their contribution is making an eternal difference. Gordon Dalbey discusses the risks and rewards of challenging men:

Most often, we draw back from challenging men to greater commitment, assuming their laziness. We then wonder why men have so little respect for the church—even as we presume so little respect for them.

But what if we told men up front that to join the church of Jesus Christ is . . . to enlist in God's army and to place their lives on the line? This approach would be based on the warrior's spirit in every man, and so would offer the greatest hope for restoring authentic Christian manhood to the Body of Christ. To be sure, it would be risky: what if the lazy men didn't come? But what if the real men did?[16]

PROMISE MEN OBSTACLES, NOT EASE

Bruce Barton writes, "The higher type of leadership which calls forth men's greatest energies by the promise of obstacles rather than the picture of rewards—that was the leadership of Jesus. By it he tempered the soft metal of his disciples' nature into keen hard steel."[17]

Jesus sent His disciples out "as sheep among wolves." He promised them arrest, floggings, betrayal, persecution, and death (Matt. 10). He constantly predicted their disloyalty. Hebrews 11 reads like Poe, with Christians stoned, skewered, and sawed in two.

There is a kind of high-octane man who will not follow unless he sees danger ahead. Jesus knew this. So did Antarctic explorer Ernest Shackleton, who posted this advertisement in 1913:

Men wanted for hazardous journey. Small wages. Bitter cold. Long months of complete darkness. Constant danger. Safe return doubtful. Honour and recognition in case of success.

More than five thousand men applied for twenty-six slots. *Precisely the kind of men who are missing in today's church!* If we want aggressive, bold, greatness-seeking men, we must do what Jesus did and promise suffering, trial, and pain. But today's Christianity is marketed like Tylenol: it's the *antidote* to suffering, trial, and pain. We've turned Jesus' approach on its head!

Now here's a strategy you probably never learned in evangelism training: it's sometimes wise to rebuff a man's first attempt to receive Christ. Certain men need to feel the back of God's hand before they will walk at His side. My friend Paul is such a man. He's one of Alaska's premier bush pilots, owner of a wilderness lodge. He's an adventurer who's made the first ascent of some of Alaska's toughest peaks. Paul was raised in church by devout parents. But for decades he ran from God, and his life was falling apart. One Sunday he approached a pastor he had known for years and asked how to become a Christian. The wise pastor looked him in the eye and said, "Don't waste my time. When you're ready to give *everything* to God, come back and see me." He turned and left Paul at the altar, stunned.

Does this sound crazy to you? Look at how Jesus handled a similar encounter: "Along the way someone said to Jesus, 'I'll go anywhere with you!'" (Luke 9:57 CEV)

Did Jesus say, "Praise God, another Christian! Welcome to the family"? No! He responded with a stern warning. Jesus said, "Foxes have dens, and birds have nests, but the Son of Man doesn't have a place to call his own" (v. 58).

In the next four verses He rebuked two other would-be followers, one for wanting to say good-bye to his family, and one for wanting to bury his father. Talk about insensitive! Yet Christ knew what we have forgotten: a man who is challenged into God's kingdom will be a follower forever. That's what happened with my friend Paul. A few weeks after the pastor challenged him, Paul flew his bush plane in to Anchorage and gave *everything* to God. He's been transformed from an unfaithful lout to the world's most doting husband. And he's turning his wilderness lodge into a proving ground for young male disciples.

DON'T BEG OR PLEAD

Jesus never begged anyone to follow Him. He never waited for anyone, never sang *one more verse* while people decided whether to follow. He barked, "Follow Me!" and kept going. Those who immediately dropped everything became His disciples; those who hesitated were left behind.

Yet week after week, especially in evangelical churches, we beg men to be saved. Problem is, the call to be saved is so familiar, men see no value in it. Don't misunderstand me: it's vitally important that we call men to follow Jesus. Men need salvation. But instead of pleading, what if our approach was: "Do you have what it takes to follow Christ?

Many say they do, but fewer than one in four will remain loyal. Are you one of the few, or when trials come, will you crumble?" What if we stopped begging men to be saved and started challenging them to follow Jesus Christ?

These approaches are risky and should be employed only with prayer. I would not use them with mixed-gender audiences. But a sharp-edged gospel may be the only way to pierce the hearts of some men.

MEN NEED TO PRODUCE FRUIT

If you want to demoralize a man, give him a pointless task. The Nazis demonstrated this by forcing certain prisoners to dig a hole, then fill it back in. Day after day: dig-fill, dig-fill. Camp doctors discovered those men died more quickly than others who were given meaningful work. To men, futility is torture, lethal as any gas chamber.

Men have to be productive. Jesus prayed we would produce an abundant crop, thirty, sixty, even a hundredfold. Yet in a typical year, just one new person comes to faith in Christ for every eighty-five churchgoers.[18] That's not even a onefold crop. This discourages a lot of men, because guys are results oriented. *A man's strongest urge is to reproduce.*

One New Year's Eve I asked my pastor a very straightforward question: "How many adults came to faith in Christ at our church this year?" The pastor, a very diplomatic man, said, "I'm not sure. I'll have to get back to you on that." But he and I knew the answer. It was zero.

I added it up. That year our church conducted 104 regularly scheduled worship services, 7 special services, some 250 adult classes, 600 committee meetings, and 1,000 small-group meetings and ran through a $750,000 budget to produce exactly zero new adult followers of Jesus Christ. We gathered. We worshipped. We loved each other. But we produced no crop. Our church was a contraption worthy of Rube Goldberg: lots of sound, motion, and fury to produce a tiny amount of fruit. At that moment I felt like Sisyphus; the church was my rock.

Even soul-winning churches can fail to produce a crop. Pastor G. F. Watkins noticed his young church was winning thousands of converts, but few were sticking around: "Like a flood people were surging in, then surging right out the back door into oblivion."[19] Jesus said our job is to produce fruit: fruit that lasts (John 15:16). When hundreds are saved but few become disciples, men are discouraged.

OK, I admit there are other ways to measure productivity besides converts and church growth. Some would say real fruit of Christianity is life change: people becoming more like Jesus. So how are we doing in that regard? Let's recap some findings I mentioned in earlier chapters: half of U.S. worshippers freely admit they are not growing in their faith. Only half say they frequently leave worship services challenged to change. George Barna finds:

> few congregants have a biblical worldview, half the people [our churches] minister to are not spiritually secure or developed, kids are fleeing from the church in record numbers, most of the people who attend worship services admit they did not connect with God, the divorce rate among Christians is no different than that of non-Christians . . . and the average congregant spends more time watching television in one day than he spends in all spiritual pursuits combined for an entire week. [20]

While some churches are producing abundant fruit, the sad truth is, many are not. I think it's safe to say most U.S. congregations are not having the impact God wants them to have. We are not reaping the crop of transformed lives that Jesus promised.

How do we conceal this scandalous lack of productivity? Some clever churches have simply changed the definition of *crop*. Churches now judge success by the standards of a family reunion: *How many people came, and did everyone get along?* A big, happy crowd equals a crop. The more meeting, gathering, and loving that take place, the more abundant the crop. This is another way the modern church reflects the feminine heart—*the people gathered, formed the body of Christ, and loved each other*. This outcome is unlikely to electrify men.

But churches that reach men have a different standard. Barna reports, "At growing churches, a program was deemed successful according to how many changed lives resulted from the outreach. This differs from the experience of stagnant churches, where a program is usually evaluated according to how many people are involved." [21]

Why do our churches produce so little fruit? Of course there are the spiritual reasons—a lack of prayer, faith, abiding, trust, etc. But even faithful, praying churches sometimes fail to produce an abundant crop because they're afraid to take a painful but necessary step: thinning their ministry programs.

Thinning: The Missing Step in Fruit Production

When I was a boy of nine I planted a carrot patch in the backyard. I followed the instructions on the seed packet, and watered every day. Within a couple of weeks, tiny green sprouts popped through the sandy loam. As the weeks passed the carrot tops got taller, fuller, and leafier. I was thrilled, certain I'd soon be munching on Bugs Bunny–sized carrots.

The seed packet said: *carrots will be ready to pick in about 90 days.* On day 90 I rose early, ran to the carrot patch, and pulled one out. I was shocked to find a shriveled, orange root less than 2 inches long. I pulled more carrots. Same thing—none of my carrots had developed properly.

I reread the instructions, and realized I had missed an important step: *plants should be thinned to a final spacing of 2" to 4" per carrot.* With so many carrots competing for nutrients it was impossible for them to reach maturity. My carrots looked good on the surface, but there was no edible crop.

Sadly, many of our churches look good on the surface, but are producing a meager crop. This is because we do too much. Over the years we plant new programs but never thin the less effective ones. So our roster of ministries grows and grows. Soon, like crowded carrots starving for nutrients, church programs begin starving for volunteers. Understaffed ministries become less and less effective. Men sense the pointlessness of it all and drop out, leaving women to do all the work.

Still we fail to scale back or eliminate unfruitful programs. Instead, we keep programs alive long past their useful lives, in order to keep people happy. But, in trying to be everything to everyone, we fail to produce a crop. Ministries wither. Volunteers labor, but produce little discernible fruit. This is a recipe for volunteer burnout, especially among men.

How do you thin your ministries? Fellowship Bible Church in Arkansas evaluates all its ministry activities for fruitfulness; it drops the bottom 10 percent each year. There are no sacred cows; any ministry that's not changing lives is subject to the chopping block. Rick Warren of Saddleback is more direct: "Kill any program that doesn't fulfill a purpose."[22] Jesus said, "He cuts off every branch in me that bears no fruit, while every branch that does bear fruit he prunes so that it will be even more fruitful" (John 15:2 NIV). Do we have the courage to treat our church programs this way?

Thinning plants is always painful. In my opinion it's the worst part of gardening, pulling those innocent little sprouts out of the ground. Thinning your ministry offerings also hurts, and you can count on resistance from well-meaning Christians. You will hear things like this: "We can't stop offering that program! Sister Bertha will be crushed. She's given her life to that ministry." This usually stops any changes, because in most churches, people's feelings are the primary consideration when taking action (more on this in chapter 20).

Why must we take the painful step of thinning our ministries? Because men need to produce fruit. If we plug men into fruitless ministry activity, they will burn out and either go passive or leave the church. The prophet Isaiah spoke for these men: "I have labored to no purpose; I have spent my strength in vain and for nothing" (Isa. 49:4 NIV). No longer will men sacrifice themselves to support an institution. But a church that's changing the world will draw men like a beacon.

What can you do? Come alongside Sister Bertha and help her to see the necessity of change. Give her a vision for what these changes can accomplish. Offer unflagging support to your congregational leaders when unfruitful programs are thinned. They're going to need it! One more thing: examine your own ministry. If you are busy for God but not really producing a crop of changed lives, it might be time to move into a more intentional program of discipleship.

It takes strong, courageous leadership to do these things. But you can do it. Make the tough choices. Lead courageously. Don't worry, Sister Bertha will be okay.

18

PASTORS AND THE MASCULINE SPIRIT

AUTHOR'S NOTE: THIS CHAPTER IS NOT JUST FOR PASTORS. LAYPEOPLE will learn how to help their pastors reach men and move the thermostat.

When I was in college, I wondered if God might be calling me to the pastorate. But when I discovered how demanding a pastor's life really is, I determined that God must have dialed a wrong number.

Pastors, I admire you. You have a complex, largely thankless job. I can't think of any profession that pulls a person in more directions than the pastorate. Leading a church is like trying to play cards in a hurricane, and seminary prepared you to preach, not lead. You may be frustrated by the lack of male participation in your congregation, or you may be uncertain how to get men involved. Here are some practical ideas to help you engage more men at your church.

MEN NEED STRONG PASTORAL LEADERSHIP

Let's make something clear: strong pastoral leadership is not dictatorship. In many churches the pastor controls everything, either because the laity is passive, or because the pastor has a controlling, type-A personality. Men want to contribute, but if the pastor calls all the shots, the men wither. John Eldredge sums it up, "You want a team, not a one-man show. If you have a one-man show, the men you'll get are going to be sheep, rather than tigers."

William Easum understands what it takes to be a good pastoral leader in the twenty-first century:

> Today's leaders focus on permission giving rather than control or managing . . . They do not give orders, or dictate how people must operate

within the organization. They cast vision that creates victory, that frees people to make on-the-spot decisions, then get out of the way. In this role they model an open and free environment in which ordinary people are encouraged and equipped to do extraordinary ministry. Their passion is to develop other leaders who will develop other leaders.[1]

You attract tigers to your church by letting them be tigers. Isn't this what Jesus did? He trained seventy-two tigers, then sent them out with all of his authority (Luke 10). Pastors, do likewise: train your men and send them out. When you get a reputation as an equipping church, male tigers will start showing up on Sunday. You may say, "This is an impossible dream; you don't know how passive my men are." Or you may say, "I've tried to lead more courageously, but the people start shooting at me."

Ah, the people. Fact is, the people in the pews often thwart courageous pastoral leadership. Why? Studies show that few Christians recognize the importance of good leadership.[2] Strong leadership always involves change, which bruises egos and feelings.

Bottom line: if we want more male tigers in our churches, we must help our pastors deliver great leadership. How can you help?

- Give your pastor time to pray, dream, and cast a vision for the congregation. Relieve him of as many responsibilities as possible (Acts 6).

- Let the pastor know that you will follow his leadership, even if he leads you into the unknown. Get your group together (Bible study, women's circle, etc.) and write your pastor a letter, telling him you appreciate his leadership and encouraging him to dream big. Let him know he has your support, no matter how God leads. What an encouragement this will be to your pastor!

- Be supportive when your pastor communicates his vision for the congregation, even if it involves change that may upset some people. Don't stir up opposition; instead help your pastor smooth any ruffled feathers.

PASTORS SHOULD BE MASCULINE, STRONG, AND RESOLUTE

There's a stereotype that pastors and priests are pantywaists. You see this all the time in movies. Cinematic pastors are low-key, avuncular souls who mumble their way through weddings and funerals. They are decidedly less masculine than the hero who's getting married or the mobster who's being buried.

Is there any truth to this? According to personality tests, "men entering the ordained ministry exhibit more 'feminine' personality characteristics than men in the population at large."[3] Pastors also tend to have lower testosterone levels than other men.[4] This does not mean pastors are necessarily effeminate; they are simply more verbal, expressive, and sensitive than the average man.

But guys disrespect men who are overly verbal, expressive, or sensitive. Let me give you an example. Budweiser aired a popular series of commercials with a talkative older gentleman in a cowboy hat. Let's call him Tex. Tex yaks and yaks while the other guys in the commercial roll their eyes. The message is clear: a man who talks too much is suspect. So is one who is overly emotional or sensitive. So is one who's quick to hug other men.

What can you do?

- Talk less and listen more. The best pastors for men are good listeners. They ask great questions and let men discover truth for themselves.

- Be judicious about emotive displays. Jesus wept publicly, but He did so at the funeral of a friend, an appropriate forum for male grief. A pastor who chokes up frequently or cries in the pulpit may endear himself to women, but may drive a wedge between himself and certain men.

MEN APPRECIATE CERTITUDE AND CONVICTION

Men want a pastor who is firm in his convictions. Listen to Jorge, a formerly unchurched man: "I visited a few churches before I became a

Christian. Man, some of them made me want to vomit! They didn't show any more conviction about their beliefs than I did." Sean's resistance to church softened after hearing a pastor who preached with certitude: "The first time I heard him, I thought, this guy really believes this stuff. I guess I really surprised Marilyn when I told her I wanted to go back for another visit." Men want a pastor who proclaims the gospel with boldness, unashamedly and unapologetically, but not with a harsh or condemning tone. Thom Rainer asked the formerly unchurched what they liked in a pastor, and he reported, "Numerous times we heard how these pastors were strong in their convictions but gentle in spirit."[5]

MEN LIKE PASTORS WHO HAVE THE TRAPPINGS OF MANHOOD

Jeri Odell's husband, Dean, was impressed with her new pastor because he wore cowboy boots when he preached.[6] I know a number of football players-turned-pastors who are very popular with men. Stu Weber, one of America's leading men's pastors, is a former Green Beret.

Pastor, you don't have to be Arnold Schwarzenegger to attract men, but the more trappings of manhood, the better. Men will judge your manhood by the clothes you wear, the car you drive, and the hobbies you pursue. (I know it's not fair, but it's true.) You don't have to wrestle alligators, but the more time you spend outdoors, the better. If you were once employed in a field other than ministry, speak of it often, especially if you served in the military or worked in blue-collar fields. Men respect a pastor with real-world experience. Richard Rohr and Joseph Martos write, "People are sick of sermons that come out of the study and into the pulpit."[7]

MEN WANT A PASTOR WHO'S A REGULAR GUY

Lee Strobel says unchurched men "prefer down-to-earth, straight talking leaders, ones who don't insist on 'Doctor' or 'Reverend' before their names." Strobel also recommends giving up perks, parking places, even the ministerial robe: "Those trappings smack of elitism and, in some cases, arrogance."[8] Thom Rainer quotes formerly unchurched Larry from Boston, who praises his pastor's authenticity: "Pat is just a real guy.

He doesn't try to pretend to be somebody he's not."[9] A pastor who speaks openly of his struggles, failings, and challenges will win points with men.

AVOID PREACHER-SPEAK

Certain Christian traditions encourage preachers to talk different when they're in the pulpit. This is called *ministerial tone.* Seminaries discourage it, but some Christians insist on it. The moment the pastor enters the pulpit, he's expected to change his speaking cadence and accent. For example, Southern preachers are renowned for calling on the name of JAY-sus or ending sentences with an uplifted *amen?* Other pastors do a lot of whoopin' and hollerin' or adopt a singsong tone in the pulpit. Mainline pastors sometimes take on a highbrow ministerial tone, draaaaagging out their vooooowels, speaking slooowly and distinctly. Once the sermon is over, the pastor speaks normally again.

The problem with preacher-speak is that unchurched men may see it as performance, not heartfelt communication. Your message may be obscured because the listener is paying attention to the way you speak and not the words you're speaking. Make your preaching delivery as conversational as possible. Passion in the pulpit is great, but avoid anything that looks like it's staged or performed. Men are looking for a pastor who's real, and if your message feels like a show, they're more likely to find you hypocritical.

THE IMPACT OF WOMEN PASTORS

America's seminaries are building an army of female pastors. Women are being ordained to the clergy in unprecedented numbers.[10] The number of women who identified themselves as clergy tripled between 1983 and 2000.[11] Most Christian colleges and some seminaries are struggling to recruit men. Some observers believe the pastorate will reach a tipping point in a generation or two when most men abandon the profession and women take their places. The revolution is already under way in the church of England: in 2005, for the first time, more women than men applied for ordination. What led to this historic shift? The number of men seeking the priesthood plunged by half between 2003 and 2005.[12] The majority-female pastorate is coming, not because women are horning in, but because men are dropping out.

A female pastor faces a number of challenges ministering to men:

- *Softness.* Generally, women are more tender and compassionate than men. A female pastor may inadvertently move the thermostat toward comfort just by being herself. Pastors of both genders believe female ministers "are more caring than men about the individual lives of members of the congregation, more pastorally sensitive, more nurturing."[13]

- *Leadership.* Men love women, but they follow men. G. F. Watkins puts it this way: "Men want a mother, but they need a father." Men want to be nurtured, but they need a good kick in the pants now and then. Female pastors may feel ill equipped to administer that kick.

- *Example to the boys.* With a male pastor, there's at least one man in the church who's left everything to follow Christ. It's now possible for a boy to grow up in church without ever seeing a man truly living his faith. This could make it even tougher to transmit Christianity to our sons, and lead to enormous gender gaps in the future.

- *Liberal views.* Female clergy are overwhelmingly liberal, while men tend to hold more conservative views. Fifty-six percent identify themselves as strong feminists compared to 24 percent of male pastors in the same denominations. The top four priorities of female ministers are "economics and social welfare, tolerance and rights, civility, and gay rights."[14] The National Congregations Study found liberal churches were 14 percent more likely to sport a gender gap than conservative ones.[15]

Maybe you're thinking female pastors just can't reach men. Well, male pastors aren't exactly packing 'em in either. Ninety-five percent of the senior pastors in America are male, but only 39 percent of the adults who show up on Sunday are male. Maybe the key isn't the gender of the pastor. Maybe it's the *spirit* of the pastor.

The word *pastor* means "shepherd." That means gentle, right? Not at all! The Bible's most famous shepherd, David, was also the Bible's most celebrated warrior. This is what men need: a pastor with a shepherd's heart and the spirit of a warrior.

Here's the real question for pastors of either gender: Can you deliver the goods to men? Can you foster a masculine spirit in the church? Pastor, are you tending the flock or leading the troops? Do you see yourself as a gentle shepherd or as a warrior out to change the world?

Henrietta Mears was a woman who could deliver the goods. She led hundreds to faith in Jesus, including Bill Bright, the founder of Campus Crusade for Christ. During her tenure as Christian education director at First Presbyterian Church in Hollywood, more than four hundred young people entered full-time Christian service, most of whom were males. Men respected her because she spoke their language. "God doesn't call us to sit on the sidelines and watch. He calls us to be on the field, playing the game," she said. Biblically faithful, she sent back to the publisher teaching material that denied the miraculous in Scripture. She lived by two words: *dream big*.

Why was Henrietta Mears so effective in reaching men? Why did Billy Graham call her the most influential woman he ever met, after his own mother and wife? Mears possessed the spirit of a warrior! She loved people enough to challenge the tar out of them! She was a woman with a healthy dose of the masculine spirit.

Ready or not, female pastors are coming. Women pastors, teachers, and lay leaders, I entreat you: become students of men. Learn their needs and expectations. Offer them challenge, not just comfort. If you make the church a more comforting, nurturing place where the top priority is making everyone feel loved and accepted, more men will depart. Begin praying now, asking God to help you deliver the goods to the men under your care.

19

TEACHING AND
THE MASCULINE SPIRIT

THE PASTOR DELIVERED A GOOD SERMON. IT WAS INTERESTING, theologically sound, and well buttressed with Scripture. At thirty-two minutes it got the congregation out in time to beat the Baptists to the restaurants.

That evening at the business meeting, the pastor opened with prayer, then asked the elders which of his three main points they thought was best. Not one of them could remember anything he'd said. The elders were embarrassed. The pastor was discouraged.

There's a lot of *teaching* going on in church, but not much *learning*. Men realize this. It's one reason men feel church is a futile endeavor. If we are going to reach men with the gospel, we must be more effective in how we communicate. If you teach men, here are some great ways to bring the masculine spirit to your teaching:

HOW TO TEACH MEN

Let Men Learn Through Personal Discovery

Why did Jesus ask Peter to step out of the boat and walk on water? Peter had heard Jesus' teaching on faith. But that stormy evening, Peter *personally discovered* what faith really was. When teaching men, ask them great questions; don't just give them the answers. Let men discover truth for themselves. Make men think! Like toddlers, men want to do it themselves.

Let Men Learn by Hands-on Experience

This advice goes for women as well. You learn to cook by cooking, to play guitar by playing guitar. Use active learning techniques whenever possible. Put something in men's hands. Use props, scents, visual aids, anything that helps men *experience* the lesson. Why do major corporations spend millions to send their mostly male executives to play team-building games or walk across hot coals? There are certain lessons a man cannot learn from a lecture or book. Men are changed by personal experiences.

Let Men Learn Through Object Lessons

Try this: after church next Sunday, ask a man what the sermon was about. Then ask him what the *children's* sermon was about. Typically, he will remember the latter more easily than the former. Why? Children's sermons are brief, less verbal, and built around an object. Teachers, if you want to reach men, take note. Jesus' most powerful messages were His parables: brief, punchy, and built around a little story or an object at hand—lessons that survive to this day *because men remembered them.*

Years ago at a men's event, our pastor used water and a copper pipe to illustrate how men are to be conduits of God's blessing to the people around them. He sent each man home with an inch-long copper tube to put on his keychain. I still see copper tubes whenever my friends pull out their keys. I ask them what it means, pretending not to know. The men quickly explain the illustration to me. Needless to say, this lesson has had a lasting impact on the men of our church.

Teachers, there's no excuse. C'mon, you're creative. Think outside the box! Object lessons are readily available in books and on the Internet. In my opinion, you should never teach men without at least one object lesson, unless you're content to have your words forgotten.

Let Men Be Real, Not Religious

When a man walks into church, he may feel like Tom Sawyer in Aunt Polly's parlor. He must watch his language, mind his manners, and be extrapolite. But if church was a place where men could be *real* and not *religious,* you'd see a lot more of them. One of the best ways to foster this environment is to . . .

Let Men Ask Questions and Challenge the Party Line

Some Christians feel we offend God with honest questions that challenge widely held beliefs. Yet Jesus did this all the time. He often taught, "You have heard it said . . . but I say to you . . ." Whenever the disciples heard this, their ears perked up because another sacred cow was about to be slaughtered! Let men ask tough questions, especially those that challenge the accepted wisdom.

HOW TO MEET MEN'S NEEDS

Men Need Dialogue, Give-and-Take, a Chance to Argue

Woody Davis says, "Men enjoy and value argumentation. If you don't believe it, go to the local café where men gather to solve the world's problems. Listen to their conversation and notice the give and take, the challenge and response."[1] But in church we offer lectures because we can restrict what is said to acceptable Christian themes. Even if we do have discussion, we often shy away from frank, salty debate, because people might get upset. Instead, we give people answers because we think it promotes *unity*. But men find this boring—and so do many women.

Men Need Simple, One-Point Lessons (and Sermons)

The U.S. Army has been training a mostly male fighting force for more than two hundred years. Their method: *tell them what you're going to tell them, tell them, then tell them what you told them.* It's often more effective with men to make one point thrice than to make three points once.

Men have an attention span of six to eight minutes, yet the average Protestant sermon is more than thirty minutes in length.[2] It has three main points and sometimes more. No wonder men can't remember what's being taught! Pastors and teachers, why not break your teaching into smaller bits so men can more easily digest what you're saying? The one time I saw Rick Warren preach in person, he taught in five- to eight-minute segments with a song, video, or drama between each segment. I heard that sermon almost a year ago, but I still remember the gist of his message—and I've applied it to my life many times.

If you really want to attract unchurched men, paint this on your sign:

HOME OF THE 10-MINUTE SERMON. Break your message into a five-minute Scripture lesson, a five-minute object lesson, and a ten-minute sermon with other elements in between. Make the same point using three different approaches. You still get your twenty minutes, but you honor men's shorter attention span. End your message with concrete action items or an optional discussion for those who want to stick around. See if that doesn't liven things up for the men.

Men Appreciate Forthrightness

Many teachers feel that every word out of a Christian's mouth must be sweet as honey, carefully considered so that no one's feelings are bruised. But men appreciate forthrightness and honesty. They respect a teacher who tells it like it is and doesn't beat around the bush. They want to get right to the point and are not impressed by diplomatic language. People were amazed at Jesus because He taught as one having authority, not as the teachers of the law. Teach as Jesus did: be direct and to the point!

Men Need Challenging Teaching

Men appreciate a challenging, direct message that prods them to action. Robert Lewis tells the story of a rough-and-tumble construction worker who approached him after a Men's Fraternity meeting. He stuck out a calloused hand and said, "Man, every time I come in here you just crush my toes. You're just livin' in my jock shorts. Everything you talk about is right were I live." Generally speaking, the more frank and hard-hitting the teaching, the more men like it—as long as it doesn't stray into condemnation or moralism. The key is to speak the truth in love. Jesus loved people enough to challenge them. Teachers, do likewise.

Men Need the Unexpected

The Bible says of Jesus: *the people were astonished and amazed at His teaching.* When was the last time you were astonished in church? Men need to be amazed by God, but our liturgies and rituals have made Him utterly predictable. No wonder men find church so boring. My advice: when teaching men, do the unexpected. Break something. Pretend something's going wrong. Do a card trick. Take them outside. Light something on fire (not inside the church, of course). Play part of a video. Challenge the party line. Astonish men, and watch them lock in.

Men Need Great Stories

Larry Crabb laments, "We are a generation of men without stories . . . we don't know who we are, why we are here or where we are going."[3] For centuries men have learned heroism and self-sacrifice through great stories, which they stored in their hearts as boys. If we want our young men to be courageous followers of Christ, we must *tell them stories of people following Christ courageously.* We used to tell the stories of martyrs and missionaries to our boys. Now we don't. Young men see Christianity as a religion, not an adventure.

Where do today's men get their stories? The cinema! Every good film has a big story behind it: a tale of selfless love, forgiveness, redemption, or heroic sacrifice. Teach men to identify the gospel hidden in the movies they watch. A film like *Braveheart* can point a man toward God if he sees the film as a reflection of the spiritual battle that's raging about him. Train your men to spot the Christ-figure who appears in many films. (He's the one who sacrifices himself so others can live.) Films can help men make sense of their world *if they know how to interpret what they're seeing.*

When teaching boys, don't avoid the gross-out stories in the Bible. The Old Testament features heads being cut off, a tent peg driven into a man's temple, and a sword buried so deep in a fat king's middle that it disappeared! I believe God tucked these tales into the Bible just for preadolescent boys. Yet many Sunday school teachers avoid these accounts because they're too violent. Then we wonder why boys read *Harry Potter* instead of their Bibles.

HOW TO APPROACH MEN

Emphasize Strength More Than Weakness

Constant exhortations to become weak, dependent, and broken are tough on guys, particularly younger ones, who still think they are immortal. Let me be clear: men must be broken before God. Apart from Christ we can do nothing. We are pitifully weak without the Holy Spirit.

That said, it is patently untrue that He would have us wallow in weakness and unworthiness. The words *strong* and *strength* appear 561 times in the New King James Version, while *weak* and *weakness* show up just 83 times.[4] We need to acknowledge our weakness in relation to God's strength, but we do not need to obsess on it. It's far more effective to speak of strength when teaching men.

Start with Real Life

Robert Lewis's approach to unchurched men is simple: "You don't teach the Bible first. You teach real life issues first, then you bring the Bible in to surprise them. Most men's ministries fail because they are Bible studies. I always start with the practical and bring the Bible in on the back end." Lewis sums up his approach this way: give men what they need disguised as what they want. Wasn't this Jesus' method? The woman at the well wanted a drink, but she needed abundant life. Jesus offered her living water. He framed the gospel to reflect her desire.

Emphasize Life Transformation
Rather Than Moral Improvement

Jesus' message was one of repentance. To repent is to do a complete turnaround. The old man dies; a new man is born. Unfortunately, many teachers focus on moral improvement instead of total repentance. This was the method of the Pharisees: changing men one sin at a time. Erect enough laws, and men will be righteous. This brand of incremental moralism makes men resentful. They see it as nagging. It's far more effective to call men to life transformation than it is to target specific sins. Once a man is following Jesus, he will accept moral instruction because of his transformed heart.

Present Teaching That Leads People Somewhere

Almost without exception, today's dynamic churches present truth you can use. Men will not get excited about a lesson from Ephesians, because most men don't know what an Ephesian is, nor do they care. But if men know where they're going and what's in it for them, they're more likely to come to church. One wise pastor preaching in Ephesians 6 titled his sermon series "Get Your Armor On: How to Slay the Giants in Your Life." He promised to bring a sword, shield, arrow, breastplate, and helmet with him as object lessons. Men showed up in large numbers because they knew where they were going, and the topic sounded interesting.

Stay Faithful to Scripture

Human opinion is everywhere. It's easy to know what CNN, *Cosmo*, or the *New York Times* think. But men want to know what God says. Men respect an argument backed by the Bible. Show me a fast-growing church, and I'll show you a church that's faithful to Scripture. George Hunter makes this evaluation: "There is virtually no market, among secular people, for new theologies or alleged 'improvements' upon original Christianity."[5]

Answer the Questions Men Are Asking

Men's ministry veterans Geoff Gorsuch and Dan Schaffer researched and identified the questions that today's men are asking. Here is their top-ten list:

1. What is true manliness?
2. What is success? The real *bottom line* of life?
3. How do I deal with guilt feelings?
4. What is male sexuality? Is purity possible for the modern man?
5. How can we nurture family life?
6. What is Christian leadership? How is it developed?
7. What are the basic disciplines of the Christian man?
8. What ministry skills need to be developed? How?
9. What is biblical business conduct?
10. What is integrity? How is it developed?[6]

Teachers, if we want to reach men, we need to answer these questions. Notice what men are *not* asking about: eternal life, doctrinal truth, and political issues are not on the list. Relationships don't show up till number 4 or 5. Look again at the top two. Might this change how we teach men?

Use Masculine Imagery and Language

I picked up a recruiting brochure for the U.S. Army the other day. Bold letters on the front cover invited me to **Rise to the Challenge**. As you read, notice the masculine imagery and language:

> If you're looking for a job that will challenge you from day one, look no further than the U.S. Army. As a Soldier in the Army of One, you'll engage in life faster and better than most people your age . . . you'll experience things that you never thought possible and go places most people only read about. You'll learn your capabilities, sharpen your skills and then push yourself to the limit on a daily basis. You'll grow stronger, physically, mentally, and feel a sense of pride you've never felt before.[7]

This ad copy can teach us a lot about men. Listen to what it promises: challenge, rising above the rest, adventure, increased competence, skill, endurance, strength, and pride. It's competitive: you'll be faster, better, and stronger than the rest. With such imagery the army attracts sixty to eighty thousand volunteers each year, most of them male.

Church teachers can use similar imagery to engage men—and women. Dorothy Cassel of Wesley United Methodist Church in El Reno, Oklahoma, noticed that most men would drop out of her *Experiencing God* class by the third session. So she decided to insert as many masculine themes as possible into her teaching. She did not change her content. Instead she expressed it in terms of *influence, belonging to a team, purpose, character, courage, discipline, power,* and *perseverance.* Attendance at her first session was 60 percent women. But by the third session Dorothy drew a crowd that was 60 percent men! Plus the class doubled in size (more men *and* women came). She's used this technique again and again and cannot believe the difference it makes. When she stresses feminine themes such as *sharing, nurturing,* and *becoming,* the response is tepid; when she stresses the masculine themes of *influence, courage,* and *accomplishment,* both men and women respond with enthusiasm.[8]

Leaven your lessons with stories and metaphors that men can relate to. Analogies from sports, battle, business, and survival capture men's hearts. So does the language of death and sacrifice.

We no longer live in a monarchy, so the word *Lord* is meaningless to men (ten lords-a-leaping?). It conjures up an image of a man in tights, with a feather in his cap. Some men may have an easier time thinking of Jesus as their Coach, CEO, General, Leader, Guide, or Boss. David James invites men to relate to God as Wildman, King, Son, Warrior, Judge, and Brother.[9] Calling God by a more relevant name can breathe new life into a man's prayer.

Finally, it's time to reacquaint ourselves with Christ the man. Read your Bible. He's there! Think of His physical power—a carpenter who worked long days with primitive tools. He had "the voice and manner of a leader—the personal magnetism that begets loyalty and commands respect."[10] Christ plows through the Gospels like a wrecking ball, smashing tables, driving people with a whip, devastating the Pharisees with a word, taming the winds with an uplifted hand, toppling a detachment of armed soldiers simply by speaking His name. He never cajoles; He commands! Christ is powerful, dangerous, and un-predictable. Teachers, present Christ the man. Men will follow.

20

WORSHIP AND
THE MASCULINE SPIRIT

WOMEN ARE TO WORSHIP AS MEN ARE TO SEX. WOMEN LOVE
to worship anywhere, anytime, and with anyone. Often it's a woman's
greatest release. Women are more likely than men to say worship is the
top priority of the church and are more likely to *experience God* during
worship.[1] I know women who attend their home church Sunday morning, but sneak off for a liaison with another congregation that afternoon
or evening. When it comes to worship, women just can't get enough.

Meanwhile, men are to worship as women are to sex. Most guys have
to be *in the mood* to really enjoy worship. A man can surrender himself
fully in worship only when he feels secure and is with people he loves and
trusts. A man is less likely to worship in a church where he knows no one.[2]
Men tend to find a church they like and stay faithful to it. If they break up
with a church, they are devastated and may never seek out another one.

What's a worship leader to do? How do you lead both men and women
into God's presence? Douglas Wilson suggests, "In a scriptural worship
service, both masculine and feminine elements will be present, but the
masculine will be dominant, in the position of leadership. When the feminine element leads or dominates, the result is that those men who are
masculine are encouraged to stay away."[3] If we want men to truly worship, allow the masculine spirit to lead. Try these practical suggestions.

MEN GET EXCITED ABOUT QUALITY

I said a lot about this earlier, but it's so important I must say it again: *if
you want to attract men, you must provide a quality worship experience.* Men

respect excellence. I'm not talking about a canned, slick sales pitch for Jesus. However, whatever is done in God's name should be done well. If your worship service feels like amateur hour, men will recoil. What a woman may see as heartfelt and homespun, her husband often sees as corny and half-baked.

A good way to identify areas for improvement is to survey the congregation.[4] Another way is to survey visitors.[5] Once the surveys are in, study the results, pray, and take action. George Barna writes, "In the user friendly churches, there was almost a passion for identifying weaknesses and developing practical and efficient solutions to those soft spots." Barna continues, "The successful churches we studied had no sacred cows. That is, everything about them was open to scrutiny and criticism."[6]

MEN GET EXCITED ABOUT FUN

Surveys indicate that when unchurched people return to the fold, they usually pick a church where they have a good time: "These are not frivolous, entertainment-style churches, but those where people have such a great time exploring their faith . . . that they experience the *esprit de corps* and the joy of discovery that makes their faith journey a blast. Getting to know God and His ways can be enormous fun."[7]

But men get the impression that fun and Jesus are incompatible. Why? Because we tell them so! How many times do our young men hear at youth group, "Okay, guys, fun's over. It's time to learn about God."[8]

Kevin Leman reminds us that *men are goofy*. There's nothing wrong with a little *goofy* during the worship service. One fast-growing church I know does something completely off the wall at least once a month, from releasing beach balls in the pews to having the pastor ride into the sanctuary on a Harley. Show me where the Bible says that a good belly laugh detracts from true worship.

Men love to laugh. They are the primary viewers of the Comedy Central cable channel, and they are the biggest fans of late-night comedians. A number of Christian stand-up comedians are delighting audiences around the country.[9] Why not book one at your church? A church that is full of laughter and fun will soon find itself full of men—and young people too.

MEN LOVE FRIENDLY COMPETITION

I've heard that some junior sports leagues have stopped keeping score. Guess what? The boys keep score anyway. Without friendly competition, men lose interest. Bill Moir warns, "Deny boys and young men the spur of competition and you risk leaving their abilities dormant."[10] For Father's Day our church always does something fun and competitive for the men. One year it was a log-sawing competition. Another year men hit golf balls at a target on the wall. The winners get silly prizes. C'mon, guys love this stuff! God is not offended by friendly competition.

SHOWCASE YOUR MEN

I did a little experiment last summer. I visited the five fastest-growing churches in our city. Every one of them showcased men in prominent roles. Men were conspicuous in every aspect of the worship service: leading worship, ushering, giving testimonies, and teaching. All five churches had male pastors. One church had an all-male praise band. One even had men in charge of the children's program! Women weren't invisible in these churches, but men were given the high-profile spots in the worship service.

Were men the majority in the pews? No, women had the majority. Nevertheless, these fast-growing churches shined the spotlight on men. Why? I'll say it again: *men follow men.* When a man sees enthusiastic men in leadership, he is likely to believe there is a place for him in church. Women also appreciate animated male leaders.

MAKE SURE THE SERVICE MOVES ALONG

Sometimes the slow, serene atmosphere of a worship service bores men. Man-friendly churches work hard to minimize dead space between proceedings. The story is told of a Scottish pastor who took a young man to the church's general assembly meeting. "Who's the pirate with the wig?" the boy asked. "That's the moderator," explained the pastor. "Moderator? What this place needs is an accelerator!" exclaimed the young man.

RETHINKING WORSHIP

The church has been embroiled in worship wars since the 1970s. Some parishioners prefer traditional hymnody, while others like contemporary praise songs. Yet neither hymns nor praise songs are a perfect fit for men. Some hymns have bold, masculine lyrics, but their old-fashioned style fails to connect. Contemporary music is more up-to-date, but the lyrics are mostly tender love songs to Jesus. I wish some composer could capture the masculine spirit of a Reformation hymn in a praise chorus; then you'd have something men would love to sing!

We've already discussed how today's praise music invites the worshipper to assume the feminine role. But it's not just the lyrics: the music itself is getting slower and dreamier. This reflects women's tastes. Market research shows that men like robust, fast-paced music with a driving beat. For example, album-oriented rock, known for its blaring guitars and bone-crushing percussion, draws an audience that's 69 percent male. Soft adult contemporary, known for its tender love songs, attracts 67 percent female ears.[11]

Many people feel the slower the song, the more *worshipful* it is. But the psalmist described worship as a cacophonous expression, replete with crashing cymbals, blaring trumpets, and (gulp) dancing (Ps. 150). When our church music is vigorous and energetic, we help men connect with God.

Two things you might not realize about congregational singing. First, there was a time when it was not even allowed in many Protestant churches. Congregational singing is a relatively new phenomenon in Christianity, historically speaking. Second, if we examine the primary activities of the early church in Acts 2, singing is not mentioned. The passage does say the apostles praised God, but it's not clear what form that praise took.

Am I suggesting we get rid of music in the church? No, but we are dangerously close to making music an idol. Rick Warren says, "Too many equate being emotionally moved by music as being moved by the Spirit, but these are not the same. Real worship happens when your spirit responds to God, not some musical tone. In fact, some sentimental, introspective songs *hinder* worship because they take the spotlight off God and focus on our feelings."[12] Douglas Wilson minces no words: "The current emphasis on *feeling worshipful*," he says, "in men produces a cowardly and effeminate result."[13]

To many Christians, singing and worship are now synonymous. One time a woman was telling me about her church. She said, "We have twenty minutes of worship, then teaching." I replied, "Really? So you stop worshipping when you close your mouths?" At first she was taken aback by my comment, but now she realizes that her definition of worship was too narrow.

Worship includes singing, but there's so much more to it! Worship leaders, you have a wonderful opportunity. Mine your Bible, and discover the many ways to give praise and adoration to God. Gary Thomas's book *Sacred Pathways* offers dozens of time-tested ideas for expanding worship beyond singing. Teach these to your people. Recovering these ancient modes of praise giving will help the church recover its masculine voice.

Here are some other ideas:

- Discuss and study worship. Rich Kingham of Promise Keepers encourages men to study and practice the forms of worship found in the Psalms.[14]
- Choose talented people to lead music. Amateurism turns men off.
- Play songs in men's vocal range. If the songs are too high, men won't sing.
- Offer more performed music and less congregational singing when targeting unchurched men. Rick Warren notes, "Visitors do not feel comfortable singing tunes they don't know and words they don't understand. It is also unrealistic to expect the unchurched to sing songs of praise and commitment to Jesus before they become believers."[15]
- Offer men-only worship opportunities. With no women in the room, men are less inhibited.
- Here's a wild idea: advertise a singing-free, purpose-driven men's retreat, and see if you reach more unchurched guys.

- If you choose to have music at men's events, select songs with masculine lyrics. Avoid rapturous love songs to Jesus or songs that stress brokenness, unworthiness, or weakness.

The Bible's greatest worship leader was David—king, outlaw, lover, and warrior. Worship leaders, you need the strength of a king, the cunning of an outlaw, the faith of a lover, and the courage of a warrior. Remember, you are leading the people into battle, not the bedroom. Put a masculine edge on worship, and watch your men come alive. John Eldredge says, "Softness cannot be the predominant quality of the worship, or the worship leader."

GET MEN OUTDOORS FOR WORSHIP

Men feel more alive when they're outdoors. They feel closer to God there. Eldredge advises, "If you want men to learn how to worship, take them outside. Take them into contexts where their heart is alive and it will come naturally." Isn't it interesting how often men's conversion stories take place outdoors?

Outreach to men—especially young men—should also take place outdoors whenever possible. Rev. David Reinhart of the Roman Catholic Diocese of Toledo, Ohio, leads more than two hundred motorcycling Catholics on a seventy-mile ride across the countryside every summer. Pastor Chip Thompson is a surfer who ministers on the beaches outside Los Angeles: "It's much more meaningful to them [than a church service would be] because it's on their own turf. I find people are more than willing to talk at the beach about matters of faith."[16] Worship planners, if you're serious about reaching men, move it outside.

MOVE WORSHIP OUT OF THE CHURCH BUILDING
TO ALTERNATE VENUES

Because going to church turns off a lot of guys, it's often smarter to take church to them. Today's growing house church movement replicates the New Testament model. Churches now meet in shopping malls, office complexes, and school gyms. More Americans are taking their faith to work, participating in employee prayer groups and swapping prayer requests via faith-based e-mail networks.[17] Steve Sonderman recommends that evangelistic men's events be held at a local hotel banquet room.[18] This makes it easier for men to invite their church-phobic friends.

If you are serious about reaching men, move as much ministry as possible out of the church building. I know it's costly to rent space instead of using your perfectly good facility. But if your goal is to reach unchurched guys, spend the money; it's worth it.

DECORATE WITH MEN'S TASTES IN MIND

Believe it or not, decor makes a difference. Many sanctuaries are painted a soft pink, eggshell white, or lavender, with cushiony pews and neutral carpet. The altar features fresh flowers while the walls are adorned with quilts or felt banners. Honestly, how do we expect men to connect with a masculine God in a space that feels so feminine?

I heard the story of a church whose prayer room was seldom used by men. It was painted a soft lavender with silk flowers, lace curtains, candles, and boxes of Kleenex everywhere. The pastor asked his men why they rarely used the room. "Because it's so feminine!" they replied. The pastor challenged the men to redecorate. They stripped the place and put up swords, shields, Celtic banners, and tomahawks! Now the guys go in there. Not surprisingly, the young women also love it. Decorators, consider the needs of men when adorning the church. It makes a difference!

HOW TO PRAY FOR (AND WITH) A MAN

Dan Schaffer says, "Women equate closeness with safety. Men equate personal space with safety." When we gather around a man and lay hands on him for prayer, we may unknowingly violate his need for space. I call these impromptu gatherings *prayer mushrooms*. You know what I'm talking about: Brother Vince happens to mention that his back is sore, and before he knows what hit him, a crowd has sprouted around him, hands extended, heads bowed, eyes closed. Not only has Vince got relative strangers inches from his nose and unfamiliar hands all over his body, but he must remain frozen for ten minutes or more while everyone has a say. Testosterone makes it hard for Vince to stay still, and despite the prayers, his back is killing him.

Most women love prayer mushrooms because closeness is comforting. But they're a little too close for a lot of men. I think this is another reason men keep their prayer requests to themselves. They don't want to end up like Brother Vince!

Is there an alternative to the prayer mushroom? Yes! Some men's groups have created a brilliant option I call the *prayer force*. Brother Vince sits or stands while the others surround him in a loose semicircle. As the Spirit prompts, people step forward to lay a hand on Brother Vince *one at a time*. Others who want to lift up brief prayers simply pray from where they stand. The prayer force has many advantages over the prayer mushroom:

- It honors Brother Vince's need for space.
- It avoids *prayer wrecks*, when two people start praying at the same moment.
- It allows Brother Vince to see who's praying for him and share a smile or wink. This promotes brotherhood.
- The one praying can speak to Vince and/or God as the Spirit leads.
- Hands are laid on, in obedience to Scripture.
- It has a more masculine feel than the prayer mushroom.

Men also appreciate brief, to-the-point prayers. So did Jesus. He said, "When you pray, do not keep on babbling like pagans, for they think they will be heard because of their many words" (Matt. 6:7 NIV). The model prayer given us by Christ in Matthew 6 can be comfortably prayed in thirty seconds. Nothing in the Gospels suggests long prayers are better than short ones.

CHRISTIANS, AVOID PRAYER-SPEAK

Have you ever noticed how Christians speak conversationally to each other, but they speak strangely to God? For example, some faith groups expect people to pray in Elizabethan English: "We beseech Thee, O

Lord, that Thou wouldst shew Thyself amongst us this day." Others repeat God's name again and again in prayer, like a mantra. "Lord, we just thank You, Lord, for this day, Lord, and Lord, we just ask You, Lord, to bless us, Lord." Would you call a friend and say, "Helen, how are you, Helen? Helen, would you like to go to lunch, Helen? Okay, Helen, see you at noon, Helen"? Helen would think you were nuts.

Like preacher-speak, prayer-speak comes across as a performance. Instead of genuine communication with God, men may see it as spiritual grandstanding, designed to make the one praying seem holy. Plus it shuts men out of prayer. Guys won't pray aloud if they must use the language of Shakespeare or repeat *Father God* again and again. The irony here is that Jesus always preferred simple, humble prayers, delivered in the vernacular. Men will talk to God if they're allowed to speak naturally.

Men need time to think before they pray. Larry Keefauver observes, "I realize that wives may expect their husbands to be spontaneous, ready-to-pray-at-any-moment prayer warriors. But husbands often like to meditate and reflect on what they pray about."[19] Remember, women, their brains are not as verbally agile as yours. Praying aloud is really tough on the average guy.

Men need focus and direction in prayer. When you say to a man, "Let's pray," he's likely to say, "About what?" Remember, men are purpose driven, so we help men when we give them concrete, specific things to pray for. As they mature and learn to hear God's voice in prayer, this need diminishes.

Men need to adopt whatever prayer postures they feel comfortable with. The predominant model today is hands folded, head bowed, eyes closed. This is a picture of meekness and passivity. I'm told this, too, is a product of the Victorian era. Before that time Christians prayed with outstretched hands, palms up, face up to God with eyes open! I've begun praying this way, and it has revolutionized my communication with God. *It just feels more masculine.* I feel more like a soldier communicating with my commanding officer.

Worship, prayer, even singing will come naturally to men if they are allowed to do these things in a way that feels right to their masculine hearts. Let the masculine spirit lead in worship and watch your men come alive!

21

WOMEN AND THE MASCULINE SPIRIT

WOMEN, YOU HAVE A WONDERFUL OPPORTUNITY. YOU CAN help move the thermostat in your church. In fact, unless you offer your support, the thermostat will probably never move because a lot of pastors and church leaders won't take the risks involved without your blessing. You must communicate clearly to your congregational leaders that you want the thermostat set on challenge, and you are willing to accept changes that will make your church friendlier to men *even if those changes make you a bit less comfortable.*

WOMEN MUST USE THEIR INFLUENCE FOR CHANGE, NOT FOR THE STATUS QUO

Back in the 1950s Carl Dudley was pastoring his first church. It wasn't long before he got a visit from the president of the women's association, who informed him, "Men sit on boards, but women run the church." Dudley notes:

> Although women held less prestigious positions or none at all, they were not without clout. They remained essential to the strength of the congregation by raising most of the money and providing much of the "manpower" (as it was called) to keep everything running, including the Sunday school, choir, prayer groups and service societies. And they retained what one woman called a "velvet veto" over expenses and programs of which they did not approve.[1]

Women still wield the velvet veto today, and they often use it to drive the masculine spirit out of the church, without even realizing it. How does this happen? Let's say there's a proposal at First Church to eliminate an ineffective evangelistic ministry that hasn't won a convert in years. The leaders who are pushing for the change want to redirect money and volunteers into a different kind of outreach that's proven effective in other churches. The problem is, the old evangelistic program is led by two dear saints who've been in the church for decades: Brother Frank and Sister Dottie. When these two hear that *their* ministry is on the chopping block, they become upset. The women (and a few men) of the church rally around Frank and Dottie. They contact the pastor and exercise their velvet veto. The proposal is canceled, and the ineffective evangelism ministry continues to meet and expend church funds. A chance to introduce a bold, new approach to evangelism (one likely to bear fruit) was scrapped. Final score: Harmony 1, Effectiveness 0.

The good news: Frank and Dottie are happy. The bad news: the masculine spirit was left standing out on the porch. The women of First Church don't see this as a defeat for the masculine spirit; they see it as a victory for peace and harmony. Women tend to consider people's feelings first. Preserving the status quo kept Frank and Dottie from being hurt, so it seemed to be the most Christlike thing to do. These women acted from the purest of motives, but they crushed the masculine spirit nonetheless.

Let me be clear about a couple of things. First, not all women think this way, but this ethos is definitely more common in women than men. Second, it's no sin to consider people's feelings, but if you allow feelings to become the *primary* consideration when making decisions, you are following something other than Christ.

Here's another example of a damaging velvet veto (based on a true story): Eric planned a night of paintball for the church's fledgling men's group. But two prominent women heard about it and complained to the pastor. "How is paintball remotely Christian?" asked one woman. "It shows support for violence," said another. "What message are we sending to our boys?" The pastor knew a time bomb when he saw it. He asked Eric to find something else for the men to do. They met at the church and studied 1 Timothy.

There you have it—the reputation of men's ministry, meeting at the church to study 1 Timothy. No wonder younger, fun-loving, competitive men don't come to church! Soon men's ministry is reduced to "six white haired guys having breakfast in the church basement."[2] Another men's ministry is neutered.

It doesn't have to be like this. Women, you can use your influence to say yes to the masculine spirit. Let change happen, even that which causes people to grieve. Allow the men to do things you may not understand or approve of. Most of all, let your pastor know you support him. If your pastor knew the women of the church wanted a more challenging, man-friendly environment, he would probably be glad to oblige you.

Let Your Church Focus on Developing Men

Chuck Stecker spoke to a woman who serves as a ministry leader in her local church, and he described her attitude: "With complete candor, she said that she would be willing to cancel every program in the church that did not relate directly to developing men into leaders. 'In the long run,' she said, 'every other phase of ministry would be much stronger if the men in the church would develop into the leaders that God has called them to be.'"[3]

Do you share this woman's vision? Are you willing to make the development of men your church's top priority? Would you be willing to cancel every program in the church if that's what it took to build godly men?

Consider Men's Needs When Planning

Women do a lot of planning in the church, so naturally, they tend to plan based on their own needs and expectations. They ask questions like these: "Are we being sensitive enough? Caring enough? Will everyone feel loved and affirmed?" Rarely do women consider men's needs when planning: "Is it challenging enough? Is it visual enough? Are there opportunities to stand up and move around?" Next time you're at a planning meeting, ask yourself: *How will the men respond to this? Does this do a good job of meeting the needs and expectations of our men?* Simply acknowledging that men are different helps move the thermostat.

WOMEN MUST BE WILLING TO LET THEIR MEN CHOOSE THE CHURCH

Maybe all it would take to get your husband/father/son to go to church is to suggest that he choose the church. Then it's no longer *your* thing; it's *his* thing. Would you be willing to switch if another church met your man's needs?

WOMEN MUST ALLOW THE MEN TO GATHER WITHOUT WOMEN AROUND

Most Christian gatherings are either women-only or coed. But guys will never open up and be themselves with women in the room. Jawanza Kunjufu says, "Men act differently if they are in the presence of women; their conversation and focus are different, their attention oftentimes is diverted, and their egos motivate them to try to impress women."[4] I'm not suggesting the church go as far as Islam and separate the sexes for worship, but men do need ministry of their own, away from women.

Still, some women object to men-only gatherings. When Russell Rainey tried to start a men-only group in his Presbyterian congregation, a few women grumbled. "They were concerned that we were going to get some patriarchal, male-dominated model that was going to steal life from them," Rainey said. He was persistent and sold the women on the idea. Today *Men's Fraternity* is the largest gathering of Christian men in Jackson, Wyoming. At a Presbyterian Church, no less! Even women who initially opposed the group now support it, having seen the change it has wrought in the men.

Had Rainey been less persistent, Men's Fraternity might never have launched. Dozens of unchurched men might never have been reached. *Women, be very careful wielding your velvet veto.*

WOMEN MUST BAND TOGETHER

Almost every Christian woman has at least one man she loves who does not go to church. Why not band together to pray for these men? Bring their photographs. Meet regularly to focus intense prayer on their behalf. See what God does.

If your church is typical, some 20 to 25 percent of the married women worship without their husbands. Numerous as these *spiritually single women* are, they often feel like lepers in the church. They can't hang out with the singles, nor can they participate in couples' events.

Fortunately, these women are starting to band together. One church offers a *Moms Without Partners* group during the Sunday school hour for single moms and those who are spiritually single.[5] Another church offers a class to equip wives to reach their husbands with the gospel. In the first three months of the class, four husbands became Christians. Research confirms that the person most likely to lead a husband back to church is his wife.[6]

WOMEN MUST STOP DRAGGING THEIR MEN TO CHURCH

If you are a strong-willed woman who compels her husband, brother, or adult son to go to church, I ask you to reconsider. Jesus never forced anyone to follow Him. You may be driving your man away from God even as you drag him into the sanctuary. There is no benefit to having a man's body in church if his heart is elsewhere.

WOMEN MUST BE A LITTLE LESS RELIGIOUS AND SAINTLY

Sam Keen observes, "It's a lot easier to be a saint than to live with one."[7] If you are strictly religious but the men in your life are not, you may actually make Christianity more attractive by lightening up a bit. Ask God or a friend for ideas on how you might be less *religious* but more *real*.

WOMEN MUSTN'T "DO EVERYTHING"

One time I was speaking to an experienced Assembly of God pastor about the problem of passive men. "Men don't volunteer in church because they know eventually a woman will step forward and take care of it," he said. How true. Many times I've seen church activities on the brink of cancellation for lack of a volunteer. At the very last moment, a faithful (and often overcommitted) woman stepped forward to save it from cancellation.

Women, don't do this. I'll say it again: don't serve in a ministry to which you are not called, no matter how urgent the need. If a particular ministry is chronically understaffed, it may be a sign from God that He is leading elsewhere. Believe me, if men lose a ministry that's important to them, they'll step forward. One time my church couldn't find volunteers to prepare coffee. The next Sunday we simply had no java. Instead, we placed a sign-up sheet on the hospitality table. Guess what? By the time we sang the benediction, we had three jittery men who couldn't wait to volunteer. I call this the *Mr. Coffee* volunteer recruiting strategy.

WOMEN MUST ALLOW THEIR HUSBANDS TO INSTRUCT THE FAMILY

In times past, men instructed their families in spiritual matters. In today's church, the pastor instructs the women, who instruct their children. Men are out of the equation, stripped of their ancient role as priest of their home. Although a lot of women would love their husbands to step up as spiritual leaders, some resist. I spoke to one woman who thought the very idea was demeaning—or laughable. Like many, she was raised in a family where women took the lead in spiritual matters; she couldn't imagine it any other way. I know of one man who'd tried to lead his family in devotions, but his wife always took over because "he wasn't doing it right." Women, let your husband lead, even if he's not as good at it as you. I'm not advocating an oppressive regime where dad does all the teaching and mom is silent—ideally both parents will contribute to their children's spiritual formation.

But what if he won't lead? I believe men don't step up because of what the job entails: a highly verbal regimen of Bible reading, devotional books, bedtime prayers, and theological discourse. Grady has no problem rolling around on the floor, tickling his kids, but he suddenly freezes up at bedtime prayers. Why? Being a spiritual leader, as we currently define it, requires Grady to get still, sensitive, and verbose. No wonder Grady feels his wife is better equipped to be a spiritual leader to the children.

Here's an idea that could help men—and it would work particularly well in small churches. Pastors, instruct the men separately for the last five minutes of the service. Allow the women to sing or visit while you address the men in another room or outdoors. Talk to them man to man, and give them a compelling story or object lesson to cement your message in their minds (use the visual, hands-on techniques we covered in chapter 19). Then let the Holy Spirit—and a woman's curiosity—go to work. As soon as they're in the car, she will ask her husband, "What did the pastor say to you guys?" The husband will tell the story or explain the object lesson to his family. He may even act it out for his family over lunch. Bingo. You have a husband instructing his family. The more comfortable a man becomes talking about God, the more faith will become a part of everyday family life.

How do we get this additional teaching to single women or women who attend alone? Type up a one-page sheet detailing the instruction you gave to the men, and hand it out to anyone who might ask. But avoid giving it to women whose husbands are in attendance.

WOMEN MUST NOT BELITTLE MEN OR ACT SPIRITUALLY SUPERIOR

Some women have noticed their spiritual superiority and lord it over men. One time I was attending a couples' Bible study. The leader asked George to look up a passage in Zephaniah. He searched for a minute or two and finally found Zechariah. In his confusion George read the wrong verse. Jenny reached over and grabbed the Bible with a dramatic sigh. She found the passage in about ten seconds and, with a look of triumph, handed the Bible back to her husband. Guess where George was next week? Not at Bible study, that's for sure. I've also heard women ridicule and patronize men, saying things like, "You boys go off and have your little retreat; do your men's thing out in the woods." Questioning a man's competence or manhood is not the way to draw him to Christ.

WOMEN MUST NOT HOLD BACK IN FOLLOWING JESUS CHRIST

Some women go too far the other direction. Not wanting to emasculate their husbands, they hold back on their own spiritual growth. This is unwise. Christ never waited for anyone. He made it clear we are to follow Him regardless of our situation.

The men in your life are watching you. As you live a vibrant spiritual life, you make the gospel more attractive. But here's the key: *you must be living an adventure.* A safe Christian life consisting of attending church, singing in the choir, teaching Sunday school, and studying the Bible probably won't capture men's imaginations. But if men see your walk with God as something exciting, something that's affecting the world positively, they may become intrigued.

I have a friend who for years lived the safe, predictable Christian life. Cindy's church résumé included Sunday school teacher, choir vocalist, committee worker, and nursery volunteer. Her husband, Carl, a burly electrician, had scant interest in church. Then God's Spirit got hold of Cindy in a big way. He led her to the African nation of Uganda, where she spent her vacation time working with AIDS orphans and abused women. She also began traveling to remote Alaskan villages, ministering in communities devastated by drugs and alcohol.

Carl was watching. He'd seen a change in Cindy. Her religious life had become a real walk with God. It was no longer duty; it was pure joy. One winter night he asked Cindy to take a walk. As huge snowflakes fell, Carl reached out a husky hand, took Cindy's in his, and surrendered his life to Christ. He followed faithfully the rest of his days.

Women, if you are going to church because of a sense of obligation (Jesus paid it all, all to Him I owe . . .), because you've always done it, or because your friends are there, don't expect the men in your life to follow you into the pew. The men who are watching you don't care how saintly you are. They don't care about your traditions. Nor do they care how busy for God you are. They want to know two things: (1) Does Christianity really work? and (2) Is it really the power of God unleashed on earth, or is it just religious activity? As men see the power of the Spirit working through your life, they will be drawn. A religious life will not capture a man's imagination; only an unpredictable adventure with Christ will do.

WOMEN MUST TRANSFORM THE FOCUS OF WOMEN'S MINISTRY

A good way to bring adventure to your walk with God is to bring it to women's ministry. The focus must shift from *learning about God* to *having*

adventures with God. Mary Frances Bowley was director of women's ministry at First Baptist Church in Peachtree City, Georgia. Her ministry took
a radical step forward when she declared that no Bible studies could
meet unless they included a component of ministry to the community.
Mary Frances scoured the community for forgotten women. She set her
women loose ministering to cashiers, food service workers, single moms,
strippers, and prostitutes. Not only were these forgotten women blessed,
but the women of the church were profoundly changed in the process.[8]

WOMEN MUST GIVE UP THEIR FANTASIES
ABOUT WHAT CHRIST WILL DO FOR THEIR MEN

A lot of women want the men in their lives to come to church because
they believe Christianity would make them into better men. The thinking goes:

- *If only my boss were a Christian, he would treat me better.*

- *If only my son were a Christian, he'd stop doing so many risky,
  dangerous things.*

- *If only my husband were a Christian, he wouldn't spend so much
  time out in the garage working on his car.*

Women, have you had these kinds of thoughts? If so, you need to
repent. Christ did not die so you could have the perfect boss, son, or
husband. Christianity is not God's plan to remake men so your life can
be more pleasant.

I asked John Eldredge about this. He almost flew out of his seat! He
said, "Women need to ask: Honestly, why do I want my man to go to
church? If this is my program for shaping him up, he will not cooperate
very willingly. What's the pure motive for wanting him to go to church?
Because God has a great battle for him to fight and an adventure for him
to live, and you are willing and ready for him to find it. No matter what
the cost may be to you. That is Eve repenting at the deepest level."

Women, be careful what you pray for. If your man encounters Christ,
anything can happen. That risk-taking son? As a follower of Jesus, he

may move to an Islamic country to set up an underground church. That car-enthusiast husband? He might start repairing vehicles for single moms and the elderly, and be gone even more. Are you willing for your man to find God, even if it doesn't make him into your ideal? Larry Keefauver points out that most of the heroes in the Bible were lousy husbands and fathers.[9] What if Christ turns Him into a *wild* man instead of a *gentle* man?

Maybe you're thinking, *But that's not what I want. I don't want a religious fanatic! I just want someone to sit next to me in church. I just want my son to straighten up and fly right. I just want my boss to say a kind word to me now and then.* If this is what you want, try Prozac. Christianity was never intended as the antidote to masculinity.

As you read this chapter, did you hear the Spirit calling you to the adventure of following Jesus Christ? Don't ignore His call. Ask Christ to set the thermostat toward challenge in your life. Give up on religion, and start following Jesus! There's no better way to reach the men you love with the gospel.

22

MINISTRY
AND THE MASCULINE SPIRIT

ALL EYES WERE ON PASTOR KEITH, WHO HAD BEEN PROMISING for weeks to make an important announcement. "As of next month," the pastor said, "we are canceling the nursery and Sunday school. We will no longer offer weddings, baptisms, baby showers, or funerals. We are dropping our choir and pulling out of our partnership with the soup kitchen. Instead, we're going to minister in a new way. Our children's ministry will be based on sports leagues. We will offer free automotive repairs to the working poor. We will provide carpentry, plumbing, and electrical upgrades to seniors' homes. We will deploy our members as security ambassadors, walking the streets of high-crime neighborhoods. And we will dig water wells in Honduras and Nicaragua."

Women, how would you feel if your pastor made such an announcement? How well does this roster of ministries match your skills and gifts?

Now you know how men feel. Very few churches offer ministry opportunities that capitalize on men's skills and experience. Men long to give of their best to the Master, but few churches want what men have got.

Roger from Ohio says, "If serving in the church was more about pounding nails and less about wiping runny noses, I'd probably be interested." As I pointed out in chapter 6, much of Christian ministry involves roles that are traditionally feminine. Over the years, we've come to define Christian ministry as the things women are skilled at— and Christians serve primarily in areas where women have more experience. So men sit on their gifts, frustrated. Dutiful men may volunteer to fill a hole in the job board, but their service brings them little joy, because they are not doing what God made them to do.

How can we unshackle our men to minister?

GIVE MEN OPPORTUNITIES TO USE THEIR SKILLS AND GIFTS

Expand ministry into areas where men excel. Why not work on cars? One Illinois church has an on-site auto repair facility for single mothers and the working poor. Even a small church can offer free oil changes in the church parking lot once a quarter. If you live in the Snow Belt, offer free tire changeovers in spring and fall.

Herb Reese of New Commandment Ministries takes a group of four men and places a widow or single mother under their care. Once a month the men do handyman projects around her house, work on her car, help her balance her checkbook, whatever she needs. Herb says, "One guy told me, 'I like this. I don't feel like a wimp or a wuss.'" Herb continues, "For a lot of men, this is the first time they really understand the love of Christ. It's practical love. It's something guys can talk about on Monday morning with their coworkers."

Want to fire men up? Give them a chance to use their talents for God.

HELP MEN DISCOVER THEIR GIFTS

A crucial first step is to administer personality tests and spiritual gift inventories to every adult in your church. These tests help men because they provide objective data showing men their areas of giftedness. (Visit my Web site for a list of organizations that offer personality tests and gift inventories for Christians.) Lee and Leslie Strobel write, "When a once-sidelined, ineffective, and stagnant Christian discovers how God has shaped him to make an eternal difference through a local church—watch out! Suddenly you can't keep him from participating in ministry!"[1]

LET MEN MINISTER

Men may feel they have to go to seminary or have extensive Bible training to minister properly, because they may have grown up in a church where the pastor did all the ministering. Let men know you expect them to minister. Give them training and feedback. Start by training one or two men, then set them up as examples to the others. Pastors, I know you've heard it a million times, but here it is again: you are not the minister. Your people are. You are the coach. God made men to be active, and are often passive because they feel unauthorized or unqualified to minister.

GIVE MEN A PATH TO WALK OR A LADDER TO CLIMB

Men must sense they are on a path that's leading them toward something, or they will run aground. The path must be explained and presented in visual form so men can chart their progress. For example, Saddleback uses a baseball diamond; your goal is home plate. Church of the Resurrection in Kansas uses a mountain diagram; your goal is the summit. Your men must know they are pressing toward a target, gaining skill and responsibility as their level of commitment increases.

GIVE MEN A FOCUS: DO A FEW THINGS WELL

Did you ever use a magnifying glass to burn paper on a sunny day? By concentrating the sun's rays, the glass produces great power. So it is with your church's ministry. As we saw in chapter 17, if you focus on doing a few things well instead of trying to be everything to everyone, more men will want to become involved.

We live in an era of specialization. America has 50,000-square-foot stores that sell nothing but pet supplies! Why are parachurch groups such as Habitat for Humanity able to engage so many guys in Christian ministry? They are focused on one thing, and they do it very well. The day is coming when churches will unite not around shared doctrine but around shared mission. Men will be at the head of that parade.

GIVE MEN EXTERNAL FOCUS

Evangelist Luis Palau says, "The church is like manure. Pile it up and it stinks up the neighborhood; spread it out and it enriches the world." Eric Swanson studies healthy churches, and without exception they are externally focused: their goal is to make a significant and sustainable difference in the lives of people around them.[2] Stagnant churches ask, "How can we minister to our people?" Life-giving churches ask, "How can our people change the world?" This change is great for men.

Fellowship Bible Church models external focus through its small group system. New members are placed in small groups for instruction and nurture. But after three years, they're kicked out into a common cause group that serves the community. Pastor Robert Lewis points out, "That's where men flourish, because men are action oriented."

So-called *liberation churches* demonstrate a specialized form of external focus. A number of urban churches have discovered they can attract men through social activism. These churches are committed to turning their economically depressed communities around through drug-treatment programs, job-training centers, and economic-development projects. Many men are reached through these churches because they see the difference they make in the community.

GIVE MEN BIG PROJECTS THAT CAPTURE THEIR IMAGINATIONS

Corporate America has learned the importance of BHAGs to motivate men. BHAG stands for *Big, Hairy, Audacious Goal.* Adam Hamilton built America's fastest-growing Methodist church by dreaming God-sized dreams. He notes, "Too many churches dream safe, easily attainable dreams. They don't risk, they don't require faith, they don't need God in order to be accomplished."[3] Bruce Wilkinson says God's people "are expected to attempt something large enough that failure is guaranteed . . . unless God steps in."[4]

Unfortunately, some successful churches are caught up in another form of BHAG, the *Better Homes and Gardens* syndrome—the never-ending quest for a bigger, better building. A building-focused church can attract men's attention for a while, but even guys eventually tire of fund-raising thermometers. New facilities are useful only as they lead to more changed lives.

GIVE MEN RISK

Sociologist Marion S. Goldman of the University of Oregon suggests, "Perhaps religiosity with risk is what is necessary to bring men back." She points to the large numbers of young Muslim men who are willing to jeopardize their lives in holy war.[5] Few Western Christians ever risk anything for their faith, nor do we call them to risk. Dallas Willard believes that "only risk produces character," but he is saddened because "we use our ability to hear God as a device for securing a life without risk."[6]

Let me say this plainly: *Christianity based on risk avoidance will never attract men.* If our message is full of *don'ts, be careful's,* and *play it safe's,* men will turn their backs. Christianity is not an insurance policy; it's abundant life!

GIVE MEN ADVENTURE

Randy was a nominal churchgoer for many years, but never really came alive in his faith until he went on a two-week mission trip to Peru to build a water project in an impoverished village. "I had no idea how real the gospel was until I went on this trip. We depended on God every minute of every day," he says. "He helped us through one tight spot after another. As we were taking off, our airplane was hit by bullets from a rebel paramilitary group. It was like being in the book of Acts!"

Randy returned from Peru a changed man. Once he realized how powerful and real God is, he began a daily walk with Him. He stepped up to leadership in church. He and his wife began praying together for the first time. Randy continued to support missions in South America, and he returned the next year with a bigger team. He shared his story with his American neighbors, and they started coming to church. *Adventures with Christ change men in a way church attendance never could.*

DEPLOY MEN IN SERVANT EVANGELISM

Traditional approaches to evangelism leave many men cold. Most men don't want to go door-to-door selling Jesus. Talk about an exercise in futility! But Vineyard Community Church in Cincinnati found that men will gladly witness by serving the community. They fix up houses, pass out drinks, clean bathrooms, and wrap packages. "They accept no donations and often utter only one sentence: *we just want to show you God's love in a practical way.*" This kind of evangelism gives the church a positive image in the community and motivates people to visit.[7]

CREATE MEN-ONLY ROLES, OPPORTUNITIES, AND EVENTS

One time I coordinated a men-only workday at our church. A woman came to me and complained that she wanted to volunteer and felt discriminated against. I took a deep breath, and the Holy Spirit spoke through me: "Nora, our church has dozens of women-only opportunities, but this is the men's one chance to do something on their own. Will you allow the men to serve you?" Nora relented. The event remained men-only, and it attracted more than fifty guys. What was more remarkable, several of the volunteers were the nonreligious husbands of churchgoing wives! Unchurched men will minister more readily in a men-only environment.

LET YOUR MEN MAKE A MEANINGFUL CONTRIBUTION

Neil Carter notes, "In a highly liturgical church like a Catholic or Episcopalian church, only the minister and one or two others get to do anything that *matters* . . . Men despise their passive role in most churches, whether they have been able to label their frustration or not."[8] William Easum writes, "Individual members of the Body of Christ find their fulfillment, not as their ministry makes them feel good, but when their ministry contributes to the health of the Body of Christ."[9]

Oftentimes all a man needs for a spiritual awakening is a chance to use his gifts for God. Thom Rainer tells the story of Steve, an unchurched husband who showed up for a church work party. After a day of hard labor and hanging out with followers of Jesus, Steve asked how he, too, might become a Christian.[10] Another pastor tells of a computer expert who met the Lord after being asked to help set up the church's network.

He saw something special in the lives of the church staff. *These men came to Christ without attending a worship service and without ever hearing a formal presentation of the gospel.* They served Christ and, through that service, heard His call.

The lesson is clear: if we want to win more men to Christ, ask them to deploy their gifts in the church, even if they are not yet *in Christ.* Of course, not every role is appropriate for an unchurched man. But bear this in mind: men are sometimes changed through *service* instead of *sermons.*

Don't Keep What Your Church Is Doing a Secret: Shout It from the Housetops!

Churches that reach men celebrate loudly and publicly what God is doing in their midst. They seek publicity. They advertise. This would seem to contradict Christ's command that we do good works in secret. I think this command applies to individuals, not churches. People shouldn't draw attention to their personal piety, but when God is moving powerfully in a church, get the word out!

Charge Men Money

If you want a man to show up for a class, retreat, or seminar, charge him something. Promise Keepers learned this lesson the hard way in the late 1990s. The decision was made to stop charging admission to PK stadium rallies in the hope that more lower-income men would attend. Instead, attendance plummeted. Why? Men equate money with value. If a man has to lay his money down, he'll perceive a value. But if a man pays *nothing,* he'll think it's worth *nothing.*

You don't have to charge a lot. My church charges ten dollars for each midweek class. This modest materials fee is enough to get men to commit, but not enough to discourage low-income folks from signing up. This practice is a far cry from setting up moneychangers in the temple. The goal is not to enrich the church, but to ensure a higher level of commitment from men.

OFFER PERSONAL INVITATIONS TO CHURCH

Don't overlook the obvious. Nothing brings a man to church or to a ministry event like a personal invitation from a man he respects. Gallup Polls report that 60 to 90 percent of church members first attended the church because of an invitation from someone they knew.[11] According to Man in the Mirror Ministries, you can triple your attendance at men's events by forming a call team responsible for phoning and inviting ten men each.[12]

RECOGNIZE THE IMPORTANCE OF ENTRY AND EXIT POINTS

Traditionally, churches have had one entry point: the worship service. But since men hate going to church, we need new methods for introducing them to the gospel. Many mainline churches are offering the Alpha Course, which is a great entry point for men because of its question-and-answer format (you can learn more about Alpha on my Web site). Other churches send their members into the community to teach life skills. By giving their expertise away, Christians earn the right to be heard.

Men's ministry may offer a number of effective entry points: small groups, large groups, seminars, men's events, sports leagues, and so forth. Men's ministry provides guy-oriented events to which men can invite their unchurched friends. These should take place off-campus ideally and should not be overtly evangelistic. Men need to meet some Christian guys and make friends before they're ready for the next step.

Once a man begins attending your church, it's often helpful to have entry-level ministry opportunities. Parking and ushering are two of the most popular ways to introduce men to ministry. But don't leave a man in an entry-level job for ten years; give him a next step to move into as he matures in faith and service.

Also, don't forget exit points. Rick Warren writes, "To resign from a ministry in some churches, you've either got to die, leave the church or be willing to live with intense guilt."[13] One of the main reasons men do not step up to minister is the never-ending commitment that's implied. But ask a man for a short-term commitment, and he's more likely to say yes. When he reaches the finish line, celebrate! As we saw earlier, this honors a man's natural cycle: plan, work, celebrate, rest.

MOST IMPORTANT:
AS MEN MINISTER, MAKE SURE THEY'RE ALSO BEING DISCIPLED

This is a major tragedy of today's church. We put men to work for God, but we do not disciple them! Pat Morley tells a poignant story from his childhood:

> My dear father and mother, who both passed away last year, joined a church for the religious and moral instruction of their four young boys. Our church had a vision for putting my Dad to work—he became the top layman by age 40. But our church had no vision for helping him become a disciple—a Godly man, husband, and father.
>
> As a result, when my Dad was 40 and I was in the 10th grade and my youngest brother was in the 3rd grade, my parents burned out. Our family left the church. My parents never returned. It put our family into a downward spiral from which we have still not fully recovered.[14]

One more time: what's our goal? *To make disciples!* But our current model—teaching people and setting them to work in the church—is not getting the job done. Men need meaningful work *and* genuine discipleship. The final part of this book paints a portrait of healthy masculine discipleship. We will learn how any church can begin discipling its men.

PART 6

MEETING MEN'S DEEPEST NEEDS

Now it's time to open door number three.

I'm going to ask you to forget everything I've written up to this point. Because if all we do is take the existing church and move the thermostat toward challenge, I fear we are just rearranging the deck chairs on the *Titanic*. We may get more men into the building, but we won't bring them to life. It's time to admit that our current model of church—go to a building every Sunday, sing songs, listen to a speech, practice rituals, write a check, smile, shake hands, and leave—does not meet men's deepest needs.

A weekly worship service is like cereal: it's a *part* of a nutritious spiritual breakfast. But men shall not live by cereal alone. Men need something more than Sunday morning worship if they are to be truly nourished. That *something* lies behind door number three.

23

EVERY MAN
NEEDS A SPIRITUAL FATHER

ON BROADWAY, ANNIE OAKLEY SANG TO FRANK BUTLER, "Anything you can do I can do better." Though Frank protested, he knew it was true.

So it is in today's church. Generally speaking, anything a man can do, a woman can do better. With the exception of the pastorate, women now dominate the spiritual work of the church. They occupy the sacred roles and are entrusted with passing the faith to the next generation. If a man does anything in the church, it's usually something practical, so his best efforts go into supporting the institution, not changing the world.

Men need a *sacred role,* one only they can fulfill.

Fortunately, God gave men such a role. God calls every man to become *a spiritual father.* This may be a new concept to you. It's a role that's not well understood because, like the Trinity, it's more implied than spelled out in Scripture. But the example of Jesus and the apostle Paul are clear; spiritual fathering is the only way to bring believers to maturity in Christ.

SPIRITUAL FATHERING:
THE MISSING LINK IN CHRISTIAN MATURITY

In the natural world, fatherlessness is devastating to men. Boys without dads are more likely to run away from home, be homeless, commit suicide, exhibit behavioral disorders, drop out of school, abuse drugs and alcohol, and go to jail.[1] Among adults, 70 percent of violent criminals and long-term prison inmates grew up without fathers.[2]

Fatherlessness is devastating in the spiritual world as well. Why are our churches filled with spiritually immature men? Because we are not fathering them. We are teaching them things, but we are not raising them to maturity. Few are becoming great men because there are few fathers to show them the way. Think this is a new problem in the church? Read the words of Paul in 1 Corinthians 4:14–15: "I do not write these things to shame you, but as my beloved children I warn you. For though you might have ten thousand instructors in Christ, yet you do not have many fathers; for in Christ Jesus I have begotten you through the gospel."

Paul was warning us: a church with many teachers but few fathers is a church in trouble. Like a wayward child, the church at Corinth was stuck in a cesspool of sin because it lacked the guidance and discipline a father provides. There were plenty of men willing to stand up and teach, but few with the guts to walk alongside men and bring them to maturity.

The founders of our faith, by word and by example, made it clear that men are to serve as spiritual fathers. Jesus was certainly a spiritual father to the Twelve. Paul called both Timothy and Titus his *sons*. The apostles Paul and James and the writer of Hebrews established *maturity* as the goal for Christians. They repeatedly begged believers to grow up—to move beyond milk to solid spiritual food. Tell me, how are children to mature without the guidance of a father? No one expects babies to raise themselves, yet this is what we expect of babes in Christ.

A spiritual father is a living example. Paul was not shy about setting himself up as an example to believers. "Therefore I urge you, imitate me" (1 Cor. 4:16). "Imitate me, just as I also imitate Christ" (1 Cor. 11:1). "Brethren, join in following my example" (Phil. 3:17). "You should follow us" (2 Thess. 3:9).

Men follow men. Boys imitate their dads. Jesus imitated His Father as well: "I tell you for certain that the Son cannot do anything on his own. He can do only what he sees the Father doing, and he does exactly what he sees the Father do" (John 5:19 CEV).

Can it be any clearer? *The Christian faith is the world's biggest game of follow the leader.* Men are perishing in our churches because they have no example to follow. Or we expect all of them to follow the pastor. That's just not realistic: Jesus personally discipled twelve men. You cannot expect your pastor—with so many demands heaped upon him—to serve as a spiritual father to every man in the congregation.

In both the natural world and the spiritual world, any man can reproduce, but it takes a real man to be a father. When we win converts without providing them spiritual fathers, it's almost like siring illegitimate children. George Barna found that a majority of people "who made a first time 'decision' for Christ were no longer connected to a Christian church within just eight weeks of having made such a decision!"[3]

Not only does every man need to have a spiritual father, but he needs to become a spiritual father. I've said it before: a man's strongest urge is to reproduce. He wants to leave a lineage and legacy. God's first command in the Garden was *be fruitful and multiply*. Jesus' last command in the Gospels was *make disciples*. A man will never be fulfilled in church until he is reproducing spiritual sons.

We become great men through spiritual fatherhood. It's how we leave our mark—how we build the kingdom of God. A rich, satisfying life is available to any man who will become a spiritual father. *Attention, men:* Christianity is not about reading your Bible, praying, and staying morally pure. You do these things to become a stronger father to the men in your care.

MY VISIT TO A CHURCH BASED ON SPIRITUAL FATHERING

In 1995 Pastor G. F. Watkins had a vision: *to build America's first church designed from the ground up to reach men.* Powerhouse Christian Center in Katy, Texas, is a different kind of church, built on the principle of spiritual fathering. Powerhouse is growing rapidly and enjoys astronomical retention, giving, and male participation. Church officials report:

- Nearly 50 percent of first-time visitors become regular attendees.
- Sixty to sixty-five percent of new converts stay in church.
- On average, 60 percent of those who attend Sunday morning services attend home groups.
- Sixty percent of the members tithe, enabling the three-year-old church to build a $4.5 million facility *without a building campaign*.

Powerhouse provides a heaping helping of the masculine spirit during Sunday morning services. Half the multiethnic congregation is male. Even more remarkable: the men seem to enjoy being there. During the meet-and-greet time I received no less than seven handshakes from enthusiastic men. Things move along, and no element of the service takes more than ten minutes. There's almost always live drama or video produced in the church's on-site studio. The sermon is brief, packed with masculine imagery and illustrations.

But the hidden strength of the church is its structure. There are no committees. Instead, the pastor serves as a spiritual father to a dozen men. Each of these men fathers twelve men, who in turn father up to twelve men, and so forth. The pastor meets with his sons weekly for prayer and instruction. They hold each other accountable. Powerhouse calls this *male mentoring*.

One of Watkins's spiritual sons is Mark Glaze, a former construction worker who joined the staff about five years ago. Glaze disciples eleven men and has a total of 109 men in his *lineage*, as he calls it. He has met them all and knows most of them by name. Whenever 1 of the 109 is in trouble, he gives him a call or sends a note of encouragement. "I used to build structures. Now I build men and raise up sons," says Glaze. "God is good."

Women meet with women for discipleship as well. And more than a thousand attend Powerhouse's Sunday evening home groups, which are whole-family affairs. Jim and Vicki Rinke invited me into their group. For the first time in my life I experienced a coed home group where the men were just as engaged as the women! Men spoke up, offered their input, and talked plainly of past struggles with drugs or alcohol. One man was just three weeks out of prison. But he was excited because, for the first time in his life, he had a male leader to follow. He was learning the Christian life by watching another man live it. Isn't this the way faith is meant to be passed on?

What Are Spiritual Fathers?

Let me propose this definition: *spiritual fathers are men who are walking with God and leading men by example to maturity in Christ.* To gain a better understanding of spiritual fathers, let's examine the characteristics of a father in the natural world. As we do, we'll meet Dave and Tom, a spiritual father and his spiritual son.

Fathers Have Ongoing Relationships with Their Children

A child will have many teachers, but only one father. A good father will stick by his children and love them the rest of their lives, even after the children leave the nest. Similarly, Dave made an ongoing, lifelong commitment to Tom. He selected Tom because he saw potential in him and wanted to call that out. Tom knows that he can contact Dave anytime, for the rest of his life, whenever he needs guidance.

Fathers Teach by Example

I've taught my kids a lot, but I've never held any classes for them. I teach them as we walk together through life. In the same way, Dave hangs out with Tom (at church and other places) and instructs him as they walk along the road.

Fathers Teach Their Boys How to Release
Their Masculine Energy in a Healthy Way

Dr. Larry Crabb says every man must learn to release the masculine energy within himself. Suppressing it leads to one of three outcomes: (1) men feel powerless, and become controlling; (2) men feel rage, and become abusive; or (3) men feel terror, and become addicted.[4] Dave shows Tom how to deal with his feelings and how to express them in a healthy way. He also guides Tom through life transitions: new fatherhood, career change, midlife crisis, and health problems. Many men face these giants alone—but not those who have a spiritual father.

Fathers Are Not Mothers

When a little boy skins his knee, his mommy runs and comforts him until the crying stops. But a father is just as likely to examine the knee and, seeing no blood, say, "You're not hurt. Get back out there and play." This toughening seems cruel, but it serves a boy well as he progresses toward manhood.

The current lack of fathers has led to a culture of self-absorption in the church. Tim Stafford observes a growing epidemic of people who are wounded by their congregations, something unknown in previous generations. In today's therapeutic church we comfort people until the crying stops. But Stafford warns, "People's expectations may be impossible, and their neediness endless. We may help them more by challenging them to serve others than by trying to fill their empty holes."[5] Self-absorbed men need spiritual fathers who will examine the wounds in their lives and, seeing no blood, say, "You're not hurt. Get back out there and play."

Fathers Discipline Their Children

A child must learn there are behaviors that will not be tolerated. Spiritual fathers may on occasion be called upon to administer discipline to a wayward fellow. Say Tom is being unfaithful to his wife. Dave has the right to intervene because of the relationship they've established. *Men change only when they are forced to change.* Dave is the unmovable rock that Tom needs when his life is spinning out of control.

The Father Names the Child

In ancient times your name was your destiny. Bible heroes such as Abram, Simon, and Saul discovered their *true* names after an encounter with their heavenly Father. Dave helps Tom find his real name, the true identity that was stolen by the evil one.

The Father Gives the Boy His Sacred Role in Life

Michael Gurian writes, "Without a sacred role to grow into, [a boy] will, as he becomes a man, be more likely to join a gang, hit his lover, abandon his children, live in emotional isolation, become addicted, hypermaterialistic, lonely and unhappy. He needs a structure and discipline in which to learn who he is. He needs to live a journey that has clear responsibilities and goals. He needs a role in life."[6]

Most men do not understand their role in life or in the local church. *Why do I exist? How can I love and serve God?* A spiritual father can help a man find his role in life and in God's kingdom. Dave helped Tom discover for himself the role God has for him.

The Father Prepares His Boys to Become Fathers

I'm looking forward to the day my son becomes a good father to his children. Spiritual fathers let their sons know they are a link in a chain and will be expected to disciple men when they are ready. Sam Keen sees manhood not as a "lone man standing tall against the sunset, but a blended figure composed of a grandfather, a father and a son. The boundaries between them are porous, and strong impulses of care, wisdom, and delight pass across the synapses of the generations."[7] What if your church were alive with rich, enduring masculine relationships? What if your congregation had a team of men like Dave, who knew their sacred role and were bringing other men to maturity? It can! It starts by giving men a vision for spiritual fathering.

WHAT YOU MUST KNOW ABOUT SPIRITUAL FATHERING

Spiritual fathering cannot be grafted onto the existing church, added like a program or class. It can't be one more thing we cram into an already overstuffed church calendar. *Spiritual fathering must become the foundation of the church*. It's time consuming, so other church activities will have to fall by the wayside. It may require a complete rethinking of how we organize our ministry. But it is the future. It's Discipleship 101.

There is a stirring in the church, and a few bold congregations (like Powerhouse) are moving in step with the Spirit on this issue. These bodies have allowed their pastors to redirect their energy into fathering a few men. They have built male mentoring into the very core of their organization. Instead of a church full of isolated men who serve on committees and pass out bulletins, you have a church where every man has a spiritual father who loves and guides him. But not just a father: a band of brothers. That's the topic of the next chapter.

24

EVERY MAN
NEEDS A BAND OF BROTHERS

DEEP IN HIS HEART, EVERY MAN WANTS TO BE A PART OF A
team that does something great. Just look at the movies men adore. A
team comes together to save the world, steal the money, or win the
championship. *The Lord of the Rings, X-Men, The Matrix, Saving Private
Ryan, Ocean's Eleven, Remember the Titans*—dozens of these movies hit
the screens each year. They feature a band of brothers who attempt the
dangerous, the outrageous, the impossible. (Nowadays there's usually a
woman on the team, but she's as angular and muscled as a man.) Each
member of the team has a specialty and makes a vital contribution.
They take turns saving each other's life.

A band of brothers. Though he may not realize it, every man longs
to be part of one. It's the model Jesus left us. If the church was offering
this kind of fellowship—united in purpose, mutually supportive, and
accomplishing great things—you would not be able to blast men out of
the church.

God looked at Adam and said, "It is not good for the man to be
alone" (Gen. 2:18 NIV). Yet evidence suggests most men are alone, isolated, and friendless—even at church. Gallup reported that 51 percent
of women had a best friend in their congregation, while only 35 percent of men did.[1] Dan Erickson and Dan Schaeffer observe, "Even in
the church, very few men have close friends. For the most part, men are
spiritually fed but relationally bankrupt."[2]

You can implement every suggestion in this book, and men will still
fall away if they do not find a band of brothers to run with. According
to John Eldredge, men need a *little platoon* where they can be real,

222

where they challenge each other in their faith, where no one gets left behind.

So how do we get men into platoons if they don't even like to go to church?

First, fight the Lone Ranger mentality in our churches. Christianity has evolved into a me-and-God pursuit: read your Bible (alone), pray (alone), come to church (alone in a crowd). This spiritual individualism is killing men.

Second, see little platoons as the basic unit of the church rather than a desirable add-on. Small discipleship groups must become the cells that form the body rather than appendages to the existing church body. Ideally, Sunday morning church should be a gathering of little platoons to form the larger redemptive community.

Finally, create an environment where men can form meaningful relationships. Pat Morley tells of a church that attracted large numbers to its men's events, but few men grew spiritually despite the great teaching: "Then the pastor decided to recruit shepherds to lead their small groups instead of teachers. When the men had the opportunity to [talk about] what was going on in their lives (instead of having someone lecture them), they began to open up. By building around relationships, the church has grown tremendously."[3] Hear that? When men started forming little platoons, the entire church grew! Masculine relationships build the church, and they build men.

RELATIONSHIPS: A MINEFIELD FOR MEN

Relationships are a sensitive area for the average fellow. Here are four things you should know about men and relationships:

1. Though Men Want and Need Relationships, They Rarely Use the Term or Think Relationally

The term *relationship* is loaded. A lot of guys have messed up every relationship they've ever had, so they associate the word with hurt, misunderstanding, and pain. In a man's mind, relationships are something men have with women, not with other men. A man has to overcome a truckload of fear and suspicion to *have a relationship* with another man.

As I said in an earlier chapter, men comprehend relationships in terms of activity. Ken has his work buddies, his fishing buddies, his football buddies, and so on. Ken would never approach another man and say, "Hey, Roger, can we have a relationship?" Such a request would arouse suspicion, because it's not expressed in terms of activity. Instead, Ken would say, "Hey, Roger, let's go fishing." Ken and Roger could go fishing every weekend for thirty years and never describe what they have as a *relationship*.

My advice: avoid the term *relationship* altogether when dealing with guys. At my church, we don't encourage folks to have relationships. Instead, we encourage them to *get partnered up*. Partnership suggests activity and a goal. It's a term that motivates men and women.

2. Women Form Relationships Face-to-Face; Men Form Relationships Side by Side

In the church we form relationships the feminine way. We put people in circles and ask them to share. But men form relationships while doing something else—driving a truck, going fishing, painting a wall, or working on a car. Have you ever noticed when a man wants to talk, he'll often suggest going for a drive? Men are intimidated by face-to-face communication.

You may say, "Our church has guys in small groups sharing their hearts every week. They communicate face-to-face." But I'll bet these are the highly verbal and relational men, or those who've been in church for years. If you want to create an environment where any kind of man can get into a little platoon, give men side-by-side bonding opportunities. The support group–style circle is just too intimidating for many guys.

3. The Deepest Male Relationships Are Formed in a Crucible

Men develop lasting friendships when they've suffered together. The bonds formed on a battlefield are enduring. One time I asked my father who his best friend was. He identified an old army buddy he'd hardly spoken to in thirty years. Men who have competed together, sweat together, bled together, and overcome adversity together are bonded for life.

For most women, relationships are easy. Put two together over lattés, and within minutes their hearts are open. But for many men, struggle is the only satisfactory backdrop for relationship. Let me give you an example. Here in Alaska, men build their relationships through outdoor activities. Two guys will plan a hunting trip for six months. They'll spend thousands of dollars on gear and transportation. Then it's a week slogging through mud, sleeping on hard ground in the cold, facing danger, deprivation, and adversity. Finally, after the pair have suffered and overcome enough challenges, the men open up and tell what's on their hearts.

4. Don't Push Men Too Far, Too Fast, or They'll Pull Away

You can't just throw men together and expect them to become brothers. It takes time. Sometimes we drive men off when we push for too much depth too soon. I have a friend who, inspired by Jesus' example, decided to wash the feet of his small men's group during their first meeting. This was too much, too soon. Most of the men were no-shows the next week. Christ waited three years to gain that level of trust with His disciples. Pushing the process will torpedo a men's group.

MEN NEED A RELATIONSHIP WITH GOD

It's not enough for men to connect with each other; they need to connect with God. Our churches are full of men who know *about* God, but *who do not know God personally.*

For men the key question is not "Am I saved, confirmed, baptized, a church member, a practicing Catholic, a believer, a Christian, or Spirit filled?" All of these things are good, but they do not get to the heart of the matter. The real question is not one of status but one of practice: "Am I walking with God? Am I following Jesus Christ today?"

Pastor Karl Clauson frequently receives worried parents in his office. They have adolescent or young adult children who are living a self-destructive lifestyle. The conversation often goes like this:

PASTOR: Is Johnny a follower of Jesus Christ?

MOTHER: Well, he went to this camp when he was twelve, and he accepted . . .

PASTOR: Wait a minute. Time out. Is Johnny a follower of Jesus Christ?

FATHER: At fifteen he went through confirmation . . .

PASTOR: Hang on. Is Johnny a follower of Jesus Christ today?

Once men are saved/confirmed/baptized/members, we tend to forget about them. We teach them principles and give them moral guidance, but we do not show them how to walk with God. The average churchgoing guy has no idea how to follow Jesus for three reasons: (1) he has never been shown how to do it, (2) he has never seen another man doing it (other than a pastor), and (3) he thinks it's about religious practice and moral living.

We call men to confirmation, church membership, and salvation because we can count these things. We can report them to headquarters. It's harder to count the number of men walking with God, but is there anything more important to the health of your church? Men need to follow Jesus Christ, but we cannot expect them to do it alone. It takes spiritual fathers and a band of brothers. *It takes a team.*

I've only scratched the surface of these important topics. If you want to learn more, visit my Web site at www.churchformen.com. For more on spiritual fathering, visit www.buildingbrothers.org.

LEAVE NO MAN BEHIND

Jack received Christ during an invitation at his local church. Two months later, he no longer went to church, had lost all contact with believers, and was not living any discernible Christian life. More than half of Christian conversions end this way.[4]

What if a spiritual father had taken responsibility for Jack? What if he'd been scooped up by a little platoon of men and discipled? With a band of brothers spurring him on, do you think Jack would abandon the faith just eight weeks later? That's the strength of a little platoon—no man gets left behind.

25

THE SECOND COMING
OF THE MASCULINE SPIRIT

BRINGING THE MASCULINE SPIRIT BACK TO CHURCH ISN'T hard. It doesn't require knife throwing or hand-to-hand combat during the worship service. We don't need a new gospel or Jesus; the originals will work just fine. The goal is not male dominance; it's male resurgence. We welcome the masculine spirit by considering men's needs, assigning them a sacred role, and letting them be men. Men need masculine imagery, vocabulary, and behaviors for relating to God. They need symbols, stories, teaching, and volunteer opportunities that affirm them as men. Most of all, men need to sense a healthy, life-giving masculine spirit the moment they walk into our churches.

God differentiated between male and female in the Garden; we must never forget that the sexes are different, immutably so, and we must treat them differently. We don't need to pander to men, but it's time to stop squeezing them into a feminine religious mold. No longer can we scorn men's gifts or bid them repent for the way God made them.

You don't *make* a plant grow. When the conditions are right, it grows naturally. In the same way, men will grow in faith if they are given the right conditions. But with the spiritual thermostat in most churches set on *comfort* instead of *challenge*, it's no wonder men are withering in the pews.

It took centuries to create Christianity's gender gap; it will not be bridged in a generation. Rebuilding a negative image takes time, persistence, and in this case, much prayer. You could create the perfect church for men, and still some would resist because the whole concept of churchgoing is so abhorrent. The sad truth is, certain men will never come to church.

Maybe they don't have to. George Barna has identified a fascinating trend among men. Between 1994 and 2004, men's church attendance was flat, *but men's participation in small spiritual groups doubled!* During that decade about *nine million* additional men joined a small group that meets during the week for the purpose of prayer, Bible study, or spiritual fellowship, apart from Sunday school or other church classes.[1]

What does this mean? Since male participation in small groups exploded during a decade when male church attendance did not increase, it seems likely that thousands, perhaps millions of *unchurched* men are getting into small spiritual groups. These irreligious men have a hunger for God, but see no need to waste their time with that irrelevant bore called Sunday worship. These unchurched men are turning to a small group to give them what the modern church system cannot—a genuine connection to God, and the camaraderie of a band of brothers.

Are unchurched men really finding God without the help of a local church? Absolutely. I know a number of men who are intensely devoted to Jesus, but who do not attend organized worship services. Robert Lewis estimates that his Men's Fraternity meetings regularly draw 100 to 150 men who do not attend church. Men are taking a Costco approach to faith, going factory direct, cutting out the middleman.

Is this good news or bad news for the church? It depends. If we want more men *in church*, this is a crisis. But if we want more men *in Christ*, this is an opportunity. If millions of men are encountering Jesus through small groups, perhaps we should be planting churches based on little platoons. It might even be time to rethink what it means to go to church.

Those of us who remain in the institutional church have to make some decisions: Will we accept these men as our brothers in Christ, even though they don't partake in church sacraments or participate in organized Christian ritual? Are we willing to admit our current model of Christian formation is not producing many male disciples? If so, will we reorganize our churches to make them more effective in discipling men?

In the meantime, the local church is not standing still. New twists on Sunday worship are having some success reaching unchurched men. I already mentioned the man-targeted church in Texas; now there are multisite churches, video churches, cowboy churches, drive-in churches, even pub and tavern churches. Churches meet in shopping malls, sporting venues, office complexes, and movie theaters. The Purpose-Driven movement has been great for men because it presents the gospel in terms a man can understand. Small groups built around 40 Days of Purpose and the Alpha Course are producing many new male followers of Jesus Christ.

Men's ministry is finally being marketed to men! Three of the top men's ministries in America bear the masculine monikers Men's Fraternity, Top Gun, and G-Men. Promise Keepers ads are becoming more masculine. In the 1990s, they featured photos of men singing, holding hands, hugging, and crying. Today those images are gone, replaced by pictures of men climbing rocks, men wielding swords, men covered head to toe in mud, with this caption: "If your idea of a men's accountability group is 'been there, done that, let's skip the hug today,' think again." The ad practically apologizes for past missteps: "We've learned a lot in 13 years. Come see the new face of men's ministry . . . Bold, dynamic, challenging, and a blast. Check out the PK Challenge conference near you."[2] Hear that? It's a *Challenge* conference!

There's been an explosion in outdoor ministry for men. Guys are coming to Christ through hunting and fishing, climbing and rafting, adventures of every kind. John Eldredge's Wild at Heart Boot Camps are booked months in advance. They are not your typical church retreats: the course is rigorous and demanding. Men love it!

Best of all, men are finally being allowed to use their talents for God's kingdom. Men are building houses for the poor. Churches are deploying men as everything from volunteer accountants to mechanics. Men are teaching life skills in the community (no big evangelistic push) just to show the love of Jesus.

What Church Professionals and Leaders Can Do

Church leaders: it's time to convene a national (or worldwide) summit on the church's problem with missing/unmotivated men. Academics, pastors, lay leaders, and men's ministry leaders should gather to pray, discuss the problem, and share solutions. (To get more men to participate, let's have it up here in Alaska in June when the sockeyes are running!) To find out more, visit churchformen.com.

Scholars: it's time to study the gender gap in depth. Dozens of studies have shown us how to get more women into the pulpit; it's time for one bold researcher to study how to get more men into the pews! Who among you has the courage to swim against the current academic tide to examine this persistent problem?

Seminaries: it's time for a new kind of pastoral training. Instead of preparing pastors for a life of study, preaching, and visitation, it's time to start preparing them to lead men. We need new courses on leadership, spiritual fathering, creation of a masculine environment, and visual communication. Perhaps an entirely new kind of seminary is in order, based more on a boot camp than a classroom. Let's be honest: today's seminary system attracts a lot of studious and sensitive men. A new kind of seminary would draw a new kind of man to the ministry—men who burn with a desire to *lead* the people of God on a great adventure.

What One Person Can Do

My hope is that I've given you lots of ideas throughout this book, but I'd like to leave you with a few practical steps you can take this week.

In the first chapter I prayed that this book would be the match that ignited thousands of conversations and millions of prayers about this problem. If you would like to be a part of an ongoing, worldwide conversation, visit my Web site, www.churchformen.com. It's a place to meet others who want to call our churches back to men. You can swap ideas, concerns, and prayers. There's also a book list (for more information on this subject) and links to ministries that are breaking through to men. Look up my speaking schedule, or book a seminar in your church. I especially encourage women to visit the Web site; there is a special area where women can share their joys and frustrations regarding the spiritual condition of the men in their lives.

Second, break the code of silence in your congregation: talk about the problem of missing men. Truly I say to you: *a lot of people in your church have never even noticed the gender gap!* Ask them: "Do you realize that less than 40 percent of the adults in our congregation are men?" I've found that once people wake up to this fact, they are more likely to see the need for action.

Third, learn to recognize and welcome the masculine spirit in your congregation. When there's talk of big changes, bold initiatives, and adventures into uncharted waters, don't be frightened. Instead, step out of the boat, as Peter did, your eyes fixed on Christ. Live the adventure Jesus intended for His followers.

JESUS SAID, "I WILL MAKE YOU FISHERS OF MEN."

Seven men clung to the sides of a crude boat as it bobbed on the Sea of Galilee. They were exhausted. They had spent the night letting out their net and drawing it back in, with nothing to show for their labors. Even the sun seemed fatigued as it struggled to push itself above the eastern shore. Peter's bloodshot eyes wandered down the familiar beach, coming to rest on a stranger who was walking toward them. "Throw your net on the right side of the boat," the stranger shouted. "You'll find some fish there." The disciples looked up, then turned to one another. Imagine their reactions:

THOMAS: Who is this stranger?

NATHANIEL: Is he crazy? Isn't the same sea on either side?

JOHN: Can it really be as simple as fishing off the other side of the boat?

JAMES: I've been a fisherman for twenty years, and I've never heard such nonsense!

PETER: Friends, we've fished all night and haven't caught a thing. What have we got to lose?

As you read this book, you may have had similar questions about me and my message. *Who is this stranger? Is he crazy? I've been a Christian twenty years, and I've never heard such nonsense! Can it really be as simple as fishing off the other side of the boat?*

Yes, it's that simple. Jesus promised to make us fishers of men, but today we catch relatively few. Perhaps it's time to drop our nets on the *masculine* side of the boat. The disciples overcame their skepticism and obeyed Christ; they were rewarded with an enormous catch. I believe millions of men are ready to walk with their Maker if only we'll put aside our doubts and welcome the masculine spirit back to our churches. *What have we got to lose?*

ABOUT THE AUTHOR

DAVID MURROW IS THE DIRECTOR OF CHURCH FOR MEN, AN ORGANization dedicated to restoring a healthy masculine spirit in Christian congregations. For more than twenty years he has produced and written award winning television documentaries, commercials, and specials. He's produced material for the Discovery Channel, NBC, ABC, Food Network, Travel Channel, Animal Planet, The Miss America Pageant, Dr. Phil, and many others. He currently directs the video team at ChangePoint, a nondenominational church, and has served as an elder in the Presbyterian Church (USA). He has a degree in anthropology from Baylor University. David and his wife, Gina, are raising a son and two daughters in Anchorage, Alaska, a city where just one in five men attends church regularly. To learn more about David and CHURCH FOR MEN, please visit his Web site, www.churchformen.com.

ACKNOWLEDGMENTS

IN THE SUMMER OF 2000 MY FAITH IN CHRIST WAS HANGING BY A thread. Three books saved me. God sent me a copy of George Barna's *Second Coming of the Church* in the nick of time. Then on an Internet search I stumbled across Leon Podles' *The Church Impotent: The Feminization of Christianity*. Finally, John Eldredge's *Wild at Heart* re-introduced me to Christ the man. Without the heroic vision of these three men you would not have this book before you today, nor would I be a follower of Jesus Christ. Thank you, gentlemen.

Thanks to my research assistants, Dorothy and Kelly; my reader, Barb; and my posse of friends, especially Dave, Peter, Sean, and Scott. Thanks to many friends and associates who believed in me and my message (even when I wasn't so sure about it myself). Thanks to the team at Nelson for taking a chance on a first-time author. Abundant praise to my three children, who gave up time with Dad so he could pursue his dream. If the book sells, we're going to Costa Rica. (The promise is in print—I can't back out now!)

Highest praise to my wife, Gina. Her unflagging encouragement, her willingness to sacrifice, and her chocolate chip cookies are the reason I got it done. There is no greater woman in the world.

NOTES

Chapter 1

1. Leon J. Podles, *The Church Impotent: The Feminization of Christianity* (Dallas: Spence Publishing, 1999), xii.
2. Barna Research Online, "Women Are the Backbone of Christian Congregations in America," 6 March 2000, www.barna.org.
3. Ibid.
4. "U.S. Congregational Life Survey—What Are the Major Challenges That U.S. Congregations Face?" 26 October 2002, www.uscongregations.org/challenge.htm.
5. I came up with this figure by taking the U.S. Census 2000 numbers for total married adults and overlaying Barna Research's year 2000 percentages of male vs. female attendance at weekly worship services. The figures suggest at least 24.5 million married women attend church on a given weekend, but only 19 million married men attend. That's 5.5 million more women, or 22.5 percent. The actual gender gap figure may be even higher, because married people attend church in much greater numbers than singles.
6. Barna Research Online, "Adults Who Attended Church as Children Show Lifelong Effects," 5 November 2001, www.barna.org.
7. Barna, "Women Are the Backbone of Christian Congregations in America."
8. Ibid.
9. UK Christian Handbook online, www.ukchristianhandbook.org.uk. This statistic was posted on the home page, 20 June 2002.
10. Barna, "Women Are the Backbone of Christian Congregations in America."
11. I conducted numerous interviews, portions of which appear in the following chapters. The people with whom I spoke included Dr. Woody Davis, August 2001; Russell Rainey, 15 November 2002; Curtis Burnam, 17 May 2002; Rod Stark, sociologist of religion, Baylor University, 9 September 2003; Larry Wayne, K-Love DJ, 5 May 2002; Robert Lewis, 6 November 2002; John Eldredge, 31 July 2003; and Herb Reece, 30 December 2003.

Chapter 2

1. Barna, "Women Are the Backbone of Christian Congregations in America."

2. Dan Erickson and Dan Schaffer, "Modern Man in Contemporary Culture," in *Effective Men's Ministry: The Indispensable Toolkit for Your Church,* ed. Phil Downer (Grand Rapids: Zondervan, 2001), 17.

Chapter 3

1. George Gallup Jr., "The Religiosity Cycle," 4 June 2002, Religion and Values Content Channel, figures from the Gallup Youth Survey of 2000, www.gallup.com.

2. Cameron Strang, "Looking for Reality," *Ministries Today,* May/June 2003, 25–28.

3. Polls from Barna, ABC News, and Gallup have consistently found approximately 20 to 25 percent more women go to church than men on any given weekend. Gallup's "The Religiosity Cycle" confirms young adults are the least likely age group to go to church.

4. Cynthia Woolever and Deborah Bruce, *A Field Guide to U.S. Congregations* (Louisville: Westminster John Knox Press, 2002), 35.

5. John Eldredge, *Wild at Heart* (Nashville: Thomas Nelson, 2001), 7.

6. Barna, "Women Are the Backbone of Christian Congregations in America."

Chapter 4

1. Woody L. Davis, "Evangelizing the Pre-Christian Male," *Net Results,* June 2001, 4, www.netresults.org.

2. Podles, *The Church Impotent,* ix.

3. Woolever and Bruce, *A Field Guide to U.S. Congregations,* 35.

4. Gordon Dalbey, *Healing the Masculine Soul: An Affirming Message for Men and the Women Who Love Them* (Dallas: Word Publishing, 1988), 179.

Chapter 5

1. Rick Warren, *The Purpose-Driven Church* (Grand Rapids: Zondervan, 1995), 123.

2. Barna Research Online, "Focus on 'Worship Wars' Hides the Real Issue Regarding Connection to God," 19 November 2002, www.barna.org.

3. Chip MacGregor, "Building a Leadership Team," *Effective Men's Ministry: The Indispensable Toolkit for Your Church,* ed. Phil Downer (Grand Rapids: Zondervan, 2001), 71.

4. Rod Cooper, "Transforming Your Men's Ministry," *Effective Men's Ministry: The Indispensable Toolkit for Your Church,* ed. Phil Downer (Grand Rapids: Zondervan, 2001), 169.

5. Ibid., 171.

6. Albert L. Winseman, "In the Last Six Months, Someone Has Talked to Me

About the Progress of My Spiritual Growth," 24 September 2002, Gallup
Tuesday Briefing, Religion and Values Content Channel, www.gallup.com.

7. Michelle Conlin, "The New Gender Gap," *BusinessWeek* online edition, 26 May
2003, www.businessweek.com.

8. Elaine McArdle, "The Lost Boys," *Boston Magazine Online*, September 2003,
www.bostonmagazine.com.

9. Alaina Sue Potrikus, "Around the World, Girls Outperforming Boys in School,"
Knight Ridder newspapers, 19 September 2003, reprinted in the *Arizona Republic*
online edition.

10. Anne and Bill Moir, *Why Men Don't Iron* (New York: Citadel Press, 1999), 127.

Chapter 6

1. "Why Religion Matters: The Impact of Religious Practice on Social Stability,"
The Heritage Foundation Backgrounder, 25 January 1996, www.heritage.org.

2. Penny Edgell (Becker) and Heather Hofmeister, "Work, Family and Religious
Involvement for Men and Women," Hartford Institute for Religion Research,
http://hirr.hartsem.edu.

3. Christian Smith and Phillip Kim, "Religious Youth Are More Likely to Have
Positive Relationships with Their Fathers," University of North Carolina at
Chapel Hill, 12 July 2002, findings based on the National Longitudinal Survey of
Youth (1997).

4. George Gallup Jr., "Why Are Women More Religious?" 17 December 2002,
Gallup Tuesday Briefing, Religion and Values, www.gallup.com.

5. Jack Hayford, "The Pastor's Role," *Effective Men's Ministry: The Indispensable Toolkit
for Your Church,* ed. Phil Downer (Grand Rapids: Zondervan, 2001), 57.

6. Steve Sonderman, *How to Build a Life-Changing Men's Ministry: Bringing the Fire
Home to Your Church* (Minneapolis: Bethany House, 1996), 176.

7. George Barna, *The Second Coming of the Church* (Nashville: Word Publishing,
1998), 80.

8. John Gray, Ph.D., *Men Are from Mars, Women Are from Venus* (New York:
HarperCollins, 1992), 42.

9. Albert L. Winseman, "In My Congregation, I Regularly Have the Opportunity
to Do What I Do Best," 30 July 2002, Gallup Tuesday Briefing, Religion and
Values Content Channel, www.gallup.com.

10. Ibid., "Religion and Gender: A Congregation Divided, Part III," 17 December
2002, Gallup Tuesday Briefing, Religion and Values Content Channel,
www.gallup.com.

11. Thom S. Rainer, *Surprising Insights from the Unchurched and Proven Ways to Reach
Them* (Grand Rapids: Zondervan, 2001), 170.

12. Barna Research Online, "Research Shows That Spiritual Maturity Process
Should Start at a Young Age," 17 November 2002, www.barna.org.

13. Ibid.

14. "U.S. Congregational Life Survey—What Are the Major Strengths of Congregations?" 26 April 2002, www.uscongregations.org/strengths.htm.

15. Renee Evans, "Sharpening Our Ministry to Children," *Ministry,* November 2002, 25–27.

16. Patrick M. Arnold, *Wildmen, Warriors and Kings: Masculine Spirituality and the Bible* (New York: Crossroad Publishing, 1991), 69.

17. Richard Rohr and Joseph Martos, *The Wild Man's Journey: Reflections on Male Spirituality* (Cincinnati: St. Anthony Messenger Press, 1996), 93.

18. Moir, *Why Men Don't Iron,* 131.

19. Boys pay more for insurance at my house. I actually have a better health history and lower cholesterol than my wife, but I pay higher life insurance rates. We also pay higher premiums for my son's car insurance than for my daughter's.

20. Raksha Arora, "Female Investors Retain Bearish Outlook," 21 October 2003, Gallup Tuesday Briefing, Finance and Commerce Content Channel, www.gallup.com.

21. Edwin Louis Cole, *Maximized Manhood: A Guide to Family Survival* (New Kensington, PA: Whitaker House, 1982), 166.

22. Dalbey, *Healing the Masculine Soul,* 29.

23. Albert L. Winseman, "Congregational Engagement Index: Life Satisfaction and Giving," 26 February 2002, Gallup Tuesday Briefing, Religion and Values Content Channel, www.gallup.com.

24. Bruce Barton, *The Man Nobody Knows* (Chicago: Ivan R. Dee, Inc., 2000), 26. The book was first published in 1925 by the Bobbs-Merrill Co.

25. Bob Horner, Ron Ralston, and David Sunde, *Promise Keepers at Work* (Colorado Springs: Focus on the Family, 1996), 111.

26. Carol Eisenberg, "Americans Who Subscribe to No Religion on the Rise," *Newsday,* December 2001.

27. Barna Research Online, "Number of Unchurched Adults Has Nearly Doubled Since 1991," 4 May 2004, www.barna.org.

28. Peter Brierley and Heather Wraight, *The Atlas of World Christianity, 2000 Years: Complete Visual Reference to Christianity Worldwide, Including Growth Trends into the New Millennium* (Nashville: Nelson Reference, 1998), 54.

29. "Go Figure," *Christianity Today,* November 2003, 23.

30. Shireen T. Hunter with Huma Malik, "Islam in Europe and the United States: A Comparative Perspective," Luso-American Foundation, Center for Strategic and International Studies, Washington, DC, 2002.

31. Charles Colson, "Al Qaeda and Converts to Islam," *BreakPoint Online,* 28 April 2004. Colson quotes French scholar Olivier Roy, who observes a trend among young adults who convert to Islam in order to "stick it to their parents." It's their way of rebelling, of identifying with developing nations.

32. "Many Black Men Leaving the Church for the Mosque," *The Tennessean,* 89, no. 234, posted on the Islamic Bulletin Web site, www.islamicbulletin.org.

33. John Eldredge, *Waking the Dead: The Glory of a Heart Fully Alive* (Nashville: Thomas Nelson, 2003), 30.

Chapter 7

1. "Myths About Worshipers and Congregations: Results from the U.S. Congregational Life Survey," 2002, www.uscongregations.org/myths.htm.

2. ABC News/Beliefnet poll conducted 19–20 February 2002 among a random national sample of 1,008 adults. The results have a 3-point error margin.

3. This statistic comes from Barna's figures on male/female worship attendance, overlaid upon the Census 2000 numbers for adult men and women in the U.S. population.

4. "U.S. Congregational Life Survey—Key Findings," 29 October 2003, www.uscongregations.org/key.htm.

5. See Chapter 1, Note 5, for an explanation of this figure.

6. Rainer, *Surprising Insights from the Unchurched,* 84, 116.

7. "National Congregations Study of 1998," University of Arizona, http://saint-denis.library.arizona.edu/natcong/. The National Congregations Study finds 8.8 percent of U.S. churches reported a reverse gender gap (at least 55 percent male attendees).

8. ABC News/Beliefnet poll conducted 19 February 2002 among a random national sample of 1,008 adults. Posted at www.abcnews.com. The results have a 3-point error margin.

9. "National Congregations Study of 1998." The study finds 92.2 percent of churches that identify themselves as "Black Christian" draw a crowd that's 56 percent or more female.

10. Edward Thompson, "Beneath the Status Characteristic: Gender Variations in Religiousness," *Journal for the Scientific Study of Religion,* 1991, 30.

11. Barry A. Kosmin and Seymore P. Lachman, *One Nation Under God: Religion in Contemporary American Society* (New York: Harmony Books, 1993), 220, as quoted in Podles, *The Church Impotent,* 26.

12. "American Religious Identification Survey," Graduate Center, City University of New York, 2001, exhibit 11. Results are a combination of the 1990 and 2001 studies.

13. Philip Yancey, *Church: Why Bother?* (Grand Rapids: Zondervan, 1998), 71–72.

14. "Myths About Worshipers and Congregations: Results from the U.S. Congregational Life Survey," 2002, www.uscongregations.org/myths.htm.

15. "National Congregations Study of 1998." I had to do this table a little differently from the others. It reflects the number of persons in congregations, not the number of congregations. The NCS database did not return any results for churches 10,000+ unless I posed the query this way. I spoke to the author of the study; he blamed it on a computer glitch.

16. Podles, *The Church Impotent,* 26.

17. Joshua P. Georgen, "Looking for a Few Good Men," LAM News Service (Mexico City), 29 April 2003, www.lam.org.

18. Podles, *The Church Impotent,* 19.

19. Ann Douglas, *The Feminization of American Culture* (New York: Alfred E. Knopf, 1977), quoting F. D. Huntington, *Sermons for the People* (Boston, 1856), 350.

20. Podles, *The Church Impotent*, 17.

21. Although this hymn was penned in 1740 by Charles Wesley, it was one of the Victorian era's most popular worship songs.

22. Douglas, *The Feminization of American Culture*, 100.

23. Anna Lee Starr, *The Bible Status of Women* (New York: Garland Publishing, Inc., 1987), 379, as quoted in Podles, *The Church Impotent*.

24. Lyle E. Schaller, *It's a Different World: The Challenge for Today's Pastor* (Nashville: Abingdon, 1987), 61–62.

25. Barbara G. Wheeler, "Is There a Problem? Theological Students and Religious Leadership for the Future," *Auburn Studies*, Auburn Theological Seminary, July 2001, 5.

26. Podles, *The Church Impotent*, xiii.

27. Kenneth L. Woodward, "A Revolution? Not So Fast," *Newsweek*, 6 May 2002, 33.

Chapter 8

1. Barna, "Women Are the Backbone of Christian Congregations in America."

2. Albert L. Winseman, "Religion and Gender: A Congregation Divided," 3 December 2002, Gallup Tuesday Briefing, Religion and Values Content Channel, www.gallup.com.

3. Ibid., Part III, 17 December 2002, Gallup Tuesday Briefing, Religion and Values Content Channel, www.gallup.com.

4. Ibid.

5. Barna, "Women Are the Backbone of Christian Congregations in America."

6. United Methodist Church Web site, www.umc.org. Figures are for 1999, rounded to the nearest thousand.

7. BSF International Web site, August 2002, www.bsfinternational.org.

8. Susan Faludi, *Stiffed: The Betrayal of the American Man* (New York: HarperCollins, 1999), 256.

9. Gene Edward Veith, "You Are What You Read," *World Magazine*, July/August 2002, 26.

10. Pat Morley, "Why Don't Men Read Christian Books? Just a Thought . . . ," 6 October 2003, Man in the Mirror Weekly Briefing e-newsletter.

11. "The Explosion of Christian Music," *Radio and Records*, 19 April 2002, 46.

12. List of stations posted 6 April 2004, www.klove.com.

13. Barna Research Online, "Christian Mass Media Reach More Adults with the Christian Message Than Do Churches," 2 July 2002, www.barna.org.

14. Barna, "Women Are the Backbone of Christian Congregations in America."

Chapter 9

1. Dr. Mels Carbonnel, telephone interview with author, July 2001. Carbonnel uses the DISC test and finds that 85 percent of Christians are either S or C dominant personalities. These are also known as *phlegmatic* and *melancholy* types.

2. Alan Philips, "Monks Fight on Roof of Holiest Place," *London Daily Telegraph* online version, 30 July 2002, news.telegraph.co.uk.

3. Ellen Barry, "In Northern Woods, Churchgoing Faces Change," *Boston Globe*, 12 May 2003, B1.

4. Barna Research Online, "New Book and Diagnostic Resource Strive to Clear Up Widespread Confusion Regarding Leadership," 5 August 2002, www.barna.org.

5. Podles, *The Church Impotent*, 8–9.

6. "A Quick Question: How Religiously Active Are Gay Men?" Hartford Institute for Religion Research, quoting a study by Darren E. Sherkat, professor of sociology, Southern Illinois University, http://hirr.hartsem.edu.

7. Dalbey, *Healing the Masculine Soul*, 174.

8. Faludi, *Stiffed*, 230.

9. John Piper, *Desiring God* (Sisters, OR: Multnomah, 1996), 73.

10. Lee Strobel, *Inside the Mind of Unchurched Harry and Mary* (Grand Rapids: Zondervan, 1993), 219.

Part 3, Introduction

1. Gallup pegged weekly male church attendance at 38 percent in late 1989, on the cusp of the Promise Keepers movement. A decade later, George Barna found the number had slipped to 35 percent. The 1989 figures come from Linda DeStefano, "Church/Synagogue Membership and Attendance Levels Remain Stable," *The Gallup Poll News Service*, 54, no. 36, 24 January 1990. Barna's numbers are from "Women Are the Backbone of Christian Congregations in America."

2. Dan Schaffer, "Can the Church Be a Safe Place for Men?" *Building Brothers Newsletter*, fall 2002.

Chapter 10

1. Moir, *Why Men Don't Iron*, 131, 139.

2. Betty Mason, "The Daddy Effect," *New Scientist*, 25 May 2002, 12.

3. Thom and Joani Schultz, *Why Nobody Learns Much of Anything in Church: And How to Fix It* (Loveland, CO: Group Publishing, 1996), 136.

4. James Dobson, *Bringing Up Boys* (Wheaton, IL: Tyndale, 2001), 25, 26.

5. Moir, *Why Men Don't Iron*, 135. His source is the *Diagnostic and Statistical Manual of Mental Disorders*, 4th ed. (DSM-IV), American Psychiatric Association (1995), 49.

6. Bruce Weber, "Fewer Noses Stuck in Books in America, Survey Finds," *New York Times*, 8 July 2004.

7. Moir, *Why Men Don't Iron*, 121, 116.

8. Suzanne Pender, "Why Do Women Talk Twice As Much As Men?" Review of *Why Men Don't Listen and Women Can't Read Maps*, by Allan and Barbara Pease, *Carlow Nationalist*, 5 March 1999.

9. Kevin Leman, *Making Sense of the Men in Your Life* (Nashville: Thomas Nelson, 2000), 241.

10. Schultz, *Why Nobody Learns Much of Anything in Church*, 136.

Chapter 11

1. Jim Castelli and Joseph Gremillion, *The Emerging Parish: The Notre Dame Study of Parish Life Since Vatican II* (San Francisco: Harper and Row, 1987), 68–69, as quoted in Podles, *The Church Impotent*, 12.

2. Barna, "Women Are the Backbone of Christian Congregations in America."

3. Judith Kleinfeld, "Women Do Deal with Stress Differently," *Anchorage Daily News*, 9 August 2003, Section B, 4.

4. Frances Dahlberg, introduction, *Woman the Gatherer* (New Haven: Yale University Press, 1981), 13.

5. Sixty-eight percent of Americans believe in the devil, according to Gallup Poll Social Series—Values and Beliefs, 14 May 2001, Gallup Poll News Service, www.gallup.com.

6. Douglas J. Wilson, *Future Men* (Moscow, ID: Canon Press, 2001), 16.

7. Ernestine Friedl, *Women and Men: An Anthropologist's View* (Prospect Heights, IL: Waveland Press, 1984), 30.

Chapter 12

1. Bob Nelson, "Dump the Cash, Load on the Praise," *Personnel Journal*, July 1996, http://www.fed.org/onlinemag/dec96/motiv.html.

2. "Noble Masculinity," *Leadership Journal*, spring 2002, 26.

Chapter 13

1. Warren Farrell, *The Myth of Male Power* (New York: Berkley Publishing Group, 1994), 106.

2. David D. Gilmore, *Manhood in the Making: Cultural Concepts of Masculinity* (New Haven: Yale University Press, 1990), 11.

3. Poll taken outside Sullivan Arena Gun Show, Anchorage, Alaska, 3 May 2003, ninety-five valid responses. I asked the men to rate twelve destinations as either masculine or feminine. Church appeared in the sixth slot; Sunday school was in the eleventh slot.

4. Patrick Arnold, *Wildmen, Warriors, and Kings, Masculine Spirituality and the Bible* (New York: Crossroad, 1991), 19.

5. Albert L. Winseman, "Congregational Engagement Index: Life Satisfaction and Giving," 26 February 2002, Gallup Tuesday Briefing, Religion and Values Content Channel, www.gallup.com.

6. Ellen Goodman, "Fathering Needs a Standing Ovation," *Boston Globe,* 17 June 2003.

7. Pamela Sebastian Ridge, "Home Store Classes Encourage Women to Take Up Tools," *Wall Street Journal,* reprinted in *Anchorage Daily News,* 1 April 2002, Section E, 8.

Chapter 14

1. Sam Keen, *Fire in the Belly, On Being a Man* (New York: Bantam Books, 1991), 140.

2. Sarah Sumner, *Men and Women in the Church* (Downers Grove, IL: InterVarsity, 2003), 97.

3. Survey taken at Grace Community Church, Anchorage, July 2002; 76 percent of women chose singing as a top priority for their large group events, while 52 percent of men did.

4. Warren, *The Purpose-Driven Church,* 259.

5. Mark I. Pinsky, "Saint Flanders," *Christianity Today,* 5 February 2001.

6. Wayne Jacobsen, *The Naked Church* (Visalia, CA: Body Life Publishers, 1998), 108.

7. Strobel, *Unchurched Harry and Mary,* 120.

8. Albert L. Winseman, "Spiritual Commitment, By the Numbers," 23 April 2002, Gallup Tuesday Briefing, Religion and Values Content Channel, www.gallup.com.

9. Michael Fanstone, *Unbelieving Husbands and the Wives Who Love Them* (Ann Arbor: Vine Books, 1994), 97.

10. Carol Penner, *Women and Men: Gender in the Church* (Scottdale, PA: Herald Press, 1998), 100.

11. Leman, *Making Sense of the Men in Your Life,* 122.

12. Linda Davis, *How to Be the Happy Wife of an Unsaved Husband* (New Kensington, PA: Whitaker House, 1987), 59.

13. Jeri Odell, *Spiritually Single: Living with an Unbelieving Husband* (Kansas City: Beacon Hill Press, 2002), 40.

14. Larry Keefauver, *Lord, I Wish My Husband Would Pray with Me* (Lake Mary, FL: Creation House, 1998), 90.

15. Shannon Ethridge, *Every Woman's Battle* (Colorado Springs: WaterBrook Press, 2003), back cover.

16. Nancy Kennedy, *When He Doesn't Believe* (Colorado Springs: WaterBrook Press, 2001), 194.

17. "Opinion of Homosexual Marriages," Gallup Poll, 15–16 December 2003, www.gallup.com; Pew Research Center nationwide survey of 1,515 adults, 15–19 October 2003, quoted on *USA Today* Web site, www.usatoday.com.

18. Mark D. Jordan, "What Attracts Gay Men to the Catholic Priesthood?" *Boston Globe,* 3 May 2002, Section A, 23. Richard Sipe, who has studied the sexuality of priests for twenty-five years, estimates that at least a third of Catholic bishops are gay.

19. David France, "Gays and the Seminary," *Newsweek*, 20 May 2002, 54. The article
    states that some Catholic seminaries are up to 70 percent gay.
20. "A Report on the Crisis in the Catholic Church in the United States," the
    National Review Board for the Protection of Children and Young People, U.S.
    Conference of Catholic Bishops, 27 February 2004, 80,
    http://www.usccb.org/nrb/johnjaystudy/index.htm.
21. John Ortberg, *Everybody's Normal Till You Get to Know Them* (Grand Rapids:
    Zondervan, 2003), from the excerpt, "Our Secret Fears About Heaven," *Today's
    Christian Woman*, July/August 2003, 38.

Chapter 15

1. Traditional hymns are still the most common type of music in most services.
   Almost 75 percent of U.S. worship services feature hymns, while just 40 percent
   feature praise music and choruses. Woolever and Bruce, *A Field Guide to U.S.
   Congregations*, 35.
2. Barna Research Online, "Research Shows That Spiritual Maturity Process
   Should Start at a Young Age," 17 November 2002, www.barna.org.
3. Ibid., "Telephoning Churches Often Proves Fruitless," 22 August 2000,
   www.barna.org.
4. Barna, *Second Coming of the Church*, 58.
5. Warren, *The Purpose-Driven Church*, 191.
6. Strobel, *Unchurched Harry and Mary*, 189.
7. Ibid., 190.
8. Bob Russell with Rusty Russell, *When God Builds a Church* (West Monroe, LA:
   Howard, 2000), 113.
9. Schultz, *Why Nobody Learns Much of Anything in Church*, 241.
10. Jawanza Kunjufu, *Adam! Where Are You? Why Most Black Men Don't Go to Church*
    (Chicago: African American Images, 1997), 61.
11. Deborah Bruce and Cynthia Woolever, "U.S. Congregational Life Survey: Fastest
    Growing Presbyterian Churches," Research Services, Presbyterian Church
    (USA), 2002.
12. George Gallup Jr., "Americans Feel Need to Believe," 15 January 2002, Religion
    and Values Content Channel, Gallup Tuesday Briefing, www.gallup.com.
13. Arnold, *Wildmen, Warriors, and Kings*, 77.

Chapter 16

1. Barton, *The Man Nobody Knows*, 23.
2. Eldredge, *Wild at Heart*, 22.
3. Leman, *Making Sense of the Men in Your Life*, 26.
4. Gordon MacDonald, "The Conquering Male," *New Man Magazine*, July/August
   2003, 29.

5. Woody L. Davis, "Evangelizing the Pre-Christian Male," *Net Results,* June 2001, 4, www.netresults.org.

6. George Barna, "Unchurched Nation," *Moody Magazine,* July/August 2003, 34.

7. The phrase "family of God" does not appear in the King James, New American Standard, or Young's Literal Translation. It appears once in the New International Version—1 Peter 4:17—but it is not a happy reference. Rather, it is a warning of impending judgment!

8. Advertisement in *New Man Magazine.* The book is called *Kissing the Face of God: Enter a New Realm of Worship More Wonderful Than You Can Imagine,* by Sam Hinn.

9. Here are the titles and writers of the songs mentioned here: "The Power Of Your Love" by Geoff Bullock (copyright 1992 Word Music, Inc. Maranatha! Music—CCLI 917491); "Breathe" by Marie Barnett (copyright 1995 Mercy/Vineyard Publishing—CCLI 1874117); "Let My Words Be Few" by Beth and Matt Redman (copyright 2000 Thankyou Music—CCLI 3040980); "Here I Am to Worship" by Tim Hughes (copyright 2000 Thankyou Music—CCLI 3266032); "Oh Lord, You're Beautiful" by Keith Green (copyright 1980 Birdwing Music—CCLI 14514); "You Are So Good to Me" by Ben Pasley, Don Chaffer, and Robin Pasley (copyright 1999 Blue Renaissance Music, Hey Ruth Music, Squit Songs—CCLI 2757944).

10. David C. James, *What Are They Saying About Masculine Spirituality?* (Mahwah, NJ: Paulist Press, 1996), 20.

11. Piper, *Desiring God,* 76.

12. Kunjufu, *Adam! Where Are You?,* 94.

13. Wilson, *Future Men,* 94.

Part 5, Introduction

1. Barna Research Online, "Focus on 'Worship Wars' Hides the Real Issue Regarding Connection to God," 19 November 2002, www.barna.org.

Chapter 17

1. Barna, *Second Coming of the Church,* 36.

2. Adam Hamilton, *Leading Beyond the Walls,* (Nashville: Abingdon Press, 2002), 160.

3. Bob Smietana, "Chicago's Holy Fire," *Christianity Today,* February 2004, 28.

4. Barna, "Women Are the Backbone of Christian Congregations in America."

5. "National Congregations Study of 1998." The study finds 60.2 percent of congregations whose senior pastor/leader was male had a gender gap, while 80.4 percent of female-led congregations had one.

6. Keen, *Fire in the Belly,* 102.

7. William Easum, *Sacred Cows Make Gourmet Burgers* (Nashville: Abingdon, 1995), 74.

8. Strobel, *Unchurched Harry and Mary,* 132.

9. Barna, *Second Coming of the Church,* 15.

10. Albert L. Winseman, "The Mission or Purpose of My Congregation Makes Me Feel My Participation Is Important," 3 September 2002, Gallup Tuesday Briefing, Religion and Values Content Channel, www.gallup.com.

11. Rainer, *Surprising Insights from the Unchurched*, 121.

12. Ibid., 148.

13. Ibid., 111.

14. Vicki Marsh Kabat, "Old Time Religion . . . Is It Good Enough for You?" *Baylor Magazine*, January/February 2003, 19.

15. Warren, *The Purpose-Driven Church*, 345.

16. Dalbey, *Healing the Masculine Soul*, 129.

17. Barton, *The Man Nobody Knows*, 57.

18. Rainer, *Surprising Insights from the Unchurched*, 36.

19. G. F. Watkins, *G-Men: The Final Strategy* (Southlake, TX: Watercolor Books, 2001), 10.

20. Barna Research Online, "Barna Identifies Seven Paradoxes Regarding America's Faith," 17 December 2002, www.barna.org.

21. George Barna, *User Friendly Churches* (Ventura, CA: Regal Books, 1991), 46.

22. Warren, *The Purpose-Driven Church*, 142.

Chapter 18

1. Easum, *Sacred Cows*, 72.

2. Barna, *Second Coming of the Church*, 101.

3. Barbara Brown Zikmund, Adair T. Lummis, and Patricia M. Y. Chang, "Women, Men and Styles of Clergy Leadership," *Christian Century*, 6 May 1998, 115, excerpted from *Clergywomen: An Uphill Calling* (Louisville: Westminster John Knox Press, 1998).

4. Andrew Sullivan, "The He Hormone," *New York Times Magazine*, 2 April 2000. Sullivan says, "Actors tend to have more testosterone than ministers, according to a 1990 study."

5. Rainer, *Surprising Insights from the Unchurched*, 127, 132, 134.

6. Odell, *Spiritually Single*, 97.

7. Rohr and Martos, *Wild Man's Journey*, 163.

8. Strobel, *Unchurched Harry and Mary*, 66.

9. Rainer, *Surprising Insights from the Unchurched*, 60.

10. Martin E. Marty, "Women Clergy: The Numbers," Beliefnet, quoting Laura S. Olson, Sue E. S. Crawford, and James L. Guth, "Changing Issue Agendas of Women Clergy," *Journal for the Scientific Study of Religion*, June 2000.

11. Linda Lyons, "Church Reform: Women in the Clergy," 7 May 2002, Gallup Tuesday Briefing, Religion and Values Content Channel, www.gallup.com.

12. Jonathan Petre, "New Women Priests to Outnumber Men for First Time," *London Daily Telegraph Online Editor*, 27 September 2004, www.telegraph.co.uk.

13. Zikmund et al., "Women, Men and Styles of Clergy Leadership."

14. Marty, "Women Clergy: The Numbers."

15. "National Congregations Study of 1998." The study finds a gender gap in 57.9 percent of churches that characterize themselves as more conservative, 67.8 percent of churches that are right in the middle, and 72.4 percent of churches that identify themselves as more liberal.

Chapter 19

1. Woody L. Davis, "Ministry to, with, and Among Men," *Net Results,* November 2002, www.netresults.org.

2. "Study shows significant increase in contemporary and diverse worship styles in Protestant churches," a study from the Ellison Group, 4 March 2004. The firm surveyed 659 Protestant ministers and found the average sermon lasts thirty-one minutes. Complete results are available at www.ellisonresearch.com.

3. Larry Crabb, *The Silence of Adam* (Grand Rapids: Zondervan, 1995), 21.

4. Results of a computer search of the NKJV posted at www.biblegateway.com.

5. George G. Hunter III, *Church for the Unchurched* (Nashville: Abingdon, 1996), 159.

6. Geoff Gorsuch and Dan Schaffer, *Brothers! Calling Men into Vital Relationships* (Colorado Springs: NavPress, 1994), 34.

7. United States Army recruiting brochure RPI 272, January 2002.

8. Dorothy Cassel, phone interview with author, September 2002. Additional material from Woody L. Davis, "Evangelizing the Pre-Christian Male," *Net Results,* June 2001, 3–6, www.netresults.org.

9. James, *What Are They Saying?,* 49.

10. Barton, *The Man Nobody Knows,* 13.

Chapter 20

1. Barna Research Online, "Worship Tops the List of Important Church-Based Experiences," 19 February 2000, www.barna.org.

2. Rainer, *Surprising Insights from the Unchurched,* 83.

3. Wilson, *Future Men,* 95.

4. Barna, *User Friendly Churches,* 66.

5. Warren, *The Purpose-Driven Church,* 211.

6. Barna, *User Friendly Churches,* 65, 77.

7. Barna, "Unchurched Nation," 34.

8. Schultz, *Why Nobody Learns Much of Anything in Church,* 141.

9. Marshall Allen, "Standup for Jesus," *Christianity Today,* 9 September 2002, 76–80.

10. Moir, *Why Men Don't Iron,* 133.

11. Arbitron Audience Composition Report, summer 2003, posted at www.arbitron.com. Exact figures: album-oriented rock: men 69 percent, women 27 percent; soft adult contemporary: men 32 percent, women 67 percent.

12. Rick Warren, *The Purpose-Driven Life* (Grand Rapids: Zondervan, 2002), 102.

13. Wilson, *Future Men,* 100.

14. Rick Kingham, "Learning to Worship," in *Effective Men's Ministry: The Indispensable Toolkit for Your Church,* ed. Phil Downer (Grand Rapids: Zondervan, 2001), 147.

15. Warren, *The Purpose-Driven Church,* 291.

16. G. Jeffrey MacDonald, "In Summer, More Clergy Use Picnic Tables As Pulpits," *Christian Science Monitor Online,* 19 August 2003, www.csmonitor.com.

17. "Faith at Work, Across the Board," *Conference Board Magazine,* November/December 2003.

18. Sonderman, *Life-Changing Men's Ministry,* 134.

19. Keefauver, *Lord, I Wish My Husband Would Pray with Me,* 23.

Chapter 21

1. Carl Dudley, "Men Sharing the Burden," Hartford Institute for Religion Research Web site, April/May 1998, http://hirr.hartsem.edu/cong/cong_dudley_398.html.

2. Pat Morley, "The State of Men's Ministry in the Church," 19 January 2003, Man in the Mirror Weekly Briefing e-newsletter. Doug Haugen of the Evangelical Lutheran Church in America identifies this as the popular stereotype of men's ministry in the local church.

3. Chuck Stecker, "Foundations of Christian Leadership," in *Effective Men's Ministry: The Indispensable Toolkit for Your Church,* ed. Phil Downer (Grand Rapids: Zondervan, 2001), 107.

4. Kunjufu, *Adam! Where Are You?,* 120.

5. Kennedy, *When He Doesn't Believe,* 189.

6. Rainer, *Surprising Insights from the Unchurched,* 70, 83.

7. Keen, *Fire in the Belly,* 171.

8. Eric Swanson, "Ten Paradigm Shifts Toward Community Transformation," *Leadership Network,* September 2002, 11.

9. Keefauver, *Lord, I Wish My Husband Would Pray with Me,* 82. Keefauver mentions Abraham, Samuel, Eli, David, and Solomon as examples of lousy fathers. The only good biblical fathers were (possibly) Isaac, Boaz, and Joseph.

Chapter 22

1. Lee Strobel and Leslie Strobel, *Surviving a Spiritual Mismatch in Marriage* (Grand Rapids: Zondervan, 2002), 216.

2. Eric Swanson, "Blueprint Research: Ten Paradigm Shifts Towards Community Transformation (Part II)," *IntoAction Newsletter,* February 2003.

3. Hamilton, *Leading Beyond the Walls,* 146.

4. Bruce H. Wilkinson, *The Prayer of Jabez* (Sisters, OR: Multnomah, 2000), 47.

5. John Dart, "Men Behaving Badly," *Christian Century,* 20 December 2000.

6. Dallas Willard, *Hearing God: Developing a Conversational Relationship with God* (Downers Grove, IL: InterVarsity, 1999), 210.

7. Hunter, *Church for the Unchurched,* 144.

8. Neil Carter, "Why Men Don't Go to Church," *House2House Online,* www.house2house.tv/articles/00014.shtml.

9. Easum, *Sacred Cows,* 45.

10. Rainer, *Surprising Insights from the Unchurched,* 104.

11. Gallup, "Why Are Women More Religious?"

12. Pat Morley and David Delk, *Ten Practical Secrets to Attract and Retain Men,* a brochure from Man in the Mirror Ministries, 2002.

13. Warren, *The Purpose-Driven Church,* 387.

14. Pat Morley, "The Distinction Between Disciples and Workers," Man in the Mirror Weekly Briefing e-newsletter, 2003, 48, www.maninthemirror.org.

Chapter 23

1. Watkins, *G-Men,* 56–57.

2. National Fatherhood Initiative Web site, www.fatherhood.org.

3. Barna, *Second Coming of the Church,* 2.

4. Crabb, *The Silence of Adam,* 47.

5. Tim Stafford, "The Church's Walking Wounded: How Should We Respond in a Psychological Age?," *Christianity Today,* March 2003, 64, 68.

6. Michael Gurian, *The Wonder of Boys* (New York: Tarcher/Putnam, 1997), 249.

7. Keen, *Fire in the Belly,* 185.

Chapter 24

1. Albert L. Winseman, "Religion and Gender: A Congregation Divided, Part II," 10 December 2002, Gallup Tuesday Briefing, Religion and Values Content Channel, www.gallup.com.

2. Erickson and Schaffer, "Modern Man in Contemporary Culture," 18.

3. Pat Morley, "Rethinking Ministry to Men: The View from 30,000 Feet," Man in the Mirror e-newsletter, 2003.

4. Barna, *Second Coming of the Church,* 2.

Chapter 25

1. Barna Research Online, "Religious Activity Increasing in the West," 1 March 2004, www.barna.org.

2. Full-page ad for Promise Keepers Men conferences in *New Man Magazine,* July/August 2003, 21.